ENDORSEMENTS

In *Hearing God Through Your Dreams*, Charity Kayembe has created an extremely powerful resource for all of us who need greater equipping in understanding the value of our prophetic dreams.

The Apostle Peter said, "We are His witnesses!" (Acts 5:32) Charity explains how even in receiving prophetic dreams we become 'witnesses' and 'observers' as one of the mechanisms through which God transforms our hearts and minds. Our practiced 'observation' of these '*visions in the night*' become revelatory portals through which we pull heaven to earth. Her explanation of this process is revolutionary!

Charity is a deeply spiritual woman with so much to impart to the body of Christ. I heartily recommend her book as an excellent resource that will open up and explain entirely new dimensions of experiencing God.

PHIL MASON
Author of *Quantum Glory: The Science of Heaven Invading Earth*
Spiritual Director of New Earth Tribe
Byron Bay, Australia

Hearing God Through Your Dreams opens up a realm of blessing to you regarding the significance of dreams, their connection to the supernatural dimensions of the Kingdom of God, and their ability to reveal the heart and message of God. Charity Kayembe and Mark Virkler invite us to embrace this wonderful way God uses to connect our heart to His. This is a great book for both personal and group study and application. It is my honor to recommend it to you.

PATRICIA KING
Founder, Patricia King Ministries

"Every night we can connect with heaven through our dreams." What a beautiful challenge stated in this book. Who wouldn't want to learn more about that? This book teaches us how to pay attention to our night visions and glean all the wisdom God wants to share with us while we dream. What a privilege to hear from the God of the universe while we step out of His way and go to sleep.

Diving into the meat of this book taught me so many wonderful concepts about hearing God through dreams and how to interpret them symbolically, while showing the clear, biblical precedents for God speaking to us this way. What a terrific list they supply of the most significant moments from the Bible that you may not have even realized happened in dreams! If God places so much importance on this as a method of communication, shouldn't we?

CHERYL McKAY
Screenwriter, *The Ultimate Gift*
Author, *Finally the Bride*

When I started to read this book I had almost never experienced God speaking to me through my dreams. I realized that I dreamt, but usually forgot the dream by the time I woke up. After starting to read this manuscript I had a dream which I clearly remembered the next day. Through the principles given in this book, interpretation came to me through the Holy Spirit in a way I never experienced before. The dream proved to be key in a major decision that had to be made a few days later.

The Holy Spirit will use this book to minister to your heart. It is biblically sound, filled with many dreams and principles to interpret them, and is certainly one of the best books on dream interpretation available. The authors write from decades of experience and share very personally how God ministers to us through dreams.

Reading this book will give you a strong desire for the Lord to reveal His heart to you through the language of the dream. I heartily recommend this book to anyone who longs to understand how God communicates to us through dreams and seeks to learn how to interpret His messages in a way that is biblical and trustworthy. I wish you many dreams from the Lord!

DANIËL RENGER, B.A., M.DIV.
Senior Pastor Evangelical Church Europoort,
Rotterdam, The Netherlands
General Secretary Assemblies of God, The Netherlands

Team Virkler has made dream interpretation easy. No more "pizza dreams." Only messages from God!

SID ROTH
Host, *It's Supernatural!*

Charity states, "You will absolutely love seeing Jesus, His heart and His personality through dream work! It is an epic adventure, and we get to live into it every single night." I couldn't say it better. With humour, joy, and love for Jesus shining through, Charity takes us on an adventure in dreaming, laying out for us the biblical principles as stepping stones to understand this language the Lord pours out in the night. If you want to experience the joyful personality of Jesus discovered in dream work, then this book is for you!

MURRAY DUECK
Founder and President,
Samuel's Mantle Prophetic Training School
British Columbia, Canada

When Charity asked me to read her new book on dreams, I was not ready for the immediate impact it would have on my life. Filled with sound biblical teaching and enlightening relevant dreams and their interpretation, this book is not a good one, it is a great one! Once it hits the shelves, everyone I know will get a recommendation from me to buy it and read it over and over. Great job Charity, you hit a homerun.

JOE BROCK
Sr. Minister, Vineyard Assembly of God
Tipton, IN

Hearing God Through Your Dreams is a book that offers solidly biblical, fresh, and creative guidelines to understand what the Lord is saying through our dreams. There is much for believers to learn in this book, and it will take you to a new level of understanding what the Spirit wants to communicate to you through the language of dreams.

GARY S. GREIG, PH.D.
The University of Chicago 1990
Adjunct Faculty, United Theological Seminary
Dayton, OH

Some books on dreams give mostly symbol interpretations and few dreams. Other books give a few dreams from people in modern life and a few dreams from the Bible along with a list of rules of interpretation. Those are all good. But what I especially like about this book is something that is quite rare: 30 Dream Interpretation Keys are used on 60 fascinating dreams—each dream by the same person.

Dr. Mark Virkler and his daughter, Dr. Charity Kayembe, co-write this book. I love their writing style—*easy* and *interesting reading*, great teachings, all coupled with thorough dream interpretation. I love it! This book will remain as a primary reference book for me for my own dream interpretations for years to come! Get this one. You're going to need it!

STEVE SHULTZ
Founder, *The Elijah List*

Understanding our dreams and visions prepares us to play a prominent role in God's end-time revival. We agree wholeheartedly with Charity and Mark when they say, "God speaks through our dreams and He does it often.... They are a portal to the spirit realm." It's in opening that realm that brings Heaven to earth. The personal wisdom, knowledge, and insights into the language of dreams that the authors have provided would normally take years to acquire. We strongly recommend this well-written and comprehensive Christian dream interpretation resource for all believers.

ADAM F. THOMPSON and ADRIAN BEALE
Authors of *The Divinity Code*
www.thedivinitycode.org

Hearing

GOD

through

Your Dreams

GOD

through

YOUR DREAMS

UNDERSTANDING THE LANGUAGE
GOD SPEAKS AT NIGHT

MARK VIRKLER *and*
CHARITY VIRKLER KAYEMBE

DESTINY IMAGE® PUBLISHERS, INC.
P.O. Box 310, Shippensburg, PA 17257-0310
"Promoting Inspired Lives."

This book and all other Destiny Image and Destiny Image Fiction books are available at Christian bookstores and distributors worldwide.

Cover design by Eileen Rockwell

For more information on foreign distributors, call 717-532-3040.
Reach us on the Internet: www.destinyimage.com.

ISBN 13 TP: 978-0-7684-0997-0
ISBN 13 eBook: 978-0-7684-0998-7

For Worldwide Distribution, Printed in the U.S.A.
2 3 4 5 6 7 8 / 20 19 18 17 16

DEDICATION

This book is dedicated with much love to my parents,
Mark and Patti Virkler.
I am so grateful you taught me how to hear God's voice
all day and all night and walk according to His Spirit.
You have always encouraged me to look
into the supernatural realm and live by what I see there.
What a priceless gift!

ACKNOWLEDGMENTS

Thank you to

Dr. MaryAnn Diorio, Ivey Rorie, and Lynn Lougen for reviewing early drafts of this book. Your attention to detail, edits, and prayers were a wonderful encouragement that helped create the best version possible of this manuscript.

Special thanks to Aminadav Badichi for your excellent insights and assistance with my Hebrew word studies.

I am also grateful to Larry Sparks, Publisher at Destiny Image. Thank you for believing in this project and working to make it a reality. You guys are the best!

CONTENTS

FOREWORD

BY DR. JAMES W. GOLL

Truths continue to unfold over time. Deuteronomy 8:3 tells us, "Man does not live by bread alone but by every word that proceeds from the mouth of God." This Old Testament truth is reiterated by Jesus Christ Himself during His historic confrontation with the devil in which He repeatedly says, "It is written…" Now that alone is amazing! The power of writing! "It is written."

Of course, this was not just another writing that Jesus was declaring. He was taking the revelatory Word from generations before and bringing it forward into His time for His personal battle with the powers of darkness, which He won by declaring, "Man does not live by bread alone but by every word that proceeds from the mouth of God!" (see Matt. 4:4; Luke 4:4).

As a part of the New Testament Sermon on the Mount, this assertion is not in the Hebrew language, as is the Old Testament; rather, it is in the language of Jesus' day. In the English transliteration, the verb tense that is used here is an ongoing active tense. So it could be stated something like this: "Man does not live only by natural bread. But man thrives on the ever-proceeding Word that has come forth, does come forth, and will come forth from the very mouth of God Himself!"

Now, that is interesting for sure. "But," you say, "how does that relate to a book on the power of dreams?"

In recent years, various leaders have often stated that "our ceiling is the next generation's floor." This is especially true when the culture of honor is present, relationships are in place, and the truth of God's Word is upheld. That is the case with the writings of Dr. Charity Kayembe. Though I do not know her personally, I know her dear father very well, and he and I have walked a path of progressive revelation together for years. Her father is none other than Dr. Mark Virkler of Christian Leadership University, author of *4 Keys to Hearing God's Voice* and a personal friend of mine.

When I was asked to consider writing an endorsement or a foreword for his daughter's book on dreams and the revelatory ways of God, I did not hesitate. In fact, I did not even pray about it. I said something like, "It would be an honor." Now, please understand that I am asked by people every week to do an endorsement or compose a foreword for a book, and my primary guideline is that I will not do it unless I have a relationship with the person. In this case, I know the father and mother, I know the legacy, and I trust the fruit! Yes, I trust the fruit that comes forth from this strong and tested tree!

Over the years I have helped shape some of today's understandings in the prophetic realms with books such as *The Seer*, *Dream Language*, *The Lifestyle of a Prophet*, *The Prophetic Intercessor*, *Angelic Encounters*, *Adventures in the Prophetic*, and many others. My writing combines three strands of truth: 1) scriptural foundation, 2) precedent in Jewish and church history, and 3) contemporary examples of current-day activity of the Holy Spirit. So while I do have some history under my belt, I could not have written this book!

Hearing God Through Your Dreams draws on the genius of science, including studies of brainwave activity, quantum physics, and so much more. Charity picks up where I leave off—my ceiling has become her floor! In the true culture of honor, she builds on my teachings as well as those of her father and others, adding revelation the Holy Spirit has given her personally that is full of truth and insight. It is intriguing, and even challenging. Don't you love a challenge?

Coming from another generation's way of receiving, analyzing, digesting, and communicating, the book in your hands states things factually that I only "dream about." In other words, her studies have taken her outside of my wonderful, and what I thought to be somewhat thorough, wheelhouse. The book is, in fact, brilliant.

So I want to thank the Lord that lineage and legacy are being established. I want to thank the Lord that progressive revelation is contained in this book. I want to thank the Lord that God still speaks and His servants are still listening!

Congratulations, Charity! I am sure you have made your mother's and father's hearts glad. This I know for sure: you have done a great job of helping us move forward with more understanding concerning one of God's historically most important revelatory languages: the art of dreams! This makes my heart glad.

I trust readers will be impacted, educated, and inspired by the writings of a next-generation revelatory voice. Thank you, Charity, for picking up the baton of forerunners and carrying the message that "God still speaks" further down the road!

Dr. James W. Goll
Founder of Encounters Network, Prayer Storm,
GET eSchool, and Compassion Acts
International Best-Selling Author

FOREWORD

BY DR. JOHN ARNOTT

Dreams, as common as they are to all of us, are nonetheless very often overlooked, ignored, or dismissed as a curious result of a double-cheese pizza the night before. Sometimes, as in the case of recurring nightmares, they can be feared or even hated.

But the Bible has much to say about dreams and visions, and it's important to understand that they have great power to change your life. I remember years ago, in the mid-1980s, as Carol and I had planted our first church in her hometown of Stratford, Ontario, I started to take dreams seriously and began studying them in Scripture. I did a word search on my primitive computer, looking for every time the words *dream* and *vision* are used in the Bible. I then printed out the whole list on fanfold paper, and it stretched the entire width of our church. It was a graphic reminder of how abundant and important dreams and visions are in Scripture. I began to take dreams even more seriously.

I remembered that Joseph believed Mary's story of her virgin conception because of a dream he had and also that after Messiah was born, Joseph fled with his family to Egypt, saving Christ's life from Herod's butchers, all because of another dream (see Matt. 1:20-25; 2:13-15). Wow!

In her book *Hearing God Through Your Dreams*, Dr. Charity Kayembe has produced a very helpful work that is like a training manual, enabling the reader to see the importance of dreams and how God uses them to speak to us about doctrine, reproof, correction, and instruction in righteousness (see 2 Tim. 3:16). It becomes an application of Scripture in our lives. Are you ready for an exciting, never-ending adventure?

Let me tell you of a life-changing dream I had over thirty years ago.

In the dream, I was told to go to Buffalo, New York, to bring home three pint-sized bottles of cream. Some of you older readers may remember when milk was delivered to your door in quart-sized glass bottles and cream in pint-sized glass bottles (for you younger readers, a pint is about half a liter). Well, in the dream, it was the best cream ever.

I woke up excited, sensing something was up. I related my dream to Carol, and together we immediately took the two-and-a-half-hour drive to Buffalo to see if God would open up anything to us. I knew only one person in Buffalo, and that was Pastor Tommy Reid from The Tabernacle. I didn't know him at all, really. I had merely said a brief "hello" to him while attending a recent conference at his church.

We arrived at The Tabernacle in the early afternoon. Pastor Tommy was not in, but we met with Gordon Spiller, who was then the dean of the newly formed Buffalo School of the Bible, a Bible school based out of this church. I was very interested in the courses of study that were shown me.

We soon met Mark Virkler, one of their main teachers, and began a friendship that has endured for more than three decades. We have since met his wife Patti and his children, Charity and Joshua, on many occasions.

Well, Carol and I returned home with a manual on "Hearing God's Voice," which turned out to be spiritual "cream" of the highest and best order. We had no idea of the fantastic journey of the heart that was being put into our hands. That dream of the cream bottles changed the course of our spiritual destiny!

We brought home what was soon to become one of our four core FIRE values that have formed the basis of our ministry: "intimacy," or hearing the voice of God. This wonderful teaching from Mark has transformed our lives. It became the fountainhead of all that we hear from the Holy Spirit, including words of knowledge, prophetic words, visions, and even dreams. It amazes me to this day that had I not had that dream of the cream bottles over thirty years ago, our ministry today would be very different indeed.

Our four core values are layered on top of a biblical, evangelical, charismatic statement of faith. They are as follows:

1. **F**—A revelation of the **Father's love**, which we received from Jack Winter (see Matt. 11:27; Luke 10:22 NIV).

2. **I**—**Intimacy**, or hearing the voice of God, a value whose discovery we owe to Mark Virkler. Our life and ministry were transformed through this dialogue and intimacy with God.

3. **R**—**Restoration**, teaching, healing and deliverance for life's hurts, with much appreciation to John and Paula Sandford.

4. **E**—And finally a power and love **encounter** from the Holy Spirit. We are so deeply grateful to Claudio

Freidzon and Randy Clark for a contagious imparta-
tion of the Holy Spirit that continues to this day. This
took everything in our ministry to a whole new level
of relationship, healing, and evangelism.

The first three, on which we worked faithfully throughout the
'80s and early '90s, are the fulfillment of my dream about the three
cream bottles. These values prepared us and our church teams for
the fourth bottle of cream: a mighty outpouring of the Holy Spirit
in power and love that would become known as the "Toronto
Blessing." God is so much more than history, tradition, and Bible
study. He pursues us for a dynamic love affair with Father, Son, and
Holy Spirit.

Dreams and their interpretations are therefore of the utmost
spiritual importance. Charity, in her book *Hearing God Through Your
Dreams,* has taken the time to write out a complete inventory of all
the dreams recorded in the Bible for discussion and consideration.
I made a point of reading and meditating on each passage she lists,
and it is a very, very interesting study to say the least.

As Charity points out, dreams are one of the main avenues that
God uses to communicate with His people. Numbers 12:6 clearly
states, *"If there is a prophet among you, I the Lord make Myself known to
him in a vision; I speak with him in a dream"* (ESV).

There is a promise from the Book of Joel that is quoted by Peter
on the Day of Pentecost. Peter says that God's Holy Spirit will be
poured out on all flesh and they will prophesy, see visions, and dream
dreams (see Joel 2:28; Acts 2:17). Dreams are absolutely the will of
God. They always have been—and so much the more now for us
who live in the last of the last days. Joel's prophecy is pointing to
you and me.

Charity does an excellent job of walking the reader through the
various kinds of dreams that one may have from the Lord. Dreams
are usually subjective, she explains, but occasionally objective and

intended for others. They are usually figurative, symbolic, and allegorical, but not always, as occasionally there are literal dreams such as the Angel of the Lord's message to Joseph in Matthew 1:20-23.

She explains how there is a symbolic language to be learned. It varies for every person, as the same symbols often mean different things to different people. If you learn this language, you'll be able to discover powerful and meaningful messages and insights from God.

Charity gives many examples of messages communicated in dreams, both from her own experience and from those of her students, as she has taught and worked with this material for many years. This is so helpful because we, as readers, do not merely want studies and information; rather, we want to enter into the blessing and benefit of having and understanding dreams from the Lord.

I strongly encourage you to read this book. Read it carefully, as a new adventure into the promises of God and new experiences with God.

This book is not the work of an inexperienced amateur. Charity has completed her doctoral degree in biblical studies and brings a wealth of knowledge and experience to this text. Additionally, I can sense in it the lifelong influence of her father, Mark Virkler, who himself is a diligent scholar who has studied dream interpretation for many years.

What a joy to see the next generation (like Charity) so full of godly values and principles and truly going full on after the life of the Kingdom. Well done, Charity, and well done, Mark and Patti. Your daughter and her book are in many ways a wonderful testimony to the faithfulness of God.

All of humanity is desperate to hear a word from God. People are seeking bizarre and unbiblical experiences. They are even searching for occult communications because so many do not know how available God really is. He truly is available to each and every one of us through dreams, through His Word, and through two-way communication with Him. Jesus said, *"My sheep hear My voice…and they follow Me"* (John 10:27).

I was greatly challenged by this book and motivated to focus again on the importance of dreams from the Lord. It helped me to change some things. I now prepare my heart before going to sleep at night, putting paper and pen beside my bed. I take care to see that my final thoughts for the day are biblical and wholesome instead of going to sleep after watching the evening news, which is full of problems and disasters. I am asking God in faith to speak to me more than ever in dreams and revelations in the night.

And do you know what? He's doing it!

Dr. John Arnott
Catch the Fire and Partners in Harvest
Toronto, Canada

PREFACE

BY DR. MARK VIRKLER

It was a Saturday, five o'clock in the evening, in the early 1980s. My Toronto seminar on "How to Hear God's Voice" was over, and I discovered that Reverend Herman Riffel was in town, teaching on Christian dream interpretation. I hurried over to hear him and listened with rapt attention, hanging on every word he spoke. I then invited him to come to Buffalo School of the Bible and be videotaped while he taught our students the art of dream interpretation from a biblical point of view. That began a friendship that lasted many years, until Herman died in his early nineties.

Herman was truly an apostle and trailblazer in the Church in the area of Christian dream interpretation. He was a Baptist pastor who, in his hunger for Christian spirituality, attended the C. G. Jung Institute in Zurich to learn about dream interpretation. Yes, God gives dreams and wisdom even to non-believers (e.g., consider Pharaoh in Genesis 41). Carl Jung was a man who examined fifty thousand dreams in his lifetime. How passionate is that!

Herman accepted those principles of Jung that lined up with Scripture. A few of Herman's principles I have adjusted over the last thirty-five years as I have worked with my dreams and conducted dream workshops. It has been a fascinating journey to discover that God counsels us nightly in His desire to break through into our lives with His wisdom, love, creativity, and protection.

I have moved from ignorance and disdain concerning dreams to honoring and receiving God's grace through them. Some denominations will not even ordain a pastor who believes in dreams. Some "Christian commentaries" say you are psychotic if you have dreams. And yet, one-third of the Bible records dreams and the actions people took as a result of their dreams! How is it possible for "Christianity" to take such a strong stand against dreams when they are found throughout the Bible from Genesis to Revelation?

I had the great privilege of teaching my daughter, Charity, how to hear God's voice when she was just eight years old, and she has not stopped pursuing a deeper relationship with the Lord ever since. She has stacks of journals recording her conversations with Him over the last thirty years, and she has lived her life out of that intimate communion.

When she was a teenager, she began passionately pursuing dream work as another way to connect with "her best friend, Holy Spirit," and has maintained that quest ever since. As a result, Charity receives and remembers dreams nearly every night, understands and interprets them with skill, and has been able to help others discover the meaning of their night visions as well. She has worked hard, and the Spirit has rewarded her with a special anointing that I am sure you will appreciate as you read this book. What a joy to have my children stand on my shoulders and go further than I have!

The bulk of this book is in Charity's voice, as she has taken approximately thirty of my keys to dream interpretation and provided sixty dreams (mostly hers) to illustrate those keys. What a treasure of practical Christian counseling! I know you will be blessed by not only the proficiency with which she interprets her dreams, but also the incredible depth of spiritual truth that is revealed through them. (Obviously I am very proud of the woman of God my daughter has become!) Enjoy her gift!

I have written the chapter on dreams and creativity since that is a subject that is especially close to my heart. In addition, I have written the appendix on hearing God's voice, as that is foundational not only for Christian dream interpretation, but also for the Christian life!

I pray that receiving God's grace through your nightly dreams becomes commonplace for you. His love is precious. His gifts are amazing. His protection, wisdom, encouragement, and creativity are unending, and they are all yours every night of your life.

UNDERSTANDING THE LANGUAGE GOD SPEAKS AT NIGHT

BY DR. CHARITY KAYEMBE

"And it shall come to pass in the last days,' God says, 'that I will pour out of My Spirit on all mankind; and your sons and your daughters shall prophesy, and your young men shall see visions, and your old men shall dream dreams.'"

—ACTS 2:17

We all recognize that it is important to pay attention to visions we receive during the day. They give us a glimpse into the spirit realm, and we know we should write them down, seek to understand them, and apply their message and insights to our lives.

In the Bible, the words *dream* and *vision* are used almost inter-changeably. In Job it says: *"In a dream, a vision of the night, when sound sleep falls on men..."* (Job 33:15). Again, in Isaiah, the same phrase is used: it *"will be like a dream, a vision of the night"* (Isa. 29:7). Scripture also says that *"the mystery was revealed to Daniel in a night vision,"* and later, *"I kept looking in the night visions..."* (Dan. 2:19; 7:13).

So dreams are essentially visions we have at night. Since that is the case, why wouldn't we want to give them just as much credence as visions we have during the day? Considering that in the night our analytical mind is out of the way, we have the potential to receive purer revelation much more readily through our dreams.

I used to compare dream life versus real life, but I don't think that is quite right. Dream life is still real. God is still speaking. We are still engaging the supernatural realm. If visions are real life, then dreams are real life. John 17:3 lets us know what life is about: knowing God and Jesus, whom He sent. So with that as our working definition of what constitutes real life, we can be confident that hearing from God and connecting with His Spirit through dreams definitely qualifies.

I love Psalm 139 and what it reveals about our dreams:

> *How precious are Your thoughts about me, O God. They cannot be numbered! I can't even count them; they outnum-ber the grains of sand! And when I wake up, You are still with me!* (Psalm 139:17-18 NLT)

When we sleep at night we are connecting to the very thoughts of God—the ones He is thinking about us right now. We know that we are with God while we sleep because David says when he wakes up, God is *still* with him.

If for no other reason than this, we want to understand our dreams because we want to know God's thoughts. We want to hear what He has to say about us, about life, about His world. We want to listen to His ideas, feel His heart, and understand His point of view.

We want to know Him, and listening to our dreams is a simple yet strategic way to do just that.

Understanding how God speaks at night is pivotal in our spiritual growth. Being fluent in the language in which someone is speaking to us obviously has profound implications on our ability to communicate effectively and build a closer relationship with that person. By learning God's heart language of dreams we demonstrate our commitment and desire for deeper intimacy with Him. Becoming proficient in interpreting His visions of the night is a game-changer in our walk with the Lord.

Let the journey begin!

Chapter 1

Bridges to the Supernatural: How Dreams Connect Us to God

"He gives to His beloved even in his sleep."
—Psalm 127:2

God does incredible things through dreams. And they count! Did you know that God gave King Solomon his legendary gift of wisdom in a dream? (See 1 Kings 3:5-15.) God also established the Abrahamic Covenant in a dream (see Gen. 15:12-21). God warned Pharaoh how to save his people from famine through a dream (see Gen. 41:1-37). God gave Jacob a creative business strategy through a dream (see Gen. 31:11-13). God directed Israel to go to Egypt and encouraged Gideon to go to war through dreams (see Gen. 46:1-7; Judg. 7:9-18).

And lest we think that such instances are confined to the Old Testament, the very first stories we read in the New Testament involve dreams and visions as well. We need look no further than Joseph, the husband of Mary. Joseph received messages from angels through his dreams, and the first two chapters of the Gospel of Matthew record no fewer than four of his life-altering night visions (see Matt. 1:20-24; 2:13-14, 19-21, 22-23). That is a significant way to kick off the New Testament!

According to First Corinthians 10:11, these are examples by which we are to live. Our lives are supposed to match this. Considering these precedents, have you ever wondered how many blessings we miss out on by not seeing dreams the way God does? Clearly Scripture illustrates that dreams are a legitimate connection to the realm of the spirit and a bridge to the kingdom of Heaven. This is why we want to learn more about dreams—if for no other reason than enlightened self-interest!

As we explore many of God's dream principles and promises together in this book we will soon find out that the whole Bible—from Genesis to Revelation—is overflowing with dreams and visions. In fact, when we total up all dreams, visions, stories about them, and actions resulting from them, we find that approximately one-third of the Bible is supernatural visionary encounter! That is equal in size to the New Testament, which demonstrates God spoke through spiritual pictures consistently and continually. Far from being random occurrences, dreams are, in fact, God's *modus operandi*.

Most exciting of all, we will discover what happened to those who were listening to God in their dreams. The ones who understood this nighttime language met with outstanding success as they awoke and acted on the divine revelations. Once we see for ourselves all the Lord accomplished through dreams, we won't want to be left out!

In our twenty-first century Western culture we have been conditioned to barely give dreams a second thought. While it may be easy to dismiss them because they don't make sense to us, they are only confusing because we haven't learned God's dream language yet. That is what we are going to discover in this book—how to understand the language God speaks at night.

More than any other reason, we want to listen to our dreams because doing so blesses God. He is a communicating God, speaking to us while we are awake as well as asleep. He told us to *"pray without ceasing,"* which means He wants to be having a conversation with us continually (1 Thess. 5:17). He wants our hearts connected with His all day and all night.

Dr. Virkler's Dream Key

SOME SCIENTIFIC OBSERVATIONS

Sleep laboratories have proven that everyone dreams one to two hours each night during a certain period of sleep known as "alpha level," which is light sleep. Every ninety-minute cycle of sleep begins with alpha, then goes into deeper sleep, which is called "theta," and finally deepest sleep, which is called "delta."

At the close of the first ninety-minute cycle each night, the individual returns to alpha-level sleep, where he has a short, five-minute dream period. The next time he cycles up to alpha, he has a ten-minute dream period. The third time in alpha, the dream period is about fifteen minutes, and so on. Thus, the average person sleeping for eight hours a night will dream for about one to two hours of that time.

Alpha-level sleep is where one has what is called "Rapid Eye Movement" (REM). REM is exactly what it sounds like: the eyes of the dreamer begin to move rapidly. It is believed that he is actually "watching" the scenes in the dream.

By observing the alpha-level sleep when REM occurs, researchers in sleep laboratories have determined when a person is dreaming and how much time is spent dreaming in an average night. They have discovered that if they wake a person every time REM begins, preventing him from dreaming, after about three nights the individual will begin to show signs of having a nervous breakdown.

Clearly dreams are an inner release mechanism that helps provide us with emotional balance and maintain our sanity. Dreams can be considered guardians of our mental and emotional well-being.

WHAT THIS BOOK ISN'T ABOUT

While many Christians believe God can speak through dreams, they consider it to be a rather out-of-the-ordinary experience. They may have felt the Lord lead them through a dream or two here or there over the years. They may have received a very literal dream where Jesus came to them and spoke clearly and gave them new direction for their life. And that is awesome!

God definitely does do that. He did it in the Bible, and He certainly continues to do that today. We all have been blessed by the incredible testimonies from former Muslims who were visited by Jesus in their dreams at night and, as a result, had their hearts softened to the Gospel and became Christians. Praise God! Those are powerful stories that are wonderful to hear.

However, that is not what this book is about. If the dream is obvious, and the message is spoken literally, and you understand exactly what it means upon awakening, then you don't need any interpretation. You comprehend the meaning, and nothing is lost in translation. And yes, every once in a while we are all blessed with such night visions. Hallelujah!

But what about all the other nights? If we sleep for eight hours every night, that is a third of our lives. Is it just wasted? Just something our physical bodies need in order to function, with no other eternal or spiritual significance? Definitely not. The Bible shows us that God is a bit of a "green" God in that He doesn't let things go to waste. Psalms says that He collects our tears in a bottle so that they are not squandered (see Ps. 56:8). Rather than allowing our pain to lack purpose, God redeems our suffering.

Similarly, how could an infinitely brilliant Creator forget about our sleep time and let our dreams be worthless? He doesn't. He speaks through dreams, and He does it often. Not once in a lifetime, not once every few years, but all the time.

Dreams are a gateway to the spirit realm, where God lives. They are regular and reliable. They are accessible and available to everyone every night, and they provide a meaningful, powerful way to hear from Heaven and connect to the very heart of God.

There is a beautiful Scripture hidden in the Song of Solomon that reveals what happens as we rest at night: "*I slept but my heart was awake. Listen! My beloved is knocking...*" (Song of Sol. 5:2 NIV). While our physical body is asleep in this world, our heart is very much awake and alive to the spirit, conversing with our beloved Heavenly Bridegroom, the Lord Himself.

Science is finally catching up with Old Testament wisdom, and we can now even study their principles to corroborate this profound understanding of our inherent duality. Incredibly, the truths dovetail seamlessly. Let's examine what quantum physics has to say about this amazing biblical revelation.

SUPER WHAT?

One of my favorite quotes is "We're not human beings having a spiritual experience. We are spiritual beings having a temporary human experience." (This quote attributed to Pierre Chardin.)

There is a term in quantum physics called "superposition," and it describes a situation in which something is fully in two places at the same time. Jesus said about Himself, *"No one has ascended to heaven but He who came down from heaven, that is, the Son of Man who is in heaven"* (John 3:13 NKJV). He was on earth and He was in Heaven simultaneously.

We also are living on earth at the same time we are seated in the heavenlies (see Eph. 2:4-6). We are spirits, and we can move in the spirit world easily by praying to God and connecting with Him. Concurrently, we are also in a physical, flesh-and-blood body, which makes it equally convenient for us to function in this tangible world.

Therefore, we are perfectly, uniquely, gloriously designed to be the bridge. We are the connectors and the conduits that bridge the spiritual realm with the material realm and bring Heaven to earth. It happens through us. And one of the most natural times it happens is while we dream.

JACOB'S LADDER

We see this clearly in Genesis 28:12-17 when the Lord reaffirms to Jacob the covenant He made with his grandfather, Abraham. In a dream, Jacob sees a ladder set on the earth with its top reaching to Heaven and angels of God ascending and descending it. When he wakes up, he declares, *"Surely the Lord is in this place, and I did not know it.... How awesome is this place! This is none other than the house of God, and this is the gate of heaven"* (Gen. 28:16-17).

This verse tells us that the house of God is the gate of Heaven. We know that in the New Covenant, each one of us, as Christ followers, is a temple of God (see 1 Cor. 6:19). We are the house in which the Spirit of God dwells, which means we are the gate of Heaven (see 1 Cor. 3:16-17). We are the doorway and the ladder that connect the supernatural realm to the natural world.

In John 1:51 Jesus enlightens Nathaniel about this revelation: *"Truly I say to you, you will see the heavens opened and the angels of God ascending and descending on the Son of Man."* We know what happened through Jesus can happen through us, and even greater works than these (see John 14:12). Jesus explained that He was the entry point allowing the presence of Heaven to flood our atmosphere, and as He is, so also are we in this world (see 1 John 4:17).

THE OBSERVER EFFECT

One reason why dreams are so important is that they give us a glimpse into the supernatural realm so we are able to see what Heaven sees. We can see ourselves the way God sees us: without limits and boundaries. Isn't that what often happens in our dreams—for example, when we are flying (*sans* airplane!)?

As we begin exploring the world of dreams, let's keep in the back of our minds what I trust you will agree is one of the most intriguing concepts of the entire unfolding revelation. Again, it has to do with quantum physics and a key feature of it. In fact, the "observer effect" is universally understood to be the most mysterious yet foundational principle in the entire field of study. A simple definition of the observer effect is that by observing something, we affect and change it.

The quantum world is a world of potential, where every possible outcome is available at any moment in time. This is the world of faith, where we know that all things are possible to them that believe (see Mark 9:23).

We see this truth established scientifically by a phenomenon called "wave function collapse." An electron or a photon (the stuff that makes up matter and light) exists in a wave of possibility; however, when it is observed, it collapses into a single particle. The simple act of being watched or measured by a scientist's equipment collapses all the possibilities that are distributed along the wave, and it becomes manifested and locked into a specific place and time as a single electron or photon.

This is a picture in the natural world of what happens when we pray. In the realm of the spirit, every possibility is available to us—for example, healing, provision, and divine perspective. We want to bring those heavenly resources into our physical dimension, to have those infinite possibilities of blessing in the spirit "collapse" and materialize in our tangible world. We want to see the heavenly waves collapse into a definite manifestation, a "particle" of healing or blessing—something that is concrete and available in our localized dimension of time and space.

How do we do this? Through vision. By seeing. Science calls it "observing," and the Bible calls it "witnessing." Once the Holy Spirit has come upon us, we are empowered to be witnesses; we are anointed to be observers (see Acts 1:8).

We observe Jesus, and we witness the spiritual world of Heaven. Jesus wants a witness to His life, the one that He is living right now. By seeing Him and His realm of the spirit through visions by day and by night, we are collapsing the waves of glory into our atmosphere. We are bringing Heaven to earth.

In summary, the observer effect demonstrates that by our very act of seeing something, we change it. The reason this is so profound and relevant to dream work is because Scripture is saturated with messages about the importance of looking and seeing: "Fix our eyes on Jesus" (see Heb. 12:2). "Look at things that are unseen" (see 2 Cor. 4:18). "Set our minds on the spirit" (see Rom. 8:4-7). "Focus our attention on the things above" (see Col. 3:1-2). And most of all: "Receive the anointing to be witnesses" (see Acts 1:8). Watchers. We have been baptized by His Spirit, who breaks open the supernatural realm for us, empowering us to be observers, lookers, and seers.

WHAT JESUS IS DOING

We know Jesus did only what He saw His Father do in the spirit realm and He only spoke what He heard His Father say from that supernatural realm (see John 5:19; 8:38). So yes, we absolutely do the same. We can look into the spirit world through dreams and visions and model what is going on there. We can copy and imitate it, and we should. That is important.

According to quantum physics, however, much more is happening than we even realize. That is, before we actually imitate and model Jesus and live into the truth we see in our dreams, before we even actively follow His lead, our very act of observation has already played a part in creating in our world what we see in His. By seeing and agreeing with the meaning of our night visions, we help bring about their messages in waking life.

We want to "change" what we observe in the dream world so that it is not just a supernatural reality, but also something that is visible in the natural realm. We want to "affect" the truth of the spiritual world so that it is evidenced in the material world, too.

Vision is a bridge that helps move the Kingdom of Heaven from the spiritual side of the realm over to the tangible side of it. Our seeing, our act of observation, effects an outcome the same way physicists have proven in their laboratories. We witness Jesus and His Kingdom while we sleep, and that very looking and listening changes our waking world by manifesting His reality on this side of the dimension.

Phil Mason, Spiritual Director of New Earth Tribe in Byron Bay, Australia, elucidates the spirit/quantum connection in his excellent work *Quantum Glory*. He teaches that God is the Ultimate Observer and that because He sees all, everything exists.[1] Every possibility is present in the spiritual realm, but God wants us to co-create with

Him and bring what exists in Heaven to earth. He has already made it available and authorized it; we just need to co-sign His check.

A powerful way we do this is by looking into Heaven and seeing what He is doing. We "measure" what is in Heaven, compare it with how things are on earth, and we realize they don't match up. We see in the spirit realm what He has available to us, and then we agree with what we see. We say "yes" to all that God intends, and that act of visual agreement becomes the bridge over which the promises of Heaven can cross. Heaven is released to earth through us, specifically through our act of seeing—through our observation, through our dreams, our visions of the night.

The resources of Heaven remain in a spiritual state of possibility until someone on earth observes them. Through that observation, the potential blessing is released to materialize in our natural world. Through our dreams we can look at a spiritual reality that is not yet tangible in this physical dimension and, by observation, cause that supernatural potential to manifest in our here and now.

Jesus is the leader whose example we follow, and He observed (see John 5:19-20). He looked (see John 8:38). He listened to the spirit (see John 5:30). So we get to do these things whether we understand the full ramifications of our obedience or not. By practicing the biblical art of dream interpretation and looking at and listening to the spirit world, we are actually partnering with God as co-creators, manifesting His Kingdom of Heaven in our physical realm of earth.

CO-CREATING WITH GOD

"The heavens are the Lord's, but the earth He has given to the sons of men" (Ps. 115:16). That's us. This is our earth that we get to make look like Heaven. In his book *Rediscovering the Kingdom*, the late Dr. Myles Munroe talks about how God wants to "colonize earth with Heaven."[2] We are the ambassadors and co-creators. We are the

observers and witnesses. God has given us a part to play. He does the work. He creates the miracles and brings Heaven to earth, but He does it with us. In us. Through us.

Dreaming God's dreams and watching His visions, both during the day and at night, are key to manifesting Heaven on earth. Observation plays an essential role in bridging the Kingdom. Once we learn how to see what Jesus sees, we will begin to heal the rift within the realm.

Pastor Bill Johnson of Bethel Church in Redding, California, teaches that whatever we are conscious of we manifest. According to him, we always release the reality of the world of which we are most aware. So if we are cognizant of the atmosphere of Heaven, the peace of His presence, and Christ Himself, we can impart Him. We can radiate His life and release His power into our world.

There is a fascinating dream saga in the Old Testament that is filled with promise and precedent. Remember the story of Jacob and his striped and speckled sheep? Jacob's father-in-law, Laban, was taking advantage of Jacob and kept changing his wages. God came to Jacob in a dream and told him what to do about it. Genesis 30 and 31 tell us how the Lord instructed Jacob that when the strongest, healthiest animals of the flock mated, he should put striped branches by the water in front of them.

Jacob acted on the revelation from his dream. The surprising result was that when the strong sheep looked upon the striped branches, they produced offspring that were striped. The best of the animals became striped just like the branches they observed. Laban had agreed that Jacob could have all the striped sheep for himself so this was how God provided a strong, healthy flock for Jacob's own possession (see Gen. 30:31–31:17).

Through a dream the Lord gave Jacob a creative business idea that blessed him financially, making him *"exceedingly prosperous"*

(Gen. 30:43). That right there is a good reason to listen to our dreams and act on them!

I had found this story a bit perplexing until I heard a pastor's teaching on how water reflects, so it is a place of reflection and meditation. This is a picture of how we are to meditate on the Word and be changed by it (see James 1:23-25). Similarly, the Lord spoke the following to my dad in his journaling several years ago: *"Whatever you focus on grows within you, and whatever grows within you, you become."*

That is what this Old Testament story demonstrates: whatever you focus on you become. This is the same revelation Paul disclosed in his epistle: as we behold in a mirror the glory of the Lord, we are transformed into the same image (see 2 Cor. 3:18). This was also the meaning of a dream I recently had.

THE DREAM OF A 3-D PRINTER

In the dream, I was in my house and went downstairs to the treadmill room. There, I got very close to my brother Josh, and he ended up sitting on my hand! As I was looking at him he took my picture. He was then going to print it using a 3-D printer.

God's message through the dream was exciting and the interpretation encouraging. The house represented me, and the action of going downstairs pictured my going down deep within myself to my heart. This is the place where I "exercise" godliness and my salvation is "worked out" (remember, I was in the exercise room of our house).

My brother Joshua represents *Yeshua*, Jesus, my elder Brother. His act of sitting on my hand is a picture of my coming into deeper covenant and agreement with Him (see Gen. 24:2-3). As I moved closer and looked at Him with unveiled face, I beheld His countenance. He took my image (picture) and transformed it into other dimensions.

We want to see ourselves the way God sees us, through His lens. His picture of us is more magnificent than we could imagine, and once we see ourselves the way God sees us, we are changed. This scene was a dream picture of Second Corinthians 3:18. I observed the glory of God, and the glory changed. It was no longer only a spiritual reality; the glory transformed me, manifesting in my physical reality. I looked upon Jesus in my dream, and as a result, He made me look more like Him. God wants to see His image in us. We are His children, and He desires a striking family resemblance!

It is significant that Scripture says, "We behold *as in a mirror* the glory of the Lord, and we are changed" (see 2 Cor. 3:18). We are not just looking at a beautiful sunrise and marveling at the glory we see there. A mirror is where we look at ourselves.

According to the observer effect, what is looked at and witnessed is what is changed. "We look as in a mirror" so we are observing ourselves and we also are simultaneously beholding the glory of the Lord in that same mirror image (see 2 Cor. 3:18). His glory is within us. As we focus on Him, His holiness, His presence, and His glory, we become transformed into that image.

If we look in the mirror and see just a person, we have not looked closely enough (see 2 Pet. 1:4). The apostle Paul admonished the Corinthians for *"acting like mere humans"* (1 Cor. 3:3 NIV). How could he say that? Isn't that what they were? No, Paul understood the revelation about which Peter and John wrote: We have the DNA of divinity (see 1 Pet. 1:23). We are the supernatural progeny of God Himself (see 1 John 3:9). We are not of this world (see John 17:16).

My dream message encapsulated these concepts specifically through the aspect of the 3-D printer. In a process that I don't really understand but know often involves light, 3-D printing makes three-dimensional solid objects from a digital file. It starts by making a virtual design of the object you want to create. This is an excellent picture in the natural for what God does with us spiritually.

At our new birth, when we were born from above by His Spirit, God made a virtual design of us in the supernatural realm as new creations in Him. Like a digital file, our spirits are invisible and intangible. However, God wants His spiritual life in us to become a tangible reality in the earthly realm too.

So through the light of His glory, in a process that is beyond our understanding, God recreates us layer by layer more perfectly into His image, manifesting the presence of His Spirit in a three-dimensional world through us. We are destined to be conformed to the image of His Son through a supernatural multidimensional upgrade (see Rom. 8:29).

This is a brief synopsis of what we do through our dreams: we observe them and their messages from Heaven, which causes the spiritual reality in them to be manifested in our natural world. Jacob in Genesis, Paul in the New Testament, the observer effect in quantum physics, my 3-D printer dream last week—they are all saying the same thing. Each one confirms the scientific, scriptural, spiritual truth that observation causes transformation.

PORTALS OF GLORY

We are infinitely more powerful than we have ever imagined. We are God's image bearers in this world, and by observing His spiritual Kingdom we help cause it to be on the earth. We get glimpses of it every night. We see snapshots of the spirit through our dreams. We look upon and witness Jesus, and that is part of how He manifests and how His glory transforms our atmosphere.

We witness and observe and agree with the truths our dreams reveal, and God uses our eyes on Him and His realm as the supernatural connection, the transfer point.

It is by His Spirit joined to our spirits released through our earthly bodies into the physical world that the Kingdom comes, that the supernatural invades the natural, that the invisible truth becomes visible reality, and that the answer materializes to His prayer and to ours: *"Thy will be done on earth as it is in heaven"* (Matt. 6:10 KJV).

Chapter 2

The ABCs of Dream Work: How to Translate the Language God Speaks at Night

"Then they said to him, 'We have had a dream and there is no one to interpret it.' Then Joseph said to them, 'Do not interpretations belong to God? Tell it to me, please.'"
—Genesis 40:8

Now that we have established the grand backdrop and incredible significance of dream work, let's get down to the nuts and bolts of it. We will be very practical and examine what dream interpretation looks like up close and personal, learning to use the "Key Question Approach" when translating dream language. We will explore each of these questions in-depth in this chapter, but briefly they are as follows:

- In the dream, what was I doing? This is the *key action*.

- In the dream, how was I feeling? This is the *key emotion*.

- How do the dream's main action and emotion match up with my waking life? In what area of my life am I experiencing a similar action or feeling? This is the *setting* of the dream.

As we begin our investigative journey, the most important principle we need to understand about dreams is that they are highly symbolic. They rarely are literal, but instead almost everything in them—the people, places, and things—usually represents something else.

For example, we have all kinds of symbols in our faith. We don't see a picture of a cross and start wondering about the type of wood out of which it is made. Instead, we immediately associate that with Jesus and our salvation. Similarly, we know that biblically speaking, a dove can be a symbol for the Holy Spirit.

Dr. Virkler's Dream Key

The symbols will come from the dreamer's life, so ask, "What does this symbol mean to me?" Or, if working on another's dream, ask, "What does this symbol mean to you?"

For example, Joseph worked out in the fields, and he dreamed of sheaves, sun, moon, and stars (see Gen. 37:1-11). These images surround a shepherd boy who lives in the fields. Nebuchadnezzar, a king, dreamed of statues of gold, which surround kings who live in palaces (see Dan. 2:31).

DANCING WITH OUR HERO

My friend Elena was born in Russia so her symbols come out of that country and culture and, as such, are totally different from mine. She had a wonderful dream, which she has graciously given me permission to share, that illustrates both the personalized uniqueness of our dream symbols as well as the beautiful heart of Jesus, the Lover of our soul. Below is Elena's dream in her own words:

> I had a different dream the other night. There was some sort of dancing party with lots of people on the dancing floor, and I was dancing with the Russian actor all of the dances. I had a strong feeling of being safe and cared for, and I knew he would not let me go and protect me from anything (now, he is a very strong, big guy). His roles in the movies are usually a brave hero who is doing the right things, protects the weak, and fights the evil and stuff like that...and I have not seen a movie with him at least since I moved to the USA.
>
> What also surprised me in the dream is that he did not care, being so famous and all, that people will see him dancing for so long with someone like me. As we were talking and I called him by name in my dream, I realized it is my husband's name—Michael! Now that has to mean something good!

HOW JESUS REVEALED HIMSELF IN THE DREAM

The main emotions experienced in this dream were feeling safe, special, cared for, and protected. The main action of the dream was being chosen to dance with a strong, brave, larger-than-life hero. This is a perfect representation of God because just like the actor had done in movies, Jesus protects us and makes us feel safe, cared for, and loved. He always does the right thing, fights off our enemies for us, and saves the day.

In addition, we may feel that we do not measure up well with Jesus, that He is totally out of our league, like a big-name celebrity actor would be. Nevertheless, He has chosen us and honored us by calling us His own children. We are the bride of Christ, and He wants to have the pleasure of a dance with us.

Elena got to experience those scriptural truths—how it *feels* to be chosen. Now she understands more what it's like to be honored and loved in that way because she just lived it in her dream. We don't know the difference between something happening in waking life or dream life. We've all experienced having our hearts race and our palms get sweaty from a scary dream. Dreams affect us! And positive dreams like this one affect us, too.

If we fall asleep and in our dreams get to dance with Jesus and be showered with attention and affection from our Beloved, that's a pretty good night's rest. We wake up from that in a much better place emotionally and spiritually. Then, when we are tempted to feel unloved or unworthy, we can simply go back to the dream. We relive it and re-experience those feelings of acceptance, of being special and set apart and cared for. We meditate on how good it felt to be chosen and let that bring us back to a place of peace and joy.

LAYERS AND LEVELS

Sometimes our dream symbols mean one thing on a certain level of interpretation and something else as another layer of meaning unfolds. It doesn't have to be one or the other. As long as both messages click with the dreamer and "seem good to that person and the Holy Ghost," then we can safely assume that dual meanings and a multi-dimensional revelation are hidden within the dream (see Acts 15:28).

Scripturally speaking, we find this principle in many Old Testament prophecies. Especially in the case of Isaiah, we can easily see how his visions from the Lord actually had at least three layers of meaning and fulfillment. They spoke of 1) the return of the Israelites from Captivity, 2) the coming of the Messiah and establishment of the Kingdom of Heaven, and 3) the Second Coming and the Final Consummation. Though varied, obviously all these levels of revelation are true.

And so it is with us. For example, in Elena's dream, the actor and her husband had the same name. On one level, the dream is reminding her of how her husband, Michael, is her knight in shining armor. It is letting her see him clearly as the hero that he is in her life and showing her how he is her protector and how he fights for her. The covenant of marriage is an epic love story, and she is the leading lady.

Another layer of meaning in that symbol of the hero who shares her husband's name can be seen in Isaiah 54: *"Your husband is your Maker, whose name is the Lord of hosts; and your Redeemer is the Holy One of Israel, who is called the God of all the earth. For the Lord has called you...with everlasting lovingkindness..."* (Isa. 54:5-8).

Elena lived these verses in her dream, feeling what it is like to be specially called out and chosen by her Heavenly Husband, the Lord.

SYMBOLS PERSONAL TO THE DREAMER

It is also significant that Jesus shared her nationality in the dream. The fact that her hero, Jesus, came to her as a Russian man is profound because it showed Elena that He is just like her. It tells her that He understands where she is coming from, that He's been there, too. I love how the Lord identified Himself with her through that special symbol.

Lastly, the ultimate message of the dream is found in the main action, in that Elena was chosen to dance with Jesus—not work for Him; dance with Him. That is what God wants—to dance with us, to love on us, and to have fun and do life together with us.

So often we are afraid God is demanding something hard or difficult, and we worry that if we surrender to Him, He will make us do work that we don't want to do. Really, the desire of His heart is relationship—conversation, attention, intimacy, friendship, love. And what is a perfectly beautiful symbol for that? A dance partner. Through the dream, God is saying, "Elena, I want to be a part of your life. What you're already doing and what you already want to do—let's just do it together."

My friend Ivey Rorie shared this amazing thought in one of her *Word of the Day* blog posts: "The prayer we prayed for salvation was not a ticket to get into Heaven. It was a marriage proposal." Yes! I love that. And that is exactly what this dream allowed Elena to experience firsthand and to feel—God's love for her. The Great Invitation of our faith is simply accepting His hand to dance through life together with Him.

Dr. Virkler's Dream Key

The dream generally speaks of the concerns your heart is currently facing. So first ask, "What issues was I processing the day before I had the dream?"

For example, Paul was wondering where to go next on his missionary journey and had a dream of a Macedonian man motioning for him to come on over (see Acts 16:6-10). Nebuchadnezzar was thinking his kingdom would go on forever, and he had a dream of a tree being chopped off at the roots (see Dan. 4:1-18).

Joseph wanted to break off his engagement with Mary, but as he considered it, an angel appeared in his dream and changed his mind (see Matt. 1:19-20). Once you know the thoughts that were on the dreamer's heart when he or she fell asleep, it is much easier to draw out the meaning of the dream.

SIGNIFICANT SETTINGS

The setting of a dream is like the legend of a treasure map: we don't understand one without the other. We need to first consider the setting of our waking life in order to find the buried treasure of our dream message.

For example, I was leading a group exploring dream interpretation and one of the ladies shared a dream that everyone was sure had no meaning. They insisted, "Not all dreams are significant. We don't have to get a message from every one—especially this one!"

However, as soon as Marie told us her dream, I immediately had an idea of what it was about and asked her, "So are you feeling like you're not ready for something? Is there an area in your waking life that you don't feel prepared for or that you're worried about?"

That was it. Both she and her husband understood right away exactly what the dream was referencing. She said her job had been making her feel anxious lately. As confirmation, the symbols and actions in her dream matched up with her work situation perfectly. She realized God was speaking through the dream, encouraging her to process her feelings of anxiety with Him rather than trying to handle everything on her own. He was calling her into His peace and inviting her to rest in Him.

This simple story illustrates one of the most fundamental principles of dream work: we must always consider the *setting*. The setting of our dream is the context, what is going on in our waking life at the time we have the dream. To determine it, we should ask ourselves the following questions: "What were we working on during the day? What had we been thinking about as we fell asleep that night? What have we been praying for?"

The contextual background of our waking life sets the stage for the dream. Once we take the setting into consideration, it becomes much easier to pinpoint the area of our life to which the dream is speaking.

Dr. Virkler's Dream Key

Next, we want to look at the main *action* of the dream. Ask the Holy Spirit to show you the symbolism of the action.

For example, if the symbol in your dream is that your car is going backward, ask, "In what way do I feel that I am going backward? How am I not moving forward in an area of my life?" If someone else is driving your car in the dream, ask, "In what way is this person driving or controlling my life (e.g., my reactions, attitudes, behaviors) at this time?" or, "How is the characteristic that this person symbolizes controlling me?" (See the section later on the symbolism of people in your dreams.) If you are falling, ask, "In what way do I feel like I am falling, losing ground, or lacking control in my life at this time?" If you are soaring, ask, "In what way, or in what area of my life, do I feel like I am flying—rising above my problems or my abilities?" If you are being chased, ask, "How and why do I feel like I am being pursued or hunted?" If you are naked, ask, "In what way do I feel like I am exposed or vulnerable?"

If you dream of dying, ask, "What is dying within me?" (This may be a good thing, for perhaps you are dying to pride, or to self, or to workaholism.) Remember, actions in the dream are to be viewed symbolically. If your dream wanted to really show you that you were going to die, it would picture that event symbolically. For example, just a few days before his assassination, President Lincoln dreamed of a casket.

Once you have used the feeling and action of the dream to identify the aspect of your life that the vision is revealing to you, the rest of the symbols will be much easier to identify.

THE GOLDEN FERRARI

I was praying about being found in Christ—really, inside of Him (see Phil. 3:8-9). I had been meditating on verses about this revelation, and then I had a dream. In it I was given a brand-new shiny Ferrari that was golden in color. I got into it and drove it, and it was awesome! Being inside that Ferrari was definitely where I wanted to be.

The main feeling of this dream was extreme gratitude, and the main action was being found inside the Ferrari and moving with it, inside of it. This reminded me of Acts 17:28: *"In Him we live and move and exist."* It also reminded me of the Israelites in the wilderness: *"The Lord was going before them in a pillar of cloud by day to lead them on the way, and in a pillar of fire by night to give them light, that they might travel by day and by night"* (Ex. 13:21). The idea is that we want to move with God, within His glory.

Why did God use a golden Ferrari as the symbol for Him and His glory? Well, gold is a fiery color, similar to that pillar of fire. It is also a heavenly color (see Rev. 21:21).

And a Ferrari—that's Italian, right? Definitely not from around here—like God's glory. It's from Heaven so it's also not from around here. The Ferrari is exotic, not to mention extremely powerful. And it is more lavish and luxurious than I need, but that's God for you—always doing exceedingly abundantly more than we could ask or imagine (see Eph. 3:20).

The message of this night vision encouraged me to see how I *am* inside of God and His glory. He *is* moving me. My prayers have been answered—and in a way that is even better and more extravagant than I had thought. This confirmation from God resulted in my feeling in my waking life exactly as I had in the dream—extremely grateful and extraordinarily blessed. I am inside of Christ! And that makes it very easy for Him to move and position me exactly where He wants me to be.

Dr. Virkler's Dream Key

Because the vast majority of dreams are about your inner self, begin the process of interpreting your dream with the assumption that it probably is about something you are or should be dealing with in your own life right now.

Isolate the *feeling* of the dream. How did you feel upon first awakening? Was your heart pounding in fear? Were you confused, frustrated, angry, rejected, or threatened? Did you feel loved, excited, happy, or content? Did you feel exposed, unprepared, or disappointed? What was the overall emotion that the dream evoked? In what aspect of your life are you also feeling this emotion?

If it is not immediately obvious to you, ask the Lord to reveal it to you.

THE SURPRISE PARTY

During my waking hours God can tell me that He has everything under control. I can read verses about the good plans He has concerning me and how His thoughts for me are full of hope, prosperity and peace (see Jer. 29:11). In addition to reading these

Scriptures, the Lord will even speak to me personally in my two-way journaling and quiet times with Him, letting me know He is definitely up to awesome things behind the scenes.

Sounds great! But what if these blessings don't seem to be playing out in my life right now? I mean, how should all these wonderful promises make me feel? It looks good on paper, but at this specific moment in time, maybe I don't feel especially thought about or well cared for. What then?

Then I go to sleep, and I dream God's dreams and sense His heart. I remember one time I was feeling a bit forgotten about and was wondering where God was in all of the goings-on in my life. Granted, I knew He was there; it just didn't feel like it.

So He graciously gave me a dream in which I was going to a reunion—at least that is what I thought. But then when I arrived, it turned out to be a huge, elaborate surprise party—for me! So many people had come for the celebration, and there were decorations galore, and delicious food, and colorfully wrapped gifts.

Totally unbeknownst to me, all this organizing had been going on for weeks. The attendees had been thinking about me all this time, and their thoughts were for good and for peace. They had been planning and working hard on how to bless me best!

I felt loved, cared for, and thought about. I was overcome by the generosity, enthusiasm, and time that were invested just to honor me. It was a special dream, and I woke up in a very good place. I got the revelation: God is arranging blessing for me. He is orchestrating great things!

I just saw it. I lived it in my dream, and more than that, I experienced the comfort of His kindness and grace showered upon me. That was the main emotion in my dream, and I realized that God was encouraging me to press on, trust His surprise celebrations, and believe in all the good things He has been preparing for me.

Dr. Virkler's Dream Key

Religion tries to get to God through developing theologies and setting one's will. God comes to man by directly encountering man's heart and spirit with His voice, prophecy, dream, vision, and anointing.

THE BRIDAL TRILOGY

As the above dream key suggests, religion is all about a believer setting his will, whereas God would much prefer to do a supernatural work of grace in our hearts. Best-case scenario, they both end up with the same results, but trying to use our willpower all the time is exhausting.

Case in point: I had been trying not to be critical of some things I was seeing in my brothers and sisters in Christ and the Church. I knew I wasn't supposed to be judgmental, but I was still struggling with it. (This was the "setting" from my waking life.) So God, in His grace and patience, decided to give me three dreams on three consecutive nights that showed me His perspective of His Church. She is His Bride, and as it turns out, He's crazy about her.

First Night, Dream One: Running over the Bride

DREAM: I almost ran over a bride with my car. I sobbed inconsolably as I prayed for her. She was fine though and went on with her life.

ACTION: Recklessness

FEELING: Fear over unknown consequences (Would I get sued? Go to jail?)

INTERPRETATION: God showed me how, with negative thoughts and words toward the Church, I was running over

His Bride. Just like a new husband on his wedding day would be, Jesus was heartbroken.

Concerning that part of the dream, God specifically said, *"You're right, it's about the Bride of Christ—My Bride, My Church. I wanted to help you so that you do not feel as often the need to rail-road her, or 'throw her under the bus.' I wanted you to see that as imperfect as she may be, she's Mine. She's whom I have chosen. She's the one I died for and the one My soul loves. Get the picture?"*

If that wasn't enough to convince me, I remember how very sad and remorseful I felt in the dream. It wasn't altruistic compassion, though; it was selfish concern for my own well-being. I was worried about what was best for me and what was going to happen to me as a result of what I had done. Good grief. God used even that by showing me in the dream how others may go on with their lives but the judgments I hold against them will negatively affect me. The bride moved on with her life while I was still crying.

I still took this as a positive and encouraging dream because if you'll notice, I didn't actually run over the bride; I just almost did. I considered this more of a warning dream of what not to do and why.

Second Night, Dream Two: Family Feud

DREAM: My husband Leo and I were in the kitchen fighting—violently.

ACTION: War within our members, a house divided against itself

FEELING: Fear, confusion, distrust

SETTING: In waking life, I had recorded the dream and journaling from the Lord about the previous night's dream. Our marriage is awesome and we were doing great so this wasn't about us personally. Remember, dreams are rarely to be taken literally.

INTERPRETATION: God was telling me, *"Yeah, that is a picture of My Church fighting among itself. It's that bad, that horrible. They don't see that they're all part of the same Body (Mine). They don't see that they're all part of the same house and the same family.*

"So I just wanted you to see it, see the division in My Body the way I see it. Everyone in the world is interconnected, quantum entangled, right? But that goes to an even deeper and more profound spiritual level when you talk about believers specifically.

"That's a big reason they're not getting further faster. They continually shoot themselves in the foot (and the arm and the face) when they entertain disunity and focus on disagreements and division and strife that separate.

"But the main thing is, I just wanted to get this off My chest. I just wanted to share with you what I'm going through and how I'm feeling about things. I wanted you to see things as I see them—see the Church the way that I do, see My Bride the way I see her. I wanted to share My heart with you because I knew you would be gentle with it."

Third Night, Dream Three: Didn't Recognize the Bride

DREAM: I went to the wedding of a friend of a friend, whom I had never met before. I had a conversation with a woman, but somehow I didn't recognize that she was the bride so I didn't say the appropriate things to her.

ACTION: Being oblivious

FEELING: Duh!

SETTING: Last two nights of bridal dreams

INTERPRETATION: One lesson to learn from this is that if I really recognized the Church as Christ's Bride whom He dearly loves, I would treat her differently.

Another truth that the Lord brought out was that she is me; I am the Church. Regarding that revelation God said: *"You got it, girl. We're hitting this picture from every angle, aren't we? The main idea was, you would have acted differently if you knew who she was, right? I mean, it wasn't that you treated her poorly at all; you were friendly and kind. But you would have treated her differently and honored her with congratulations if you recognized who she was.*

"And so it is with you. You are My bride so please regard yourself as such. The promised bride of the Son of God? That's you! That's how I see you. The dream was meant to show you that when you realize who you really are, you will act differently. I want you to see you the way I see you—as a princess, My princess. This is the revelation I want you to own of who you are and whose you are: My love, My bride."

This series of dreams gave me powerful glimpses into the heart of God. Sure, I was familiar with the concepts of being the Bride of Christ and being in the family of God, but experiencing the emotions of the dreams made the Scriptures go deeper. They made it a living reality, and the truths became that much more a part of my heart so I could live out those revelations during my waking life.

NOW IT'S YOUR TURN

You may have already noticed I have a special method that organizes dream work, and I encourage you to use the same technique. Simply record the *dream, action, feeling, setting,* and *interpretation.*

First we write down or type up a short summary of the dream. Then we zero in on the main action of the dream as well as the strongest feeling the dream evoked within us. Next we look at the setting and what we were processing in waking life when we had the dream. Often this is enough to give us at least a preliminary understanding of the interpretation.

However, we don't want to stop with just what we think the dream means; we always want to know everything God is speaking so we make sure to ask Him and record what He tells us, too. It is essential that we hear directly from Him what He wants to say to us because the interpretation of dreams belongs to God (see Gen. 40:8). If having such conversational dialogue with the Lord is new to you or if this type of two-way journaling is not something that is part of your daily spiritual life, you can find out how we do it in the appendix.

Next we will look at how dreams worked in the Bible, and then I'll show you how they can work the same way in your life, too.

Chapter 3

SCRIPTURAL PRECEDENTS: EXPLORING DREAMS AND VISIONS IN THE BIBLE

"My eyes anticipate the night watches,
that I may meditate on Your word."
—PSALM 119:148

God has chosen to connect with mankind through dreams. He guides and counsels us through our dreams. He establishes covenants with us through our dreams. He grants us gifts in our dreams. The Lord used dreams and visions throughout Scripture and declared that He would continue to use them in the last days (see Joel 2:28).

As we have already mentioned, when we examine the Bible from Genesis to Revelation and total up all dreams and visions, and all the stories and actions that came out of those dreams and visions, we have about *one-third* of the Bible. Obviously dreams are a central way God communicates with us! As such, they must be given great weight.

In this chapter we are going to explore many of these often overlooked portions of Scripture to find out what God Himself says about dreams, how He desires to work through them, and what all these biblical precedents have to do with us.

Dr. Virkler's Dream Key

SEVEN REASONS TO LISTEN TO OUR DREAMS

1. In the Old Testament, God declares that He *would* speak through dreams and visions.

    And He said, Hear now my words: If there be a prophet among you, I the Lord will make Myself known unto him in a vision, and will speak unto him in a dream (Numbers 12:6 KJV).

2. In the Old Testament, God declares that He *did* speak through dreams and visions.

    I have also spoken by the prophets, and I have multiplied visions, and used similitudes, by the ministry of the prophets (Hosea 12:10 KJV).

3. In the New Testament, God declares that He *will* communicate through dreams and visions.

    In the last days, God says, "I will pour out my Spirit on all people. Your sons and daughters will prophesy, your young men will see visions, your old men will dream dreams" (Acts 2:17 NIV).

4. God declares that He *will counsel* us at night through our dreams.

I will bless the Lord who has counseled me; indeed, my heart instructs me in the night (Psalm 16:7).

5. Rather than our dreams being fatalistic, they are calling us to change *so we will not perish.*

*For God speaketh once, yea twice, yet man perceiveth it not. In a dream, in a vision of the night, when deep sleep falleth upon men, in slumberings upon the bed; then He openeth the ears of men, and sealeth their instruction, that He may withdraw man from his purpose, and hide pride from man. He keepeth back his soul from the pit, **and his life from perishing** by the sword* (Job 33:14-18 KJV).

6. God does very significant things *within* dreams. For example, He established the Abrahamic Covenant in a dream.

*And when the sun was going down, a **deep sleep** fell upon Abram; and, lo, an horror of great darkness fell upon him. And [God] said to Abram.... In the same day the Lord **made a covenant** with Abram, saying...* (Genesis 15:12-13,18 KJV).

7. God grants supernatural gifts *through* dreams.

In Gibeon the Lord appeared to Solomon in a dream by night: and God said, "Ask what I shall give thee....Give therefore Thy servant an understanding heart to judge Thy people, that I may discern between good and bad: for who is able to judge this Thy so great a people?...Behold, I have done according to thy words: lo, I have given thee a wise and an understanding heart; so that there was none like thee before thee, neither after thee shall any arise like

> unto thee...." *And Solomon awoke; and, behold, it was a dream* (1 Kings 3:5,9,12,15 KJV).

BARLEY LOAVES AND BOWING STARS

God is the same yesterday, today, and forever (see Heb. 13:8). Most all of us have "strange" dreams that are full of pictures and symbols. When viewed literally, they don't make sense, so there must be a more figurative understanding.

We have stories of God giving the same kind of symbolic dreams all throughout Scripture. The only difference between then and now is that they knew how to interpret them. Let's take a look at Genesis 37 and see what happened when Joseph told his family about the dreams he had been having:

> *Then Joseph had a dream, and when he told it to his brothers, they hated him even more. And he said to them, "Please listen to this dream which I have had...we were binding sheaves in the field, and...my sheaf rose up and also stood erect; and behold, your sheaves gathered around and bowed down to my sheaf." Then his brothers said to him, "Are you actually going to reign over us? Or are you really going to rule over us?" So they hated him even more for his dreams and for his words.*

> *Now he had still another dream, and related it to his brothers, and said, "Lo, I have had still another dream; and...the sun and the moon and eleven stars were bowing down to me." He related it to his father and to his brothers; and his father rebuked him and said to him, "What is this dream that you have had? Shall I and your mother and your brothers actually come to bow ourselves down before you to the ground?" [And] his brothers were jealous of him, but his father kept the saying in mind* (Genesis 37:5-11).

68

Joseph saw the sun, moon, and stars bowing down to him. Because we are familiar with his dream, its setting, and the interpretation of it, it might not sound that weird to us. But really, stars? Bowing? I can't picture what that would even look like, but that is what he dreamt.

What is most interesting to see is his family's reaction to his dreams: they freaked out. Why would they be so upset over some celestial activity? Obviously they did not take Joseph's dreams as literal agricultural or astronomy lessons; they took them figuratively. They immediately looked at the dreams symbolically and understood that the sheaves and stars represented themselves. We can learn much from a people whose culture understood and honored their dreams!

Fast-forward several years and we find that Joseph has become one of the most influential political power players of his day. He was promoted to second-in-command ruler over Egypt—for none other than his outstanding ability to interpret dreams! Eventually, his relatives did literally bow down to him when they asked for food in a time of famine. His dreams came true.

If we did not know the backstory about Joseph, and we did not already read the end of the story where his brothers bowed down to him, his sheaf and star dreams would not make sense to us. The same thing goes for the dreams we have every night: if we do not consider the setting of our dreams and obtain God's interpretations of them, they are going to continue to seem strange. But once we get those pieces in place, the puzzle of our dream starts coming together and the picture God is showing us finally comes into full view.

God is still working in the same way He did with Joseph so we should not let Scripture feel so far removed from us. Let's look to see how it actually fits together perfectly with our lives. Everything God was doing in the Bible He is still doing for us now, in our days and in our nights.

Dr. Virkler's Dream Key

The vast majority of dreams for most people will be subjective, meaning they will be about concerns specific to your life. These could include sanctification issues, spiritual issues, emotional issues, or health/bodily issues. I would suggest that ninety-five percent of our dreams are subjective dreams, and often an easy way to determine this is by noticing if we are active participants in the dream.

If we are an outside observer and we're watching the dream play out like a movie, that is a clue it might possibly be an objective dream. The messages of objective dreams may involve other people and have a more literal interpretation. Extremely right-brained prophetic visionaries and intercessors are usually the types of people who receive more literal, objective dreams. The rest of us are almost always dreaming of our own personal heart issues and lives.

CLUES THAT MAY INDICATE YOUR DREAM IS OBJECTIVE AND ABOUT OTHERS

1. You are only an observer of the activity of the dream. If, on the other hand, you play an active role in the dream, it is likely a dream about you.

2. The dream just does not fit your life. You should always first ask God, "Lord, show me any way the events in this dream are revealing struggles that my heart is currently facing." If you have examined the dream carefully, in full reliance upon the Holy Spirit to bring the interpretation, and you cannot see how the symbols of the dream apply to you, seek the input of your spiritual counselors. They may be able to

see your blind spots and recognize the message your heart is trying to give you. If your counselors agree that the dream does not apply to your inner life, you may then consider the possibility that it is a dream for or about others.

The following are some biblical dreams that demonstrate this principle: If you are an active participant in the dream, the dream is about you; if you are an observer of the action, the dream is about others.

- Genesis 15:1-21: Abraham meeting with God = dream about himself

- Genesis 20:1-18: Abimelech warned by God = dream about himself

- Genesis 28:10-22: Jacob being spoken to by God = dream about himself

- Genesis 31:10-29: An angel of God instructing Jacob = dream about himself

- Genesis 37:9-10: Sun, moon and 11 stars bowing to Joseph = dream about himself

- Genesis 40:1-23: Cupbearer and baker serving Pharaoh = dreams about themselves

- **Genesis 41:1-49: Pharaoh's dreams of cows and grain = dreams about others**

- Genesis 46:1-7: Israel in dialogue with God = dream about himself

- I Kings 3:5-28: Solomon converses with God = dream about himself

- **Daniel 2:1-49: Nebuchadnezzar's dream of a statue hit by stone = dream about others**

- Daniel 7:1-28: Daniel's dream of four beasts = dream about others

- Daniel 8:1-27: Daniel's dream of a ram and a goat = dream about others

- Daniel 10:1–12:13: Daniel's terrifying vision = dream about others

- Matthew 1:20-25: The angel of the Lord speaks to Joseph = dream about himself

- Matthew 2:3-15: Joseph warned by God to go to Egypt = dream about himself

- Matthew 2:19-21: Joseph led by God to return to Israel = dream about himself

- Matthew 2:22-23: Joseph warned by God to avoid Judea = dream about himself

SUMMARY: THE MAJORITY OF DREAMS ARE ABOUT THE DREAMER HIMSELF. YOU CAN EXPECT THE MAJORITY OF YOUR DREAMS TO BE ABOUT YOU.

Two important observations may be made from these biblical examples:

1. The dreams for or about others were prophetic in nature and were all given to kings or kings' advisors concerning the future of their kingdoms. The principle which may be drawn from this is that dreams (and indeed all revelation from the Holy Spirit) are given to us only if they apply to our own area of responsibility. We do not hear from God about people over whom we have no influence, authority, or accountability.

2. Dreams about self may be for the dreamer and his descendants. Again, the revelation of the dream was

not given to any random individual but to one with authority and influence. Intercessors may be given revelation of others so they can pray for them. It is also vital to understand that all kinds of dreams can contain symbolic language, literal language, or a combination of both.

WHEN A SYMBOL IS NOT A SYMBOL

A fundamental principle we must always remember about dreams is that they are not often literal; they are symbolic. They are pictures that represent something else and thus need to be interpreted. That is true with almost all dreams and with almost all symbols, *except* for numbers.

In the Bible, every time someone has numbers in their dreams, those figures represent the exact same number in waking life (e.g., seven cows means seven years in Pharaoh's dream)—no interpretation required.

Biblical numerology is interesting, and waking visions in Scripture often contain symbolic numbers (such as the 144,000 of John's vision in Revelation) so we know there is always a possibility that numbers in our dreams might be viewed metaphorically. However, to keep it easy as we're first starting out, we can simply go with scriptural precedent and the way God interprets dreams in the Bible: the number equals the number. If we find that a literal understanding doesn't make sense, we can always pray to receive a revelation of what the number signifies.

AN OBJECTIVE PROPHETIC DREAM WITH NUMBERS

One night I had a dream that my mom was upset because she and my dad had just lost 182,000 dollars. While she was telling me about it, she got a call from my dad, who had suddenly realized that he had spent ten thousand dollars the previous day on food and could not understand how he could go through that much in just one day.

Obviously, this dream involved food. It was about losing money and gaining debt. It had to do with my family—specifically, a guy I love and to whom I am related: my dad. I was not an active participant in the dream but instead just listened and watched it play out. The numbers in the dream were 182, 10, and 1.

Imagine my surprise when I awoke from this dream to find my husband Leo (a guy I love and am related to) lamenting the fact that his weight was all the way up to 182 pounds. He just checked the scale and could not believe he had gained *ten* pounds in only *one* week! The subject matched that of the dream in that it involved food. The action matched that of the dream in that something unwanted was gained (debt/weight) in a short period of time. And the feeling matched that of the dream in that Leo was similarly incredulous over the realization.

Because the dream was focused on someone other than myself and I was just an observer, we know that means it was most likely objective. The dream was filled with symbolism: the dollars represented pounds, and my father represented my husband. However, the numbers were all literal: a single day in the dream represented a single week in my husband's waking life, and the amount of money corresponded exactly to the amount of weight.

Lastly, the dream was prophetic in that it was about something that was to come. I had no idea that Leo would be weighing himself and have such a reaction to what he discovered. This is a fun example of a dream that helps us recognize some important principles of dream work and not easily forget them. Remember that numbers are a common "symbol" that may or may not be symbolic. Try it on literally first, and if that doesn't fit, ask the Lord to show you what the number represents.

Dr. Virkler's Dream Key

Numbers in dreams generally represent the identical number in waking life. However, the number will probably be linked to something that needs to be interpreted symbolically. For example, when Joseph dreamed of eleven stars, the eleven was literal but the stars were symbolic and actually represented his brothers. Joseph was dreaming about his eleven brothers (see Gen. 37:1-11).

Likewise, the cupbearer's dream of three branches stood for three days, and in the chief baker's dream, the three baskets represented three days (see Gen. 39:12,18). In Pharaoh's dream, the seven cows were seven years (see Gen. 41:26). So expect the number you dream to mean that exact number of something in life.

GIDEON'S BREAD

The story of Gideon and the dream he overheard is fascinating. Judges 7:9-18 tells us how Gideon was pretty nervous about taking his little army of three hundred men to fight against the Midianites, who were *"as numerous as locusts; and their camels were without number, as numerous as the sand on the seashore"* (Judg. 7:12).

God wanted to encourage Gideon and told him to go down to the camp because He had given the enemy into Gideon's hands. God said, "I know you are afraid so go and listen to what they say, and afterward your hands will be strengthened and you will be confident to go to war" (see Judg. 7:9-11). When Gideon and his friend arrived, they overheard a conversation between two Midianites, as one was recounting his dream to the other:

> *...And he said, "Behold, I had a dream; a loaf of barley bread was tumbling into the camp of Midian, and it came*

to the tent and struck it so that it fell, and turned it upside down so that the tent lay flat." And his friend answered and said, "This is nothing less than the sword of Gideon... God has given Midian and all the camp into his hand."

And it came about when Gideon heard the account of the dream and its interpretation, that he bowed in worship. He returned to the camp of Israel and said, "Arise, for the Lord has given the camp of Midian into your hands" (Judges 7:13-15 NASB 1977).

There are so many great lessons for us in this short story. To begin with, we notice again how the culture of that day clearly believed in dreams. None of the three men who heard the dream thought it was strange or suggested that the dreamer must have eaten Mexican food right before bed to see something so crazy in his night visions. They all took it as a true prophetic message.

Another interesting thing to notice is that, just like Joseph and his family, they also easily interpreted the dream right off the bat. I mean, a barley loaf? Where did that come from? To our literal Western minds it doesn't make any sense. But upon hearing the dream, his friend immediately offered the clear interpretation. In Bible times, people knew how to interpret even the most symbolic (read: weird) dreams.

Lastly, and this is the most important key of all: they acted on the dream. Gideon did not say, "Oh, that's not for us. It's just a dream; it's not real." Instead, what did he do? He immediately got down and worshiped God, praising Him for the encouragement and the deliverance he was now thoroughly convinced would come. Then he got his army together and made the dream come true.

BREAKING IT DOWN

Next we will take a look at how the dream was interpreted and unpack the symbolism to see how the message was understood. We know we have to start by asking, "What was the main action in the dream?" Well, something came into the camp and struck the tents down flat. That is what Gideon wanted to do in waking life—enter the camp and strike down the enemy. So that part is literal.

But what's up with the loaf of barley? Like wheat, barley is a grain. We know that before Gideon ever became a mighty man of valor, he was first a scaredy-cat thresher of wheat (see Judg. 6:11). God used the symbol of grain from his waking world to say, "Even though you see yourself as a fearful grain crusher, I see you as a bold enemy crusher. Even though you identify yourself with ordinary things, I have destined you for greatness."

This was where the dream became heavily symbolic. There are a few reasons Gideon's sword and his army were represented by a loaf of barley bread. For one, a loaf of bread is small, and that is exactly what Gideon's army was—positively tiny compared with the enemy's. God was showing that even though He had whittled the number of soldiers down, making Gideon's army small in size, He was still going to show up big and show off, destroying Midian with the most unassuming of forces.

Another thing that is small but could be dangerous is a brick. God did not use the image of a brick because that could still be used in a violent way. Instead, God used a loaf of bread, which is soft and weak—the opposite of a hard, strong brick. A brick could be threatening, but a loaf of bread? Never.

Again, the specific symbol the Lord used was meant to tell Gideon, "Yeah, I know that you feel small. I understand that you see yourself as weak and as no threat to the enemy. But let Me show you how I will use you."

I once heard a pastor explain that in those days, barley was not a very esteemed grain; it was the cheapest kind. If you were well-to-do, you would never eat it, as it was kind of looked down upon. I got the impression that it was the ramen noodles of that day. The barley, then, is speaking to Gideon's fears and most likely his enemy's pride—that everyone was looking down on Gideon and his army. Nobody thought he was good enough to stand against the Midianites with just three hundred men. He was not respected as a threat, nor was he highly regarded; instead, he was disdained and underestimated in every way.

God was showing all of them through the dream what He could do through a small loaf of bread—and a small loaf of barley bread at that: He could take out an army, and He did.

Dr. Virkler's Dream Key

Never make a major decision in your life based only on a dream without receiving additional confirmation from God through the other ways that He speaks to us and guides us (peace in our hearts, the counsel of others, illumined Scriptures, His still small voice, prophecy, anointed reasoning, etc.).

ACTING ON OUR DREAMS

As we have seen, in the Bible, God gives clear direction to people through dreams, and they act on it. They live out of their dreams and make them come true. The following is an example of a prophetic dream that prepared me for a job opportunity I did not see coming.

While the dream was not the only factor in my decision to accept the promotion, it played a key role. Just like Gideon, before I received the dream God had already spoken directly to me with His guidance and instruction (see Judg. 7:9).

In addition to the dream and journaling conversations with the Lord, I also had peace in my heart and the confirmation of my spiritual counselors. But this dream was certainly the icing on the cake that encouraged me to move forward in the direction God wanted me to go, just like Gideon's was for him.

WHO IS THE LEADER?

One thing I never used to be a big fan of was responsibility. I was happy to be a follower, as there seemed to be much less pressure in that position. God turned all this around for me one night through a dream when He explained that I can be a follower and a leader at the same time.

He showed me how He is the leader and I am always following Him, and then if anyone else wants to follow behind us, great. There's no pressure on me, though, because even if it may seem like I am leading, I'm really not. People just might not see Who it is I am following.

DREAM: I was a firefighter living at a firehouse.

ACTION: Our job was to put out fires; we were the first responders who saved lives.

FEELING: Huge sense of responsibility, but it did not weigh on me because I knew I was in the safest place.

INTERPRETATION: The safest place is the place of most responsibility. Firefighters have tremendous responsibility, but you do not often hear of their fire stations burning down. They have everything they need to fight the fires. Likewise, I have been equipped for every good work through Christ so I can be confident in any situation (see Heb. 13:20-21).

God said, "*So Char Bear, about that mantle of responsibility... here's the deal: It's not yours to wear because it is too big and heavy for your little girly shoulders. It's for Me. The mantle hangs perfectly on My shoulders. It's MY size. Leadership, responsibility—they're My mantles, My cloaks, My armor, Mine to wear. You don't have to. You just have to find yourself hidden in Me. And you can be littler, and you can be the follower (which is all I've ever asked you to be—a follower of Jesus).*

"Your life is hidden in Mine. So you are the littler one inside of Me, the Big One. And it's Me who is wearing the big cloak and mantle, and you're being covered by it because you are inside of Me. But you are not feeling the pressure or stress or weight of that mantle because you're hidden inside of Me.

"I got you. I got this. There's no pressure on you, no stress. I am the Mantle Holder, the Responsibility Carrier, the Leadership Wearer..."

SETTING: This was a slightly prophetic dream that prepared me for what was going to happen the very next day. I awoke, went to work, and was offered a new job position, which, as you can imagine, involved a great deal more responsibility.

Normally I would have been hesitant, but because of the message God gave me through the dream the night before I accepted the promotion and found once again that the safest place to be is in the center of God's will. It just may also happen to be the place of greatest responsibility.

HOW GOD SEES DREAMS

What happens in our night visions has significance and staying power with God. In His Book, He never once says, "It's *just* a dream." In fact, He does the opposite.

At the end of Solomon's life, God says, "You know, it's really too bad you messed up, especially considering I came to you twice" (see 1 Kings 11:9). The first time the Lord visited him when he was at Gibeon and gave him wisdom in a dream (see 1 Kings 3:5).

The other time Scripture says, *"The Lord appeared to him a second time, as He had appeared to him at Gibeon"* (1 Kings 9:2). So here we see God is actually holding Solomon accountable for his dreams and what happened in them. How's that for a paradigm shift?

A LISTENING HEART

The wisdom Solomon received through his dreams is the same wisdom we can receive every night through our dreams. The Hebrew word for what Solomon asked for and received is *shama*, which is a "hearing" heart (see 1 Kings 3:9,11). He asked for a listening heart, one that could clearly hear the Lord's direction and guidance.

Solomon wanted to go back to the way it was in the Garden of Eden. Adam and Eve initially lived from their hearts and spiritual communion with God. That is how they knew good from evil—because God told them (see Gen. 2:16-17). They were dependent on His voice and lived out of relationship with Him. Their sin was to choose independence and to use their own minds to discern good and evil (see Gen. 3:5).

Solomon wanted to go back to God's original intention and chose the opposite of Adam and Eve. Solomon did not want to rely on his own mind's best guess. He wanted to return to the lifestyle of Eden, not making decisions by what his physical eyes saw or his natural ears heard but instead ruling with righteous judgment (see Isa. 11:3-4).

It was the Spirit of Wisdom, the Holy Spirit, with whom Solomon connected, just like Adam and Eve had done long before. Through his dream, the spiritual portal was opened and he had the chance to access anything he wanted. What did he choose? He chose God. He chose to hear God. He asked that his heart be reconnected to God's heart so he could live out of fellowship with Him.

Solomon did not just receive a pile of detached information for his brain. That could have made him knowledgeable, but it would never make him wise. Instead, he was given the gift of being able to listen in to the spirit realm and hear the counsel of Heaven. He was given the gift of restored communion and intimate relationship with the Spirit of Wisdom Himself (see Isa. 11:2).

And just as God said, there was no king who could rival the wisdom of Solomon—until the King of kings came to earth (see 1 Kings 4:30). Jesus was baptized with the Holy Spirit, the Spirit of Wisdom, and He, too, lived out of the supernatural. He did nothing on His own initiative based on what He saw in this natural world (see John 5:19,30). We know He did only what He saw His Father do and spoke only what He heard His Father say (see John 8:26,38).

Solomon and Jesus both relied on the spirit realm to reign in life, accessing the wisdom of Heaven through their dreams and visions. We can do that, too.

Dr. Virkler's Dream Key

WARNINGS ABOUT DREAMS AND VISIONS?

1. There are no warnings in the Bible to beware of your own dreams, with the possible exceptions of Ecclesiastes 5:3,7. These verses don't really make sense in reference to "sleeping dreams" and are probably best understood as concerning daydreams. Since all other references to dreams in the Bible are positive, we need to seek to understand any anomaly in light of the volume of favorable references to dreams.

2. The only biblical caution concerning dreams, then, relates to listening to another's dream. That person may be trying to lead you astray to go after other gods (see Jer. 14:14; 23:16, 25-27,32; Ezek. 13:1,7; 12:24; Deut. 13:1-5; Jer. 27:9-11; Zech. 10:2).

BIBLICAL RESEARCH CONCERNING DREAMS AND VISIONS

The best way to gain an enlightened appreciation of dreams is to examine the 220 references to dreams and visions in the Bible. Many of these references unfold an entire story concerning a dream, including the resulting revelation and action. We have only looked at a handful of them.

To build a solid framework for Christian dream interpretation we encourage you to explore the sixty dreams and visions recorded in Scripture to see how God speaks through them and how He interprets the symbols in them. In the recommended companion workbook, *Hear God Through Your Dreams*, guided self-discovery helps you ask the right questions about each dream in order to unlock its meaning and understand what the Lord was speaking through it.

Below is a list to get you started!

1. God promises Abram as many children as there are stars in the heavens (Genesis 15:1-11)

2. God enters into covenant with Abram while Abram is in a deep sleep (Genesis 15:12-21)

3. God warns Abimelech of Abraham's treachery (Genesis 20:1-18)

4. God reaffirms His covenant with Jacob (Genesis 28:10-22)

5. Jacob receives a creative business idea (Genesis 30:31–31:17)

6. Laban's dream concerning Jacob (Genesis 31:24-29)

7. Joseph's dream of bowing sheaves (Genesis 37:5-8)

8. Joseph's dream of bowing stars (Genesis 37:9-11)

9. The cupbearer's dream (Genesis 40:1-15)

10. The baker's dream (Genesis 40:1-8; 16-23)

11. Pharaoh's prophetic dreams of plenty and drought (Genesis 41:1-37)

12. Jacob encouraged to go to Egypt (Genesis 46:1-7)

13. God's declaration concerning dreams (Numbers 12:6-8)

14. A description of the prophet Balaam (Numbers 24:3-4)

15. Laws concerning judging dreams (Deuteronomy 13:1-5)

16. Dream encouraging Gideon (Judges 7:9-18)

17. Saul expects the Lord to answer him in a dream (1 Samuel 28:6)

18. Solomon's wisdom given in a dream (1 Kings 3:5-28)

19. Eliphaz receives a vision of the night (Job 4:12-21)

20. Elihu's declaration concerning dreams (Job 33:14-18)

21. Solomon's proverb concerning vision (Proverbs 29:18)

22. Isaiah's vision concerning Judah and Jerusalem—judgment for sin (Isaiah 1:1-31)

23. Isaiah's vision concerning the last days (Isaiah 2:1-22)

24. Isaiah's vision of the Lord on His throne (Isaiah 6:1-13)

25. Isaiah's vision concerning Babylon (Isaiah 13:1-14:22)

26. Isaiah's vision concerning the nations (Isaiah 21:2ff)

27. Jeremiah's vision of the almond tree (Jeremiah 1:11-12)

28. Jeremiah's vision of the boiling pot (Jeremiah 1:13-19)

29. The false dreamers (Jeremiah 23:25-40)

30. More about false dreamers (Jeremiah 27:9-11)

31. Ezekiel's visions of God (Ezekiel 1:1-3:13)

32. Ezekiel's visions of abominations and slaughter (Ezekiel 8:1-12:6)

33. Daniel understood all kinds of dreams and visions (Daniel 1:17)

34. Nebuchadnezzar's forgotten dream (Daniel 2:1-49)

35. Nebuchadnezzar's dream of a great tree (Daniel 4:4-37)

36. Daniel's night vision of the four beasts (Daniel 7:1-28)

37. Daniel's vision of the ram and the goat (Daniel 8:1-27)

38. Daniel's terrifying vision (Daniel 10:1–12:13)

39. God's review of Old Testament history (Hosea 12:9-10)

40. The promise of the Spirit (Joel 2:28-29)

41. Obadiah's vision of Edom's destruction (Obadiah 1)

42. Nahum's vision of God's vengeance on Nineveh (Nahum 1:1-3:19)

43. Habakkuk's vision of judgment on the Chaldeans (Habakkuk 2:2-20)

44. The diviners' lying visions (Zechariah 10:2)

45. Lying prophets will be ashamed (Zechariah 13:1-5)

46. Joseph encouraged by an angel of the Lord in a dream (Matthew 1:20-25)

47. The magi warned by God in a dream (Matthew 2:11-12)

48. Joseph instructed in a dream to move to Egypt (Matthew 2:13-15)

49. Joseph told in a dream to return to Israel (Matthew 2:19-21)

50. Joseph warned by God in a dream to avoid Judea (Matthew 2:22-23)

51. The vision on the Mount of Transfiguration (Matthew 17:1-9)

52. Pilate's wife dreamed of Jesus (Matthew 27:19)

53. Prophecy concerning the last days (Acts 2:17)

54. Saul's vision on the road to Damascus (Acts 9:1-9)

55. Ananias sent to minister to Saul in a vision (Acts 9:10-19)

56. Cornelius' vision of an angel of God (Acts 10:1-8)

57. Peter's vision of unclean animals while in a trance (Acts 10:9-48)

58. Paul's vision in the night of a man of Macedonia (Acts 16:6-11)

59. The Lord encourages Paul in the night by a vision (Acts 18:9-11)

60. The visions of John (Book of Revelation)

Chapter 4

SNAPSHOTS OF THE SPIRIT: GAINING HEAVEN'S PERSPECTIVE THROUGH DREAMS

"I will praise the Lord, who counsels me;
even at night my heart instructs me."
—PSALM 16:7 NIV

"Let's go on a fast this January," my husband Leo suggested shortly before Christmas one winter. "Sure!" That sounded great to me. We usually like to begin the new year with a fast of some kind, for both the spiritual and the physical benefits.

We try to "power down" on weekends and evenings after work, not watching movies or spending time online but instead really getting into the Word and spending time in God's presence. Not having to think about planning meals and not spending hours grocery shopping, preparing food, and doing dishes frees up all kinds of time to focus on the Spirit, which is by far my most favorite part of fasting—more time with Jesus.

Now I am not going to share how long we fasted because you're not really supposed to broadcast your secret-place sacrifices to the world. (OK, I'll tell you. It was forty days.) However, only a couple weeks into it Leo decided that since we are not under law but live by grace he could eat a little food in order to be able to keep up his demanding cardio and weightlifting regimen. *Awesome.*

Well, I'm not under law either, but God was still clear that I should stick with the fast. And it was hard. We had done various fasts before, but this one was different. It involved constant temptation and struggle—not only physically, but spiritually and emotionally, too. Ugh. Whose idea was this again?

As I mentioned, my husband and I appreciate the physical benefits of fasting. I also never want to "waste" a fast. Usually (and when I say "usually," I mean *always*) when I had fasted before, I fasted for something—like for a physical healing, or for a friend's prodigal child, or maybe for favor or promotion at work. There was always something we were focused on seeing in the natural world as a result of our spiritual discipline.

The few people who knew what we were doing asked, "So what are you fasting for?" because they also understood it to be a way of releasing blessings from the spirit realm into the physical world. Which is true—fasting definitely works well for that.

But this time was different. This time I really wasn't looking for anything to happen in my physical reality or for something to change in my natural world. I borrowed the phrase from C. S. Lewis and told those who asked that we simply wanted to go "further up and further in."[3] That's all we were really going for—to get further into the Kingdom of Heaven, deeper into the spiritual realm.

Would I have anything to "show" for my fast? Any obvious outer sign that "proved it worked" and that it was "a success"? I actually didn't care, which was a first for me. Not having to authenticate or substantiate my walk in the Spirit with physical world validation turned out to be an exercise in extraordinary freedom. And little did I know then that that would actually change everything.

ORIGINAL INTENTION

During this fast, God began opening up my heart to understand that the way we live now is not according to His original intention. I love the first few chapters of Genesis because they give us a clear picture of how God actually wanted the world to be: unbroken. Everything in the Garden was "good," but what we see around us now is a world corrupted by sin (see Rom. 8:20-21).

I was excited as Holy Spirit began showing me how in the Garden, Adam and Eve had supernatural eyesight. They were created in God's image and He is Spirit (see John 4:24). So as spirit beings they engaged God easily and walked and talked with Him in the cool of the day (see Gen. 3:8). They also effortlessly interacted with other spirit beings, such as in that long-ranging conversation with the devil, who is a fallen angel (see Gen. 3:1-7).

That is why I find it so interesting that they were tempted by the words *"your eyes will be opened"* (Gen. 3:5). From what we read in Scripture, their eyes were already wide open! They were interacting with other spirits in the spirit realm—angels, God Himself—so their eyes were obviously already open to see and hear in the supernatural realm naturally and easily.

A RIFT IN THE REALM

So what happened then when they sinned? The Bible says that *"the eyes of both of them were opened,"* but to what were they opened (Gen. 3:7)? What did they see that they hadn't been aware of before? Their humanity, their nakedness, their physical bodies.

As soon as their eyes were opened to the natural world, it was as if they were simultaneously closed to the spiritual world—at least during the day. They did not talk with angels, fallen or otherwise, and they did not enjoy fellowshipping with God in the Garden anymore either.

They had been effortlessly living in a world where the spiritual and physical co-existed beautifully and perfectly, but all of a sudden, there seemed to be a separation and a falling out. Previously, the world they knew was unbroken. Now their perception was altered, and all of a sudden it appeared to them that there was a rift in the realm. From their sin-tainted point of view, it looked as if there were two distinct worlds inaccessible as one unified dimension.

How they saw everything changed: there was a division that wasn't there before. Their new reality seemed fractured, as though Heaven was no longer within reach but was somehow distant and disconnected from the earth. And when their perspective changed, that changed everything. The supernatural realm immediately became something from which they felt far removed, and the finite natural realm became their new reality.

WE WEREN'T MADE FOR A BOX

Just like that, the world in which they lived while awake became very small. They chose not to live out of the spirit realm and dependence on the Holy Spirit, so all of a sudden there were limits and boundaries. Before, they could eat from the Tree of Life, which meant they would live forever. God had created "time" in that there was evening and morning, but Adam and Eve had infinite amounts available so essentially for them time didn't exist—until that moment. The moment they sinned the countdown started and their time on earth began to run out.

Adam and Eve chose rules over relationship when they chose sin instead of the spirit. As a result, they became blinded to the supernatural dimension, in which there is no distance. Their world started closing in on them, confining them within the boundaries of space and the limitations of time.

THE MATRIX

It reminds me of that old Keanu Reeves movie *The Matrix*. There are so many spiritual principles and parallels in that film, but the main idea is that the characters' world is actually an illusion and they had misunderstood what their lives were even about. Everyone was moving through their days believing they were living, but it was just an artificial environment, not the real, true life they could have been experiencing.

Unfortunately, as Adam and Eve's descendants, we seem to have unwittingly found ourselves in a similar situation because after the Fall, we were all born into the illusion that the confines of this four-dimensional "Matrix" are actually a limit to us. We all simply believe that our world is only made up of what our natural eyes can see and our physical ears can hear.

However, God says, "Do not look at this natural world and the things that are seen. Look at the things that are unseen, because the things that are seen are temporary and the things that are unseen are eternal" (see 2 Cor. 4:18).

That is what we are exploring in this book—escaping the artificial reality of the Matrix and living into all the miraculous possibilities available to us simply by stepping into the supernatural and into the world of dreams. Through our visions (both in the day and at night while we sleep), we get a taste of how life was originally intended to be—and can be again. By connecting with Heaven, we know no limits or boundaries. We press into the spirit realm and move further up and further into it.

One evening as I was meditating on this revelation, I fell asleep and had a dream.

"FURTHER UP AND FURTHER IN"

DREAM: Leo, my brother Josh, then me, then Mom, then Dad were climbing a steep ladder/staircase behind a curtain on the right side of an auditorium. The rungs of the ladder were very wide and far apart. On our left were two ushers with their shoes off cleaning up the seats and aisles.

We passed them, and at the top it was bright and full of light on the rooftop veranda, although there were some walls, too. I tried to take Mom's picture. I took time to frame the shot well so that it included a picture hanging on the wall behind her, a big strong stone hearth on her right side, and a bunch of bananas on her lap. My camera viewfinder was shaped like a heart.

SETTING: In waking life I had sent two emails to my family with my newest understandings of the correlations between quantum physics and the spirit realm, and I was really excited. However, none of them had replied to my messages, and it had been an *entire* forty-eight hours. That felt like an eternity! So I began to feel unsure about the revelation, wondering how to make it as real to them as it was to me.

SYMBOLS: The following is how I broke down the symbols to understand God's message to me through the dream:

- **Leo leading** = He initiated the forty-day fast. Forty = 4-D. They sound the same. So Leo's presence in the dream speaks to our freedom from four-dimensional living, our ability to break out of the space-time box. That's why I needed to tell you how long we fasted—so you could see the 4-D matrix and understand the way it looked to me.

- **Josh ahead of me** = He sent me an email about this being a quantum year.

- **Mom right behind me** = I feel her support and encouragement.

- **Dad last** = He's the most logical and analytical thinker of us all; he represents himself and, on another level, represents my own mind, the thinking part of me.

- **Behind the curtain** = Behind what we can see (the 4-D world), the invisible, the spirit realm, the backstage where everything actually takes place. The real *is* the backstage. What's on stage comes from what is backstage. The visible comes from what is unseen (see Heb. 11:1,3).

- **Climbing up a steep ladder with spread-out rungs** = Further up—stretching us, pushing us; almost need to take small jumps to get from one rung to the next—that is, quantum (tiny) leaps

- **Auditorium** = Further in—inside. "All the world's a stage." Four-dimensional (4-D) living is a shadow reality that is put on by the "more real" eternal world of the spirit.

- **Ushers with shoes off** = Angels (One of the Greek words for *angel* is *diakonos*, which is where we get our word *deacon* from. We can view some angels as deacons of the spirit world.); idea of being ushered to a place of holy ground (see Ex. 3:5).

- **At first it's dark, but then at the top there's a bright light** = When I am trying to find my way in and through the supernatural realm, it may seem at times like I'm feeling around in the dark, but it gets brighter and clearer and easier (see Prov. 4:18).

- **Taking a picture of Mom** = Mom symbolizes the spirit (whereas Dad represents the mind in this dream)—I'm trying to take a picture of the spirit realm. I'm trying to capture it. I want to be able to express it and share it in such a way that it seems real and observable and concrete.

- **Framing the picture** = What pictures and words should I use to "frame my argument"?

- **Picture behind Mom on the wall** = Trying to get pictures to line up, to find corollaries in the material world that make sense and match the spirit-realm truth.

- **I make sure to include the big, ornate, sturdy stone hearth in my shot** = I want to show how solid the spirit world is—how strong, tangible, and "brick-and-mortar" it is.

- **Bunch of bananas** = Fruit of the Spirit. Love, compassion, and God Emotion are the revelation Holy Spirit has been communicating to me, and that is what I'm trying to capture and show.

- **They were all right there with me** = I don't have to prove anything to them! They're with me in this, and they see what I'm trying to say. They already see it for themselves so I don't need to worry about framing my "argument" because there's nothing to prove.

- **My heart-shaped camera viewfinder** = I was taking a picture of the spirit realm through the lens of my heart. That is how we view the supernatural realm—through our heart.

INTERPRETATION: The dream showed me how my whole family was in this together. We were all collectively moving further up (the ladder) and further in(side the auditorium). It was a holy adventure, and angels were ushering us in. There was glorious light as we reached a higher plane of revelation. I felt extremely encouraged and excited about this dream, and it motivated me to continue pressing into the supernatural to discover all that God has for us there.

SEEING IN THE SPIRIT

I want to live into Heaven, all day and all night. I want to be like Adam and Eve and see God and talk with angels. And you know what? I do. But that seems to be a bit of a stretch for some people. Dreams aren't though. Lots of people will tell you that they have never had a vision. However, those same people dream—and often. So even though it might be a little challenging for you to see visions during the day, be encouraged! Because you are already seeing visions at night.

Scripture actually uses the term "night visions" as another way of saying "dreams" (e.g., *"in a dream, a vision of the night"* [Job 33:15]). So you are already connecting with the realm of the spirit through your dreams. You are already getting glimpses of the Kingdom, seeing God's perspective, and feeling His heart every night when you lie down and fall asleep. And that's a great place to start!

It is awesome. It is huge and amazing. You are already hearing from Heaven! Now all you need to do is master the language. And that is what you have begun to do through this book. We will continue to look at examples of how God has used dreams to speak into people's lives so that you can get a feel for how dream language sounds.

I realize there are skeptics out there who don't understand their dreams and therefore may question these ideas, asking, "What if you're wrong about all this?" My favorite response to the wondering heart is "But what if I'm not?" What if I am actually right? What if we do connect with the spirit realm each night, and what if Heaven really is just a dream away?

That idea doesn't drive me, but it does draw me. It inspires and excites me. It welcomes me and attracts me with the great invitation to explore God's Kingdom and His presence I feel so strongly there.

GOD'S CONTINGENCY PLAN

Adam and Eve determined with their minds not to live out of the supernatural realm and dependence on God. They decided to live from their heads rather than their hearts, but God did not give up on humankind that easily. When our minds rest at night, our spirits still fellowship with God.

Dreams are God's contingency plan. Even though we abandoned relationship with Him and chose to live out of our minds during the day, God knew He could still reach us at night through our dreams. This was His back-up plan.

God is relentless in His pursuit of our hearts. Song of Solomon 5:2 says, *"I slept but my heart was awake. Listen! My beloved is knocking..."* (NIV). Our Beloved is knocking on the door of our hearts while we sleep, and He longs for that intimate communion He created us to share with Him.

You will absolutely love seeing Jesus, His heart, and His personality through dream work! It is an epic adventure, one that we get to live into every single night.

A DATE WITH HOLY SPIRIT

The next interpretation story is a great example of how we are able to feel God's heart for us through our dreams, how we get a glimpse of the way He sees us and what He thinks of us, and how by gaining His perspective, that can change everything.

I think out of all the members of the Trinity, sometimes it is the hardest to picture Holy Spirit. What does He look like? We have dads so Father God isn't that hard to visualize. Jesus lived as a man on earth so He is fairly easy to envision, too.

But Holy Spirit? I don't really have a grid for spirits and ghosts, holy or otherwise. When I was seeking to know Holy Spirit better, I had a dream, and I still remember how I felt while I was experiencing this dream. The sequence of scenes was simple, yet the emotion it stirred deep within me was transformational.

In the night vision, I was with Holy Spirit. He was unfamiliar to me in appearance (which makes sense since I was having trouble picturing Him. This was also good because "familiar spirits" are bad and we shouldn't be consorting with them [see Lev. 19:31 KJV]!)

He was very intriguing and mysterious, which immediately made me want to hang out with Him and get to know Him more. Honestly, in this dream, He wasn't that good looking, but there was something about Him that was magnetic. Something drew me to Him, and I did not want to leave His presence.

So in the dream I stayed with Him. Wherever Holy Spirit went, I did, too. And the best part of all, and what I still remember to this day, is that He laughed at my jokes! In waking life, this translated into my settling down even deeper and more securely into our relationship, into His love. He gets me! He *likes* me! He thinks I'm funny and fun to be with.

That one dream took my relationship with Holy Spirit to another level, and I am so grateful He gave me that picture and allowed me to *feel* His love and acceptance in such a meaningful way.

Now, if I stopped right there, I trust you would agree that it was an awesome dream. The message thus far has been so clear that I hesitate to tell you the rest, but I want you to see this in the context of how a real dream often looks.

I could get into more details of the dream, such as how the guy representing Holy Spirit was cleaning out someone's car. While He was doing that, the rest of us were all playing a board game. Then, while we continued playing, He was going to run some errands for the person whose car he had been cleaning. I excused myself from the game and offered to go along too, because I didn't want to be away from Him.

In analyzing this dream story, some of us might question and wonder: "God's cleaning out a car? God is running errands? I'm not sure that's very spiritual. Where is that in the Bible? And how do you even know it's Holy Spirit?"

Very true! Running errands and cleaning cars are not depicted in the Bible. However, the Bible does say Holy Spirit's work is to convict the world of sin, righteousness, and judgment (see John 16:8). How would you create a dream snapshot for that? What simple picture could that end up looking like?

God is in the business of making the hard things easy and uncomplicating the complex. I mean, I have a car. Sometimes I even clean it out. So that is going to be a good symbol for me to understand: He works to get the junk out of our lives.

When I considered the dream, I immediately saw the juxtaposition of working versus playing and knew that the man represented Holy Spirit, who is working in our lives to will and to do His good pleasure (see Phil. 2:13). He is the One who is actively performing a sanctifying, cleansing work in our hearts (see 1 Thess. 5:23).

God is going to take those great big concepts and make a movie in the night about them that is simple enough for even a child to understand. We are God's children, and He wants to break it down in ways that make sense to us. God wants us to understand

His messages through our dreams even more than we want to understand them.

Next, we'll look at a familiar activity to see a fun analogy of how dreams keep us on course.

BUMPER BOWLING

I adore my nieces, and every year when their birthdays come around it is usually a toss-up for what they want to do for our family celebration between bowling and roller skating. If bowling wins, we usually reserve two lanes—one regular lane for us "big kids" and an adjacent lane with "bumpers" for the three kiddos.

Have you seen those barriers they use on the gutters? They cover the edges so that wayward bowling balls will stay on the lane and not go off track. The balls just bounce against the bumper a little and then all of a sudden are back on course, heading in the direction of the pins, moving where they are supposed to be going—a super helpful invention, especially if you're five years old.

Those bumpers are a great picture in the natural of what dreams do for our spiritual lives. We are on course; we are in our lane moving in the right direction, but then we just get a little bit off course and so, *boom*—a dream bumps us back on track and keeps us headed where we are supposed to be going.

This principle is discussed in some amazing verses found in the thirty-third chapter of Job:

Why do you complain against Him That He does not give an account of all His doings? Indeed God speaks once, Or twice, yet no one notices it. In a dream, a vision of the night, When sound sleep falls on men, While they slumber in their beds, Then He opens the ears of men, And seals their instruction, That He may turn man aside from his conduct, And keep man from pride; He keeps back his soul from the pit, And his life from passing over into Sheol (Job 33:13-18).

We are rolling along in life but end up straying just a bit. God speaks over and over again in an effort to turn us from those wrong directions—to keep us in the center of His will and Kingdom; to keep us back from the pits and gutters on either side of the narrow path He has us on.

When does He do that? When sound sleep falls and we slumber in our beds. Then He opens our ears and seals our instruction. In our dreams, in our visions of the night. An example of what this principle looks like can be seen in the following story.

MIRANDA WHO?

God "bumped" me back on track one night when I dreamt of an old friend named Miranda. She and I had spent a summer ministering together in Nicaragua in the early '90s but hadn't seen each other in years.

While the action and feeling of this dream played a small role, the key to unlocking it was her name. As I prayed into an understanding, Holy Spirit showed me what a loaded word *Miranda* really was to me. The revelation ended up being about Miranda rights: "You have the right to remain silent. You have the right to legal counsel. You understand that anything you say can and will be used against you…"

Pretty serious stuff! God got my attention and showed me through this dream that I must be shrewd in waking life and seek His counsel. I should be more aware of whom I allow to get close to me and what I share with them.

This fit perfectly with the setting of the dream and the waking-life question my heart had been pondering. As I slumbered in my bed, God spoke clearly, turning me aside from careless conduct and keeping me back from the pit and gutters of misplaced confidence. Through this vision of the night He opened my ears and sealed my instruction with His wisdom: *"Be careful and watch what you say! Not everyone is to be relied upon, and in this specific situation you should reconsider where you place your trust."*

SYSTEM REBOOT

Another way to see dreams is to understand they're a bit like a computer reboot, which helps us "defragment" our inner hard drive from the emotional clutter of the day and thus run more efficiently.

Just as dust can collect for no reason other than that time has passed, so, too, can "dust" collect in our hearts. Dreams are a way for God to wipe away the "dust"—the cares of this world, the distractions—and make us clean and unbroken, ready to start a new day. His mercies are new every morning, and one of those mercies is the way we can be cleansed and changed through our night visions to be more like Him (see Lam. 3:22-23).

We have so much going on during the day, so many programs running, that we benefit greatly from a system reboot in the night. Physically, spiritually, mentally, emotionally—dreams recalibrate us in every way. Often it is not just that dreams show us where we are off; they also encourage us that we are doing great and are on the right track.

Sometimes the dust from the day is just a little bit of worry or wondering: *Am I really in the right place? Am I doing the right thing?* We recognize when God tells us through our two-way journaling or Bible study time that we are doing well and should just stay the course. But it's important to also realize that if we go to bed a little bit "off" or struggling with doubt, God can address that and heal it up for us during the night.

Dr. Virkler's Dream Key

Most dreams are symbolic (including biblical dreams) so view them figuratively, the same way you would view a political cartoon. Throw the switch in your brain that says, "Look at this symbolically."

A simple illustration of this dream key and of system reboot is that, for me, dreaming of being on the mission field is a sure sign I am in God's perfect will and plan. It is not literal—He is not telling me I should sign up for a mission trip. Rather, it symbolizes that I am already where He wants me to be today. I am putting my time into the projects that are His priority. I am pleasing Him in my decisions and relationships.

That is a custom-made symbol for me because when I was a teenager, I would go on short-term mission trips every summer and Christmas. I would pray hard and ask God to direct me to the places in the world He wanted to send me, and I would know for sure exactly where He desired me to be and would go there for a month or two. It was always an incredible time of powerful ministry, salvation, and healing.

When I was overseas in waking life I knew I was where God wanted me to be in that moment, so for me, being on the mission field in my dream is the quickest, easiest picture for Him to use to say, *"Charity, you're on the right path. You're in the right place. Regardless of whatever may or may not be happening in the physical realm, look at it through the lens of My Spirit and see that I have you exactly where I want you for My reasons during this specific season."*

Through this example we see how dreams connect us with God's thoughts and feelings. That's what we want—oneness with the Lord. What follows is a series of three dreams I had three nights in a row that demonstrates how God uses dreams to help us live more effectively into our unity with Him.

INSIDER SECRETS

SETTING: In waking life, I had been meditating on the observer effect principle of quantum physics and how it integrates with living by the Spirit. *"God is Spirit,"* and we are created in His image so we are spirits, too (John 4:24). That is who we are, where we come from, and how God intends for us to live—not in the artificial "Matrix" of a space-time box, but rather in the unified dimension of spiritual and physical world. The baptism of the Holy Spirit enlightens the eyes of our hearts and takes us back to Eden, restoring the "super" to our "natural" (see Eph. 1:17-23).

DREAM: I am privy to a huge insider secret. As the higher-ups are taken away, they commission me to break the story so that the truth gets told. They make sure I have the Eyewitness News reporter's contact information so the world can hear what really happened.

ACTION: Being given instructions

FEELING: A great responsibility has been entrusted to me

INTERPRETATION: This dream reminds me of Acts 1:1-8. There we find Jesus being taken up to Heaven (the higher-ups being taken away), but first He ensures that His disciples are equipped to get His message out (connected with the "Eyewitness" News reporter). When Jesus left earth, He said, "Wait for the promise of the Father: the Holy Spirit coming upon you and baptizing you. That is what you need to be eyewitnesses and observers of Me" (see Acts 1:8).

God wants me to share His perspective with others on how living in the confines of a four-dimensional world is not a life

He ever meant for us to live. The great responsibility I have been instructed to share is that what Adam and Eve lost in the Garden—the ability to see and participate in the spirit world—Holy Spirit restored at Pentecost.

By anointing the eyes of our hearts to see and be witnesses and observers of Jesus, Holy Spirit empowers us to perceive and live out of the supernatural realm that surrounds us. He opens our eyes to the spiritual world, returning us to the unbroken dimension of Eden, the unified realm of God. We are commissioned by Holy Spirit to be witnesses and watchers, observing the Kingdom of Heaven and manifesting it on earth, just as Jesus did (see John 5:19-20).

Awesome. That was a cool dream! God was confirming what He had been telling me for weeks—that He had given me an assignment and it was time to get started.

CONFESSIONS OF A RECOVERING PERFECTIONIST

Now just to clarify some things: if you were to ask me whether I am afraid of anything, I would say, "No way!" I pride myself on not living in fear. I'm not afraid of snakes, skydiving, or speaking in public. I know *perfect love casts out fear* and that fear is faith in the enemy (1 John 4:18). I could teach ten messages on not being afraid.

Well, that is all well and good, and it's true. What is also true is that pride comes before a fall, and if I ever stand arrogantly, I better take heed lest I fall flat on my face (see 1 Cor. 10:12). So in a dream, God, in His exceeding graciousness and patience, gave me a snapshot of how He saw my heart. *My* heart. The awesome, fearless, confident heart I was so sure was full of faith. Turns out that wasn't quite the case.

Because I am a first-born, Type A, goal-oriented perfectionist (read: control freak), I have always figured if something is worth doing, it is worth doing perfectly. While that is somewhat reasonable, that actually leaves me doing nothing at all if I'm worried and unsure I'll be able to get it "just right."

In his book *Dreaming with God*, Pastor Bill Johnson talks about having a spirit of excellence versus a spirit of perfectionism. He writes, "Excellence is the high standard set for personal achievement because of who we are in God, and who God is in us. It is not the same as perfectionism. Perfectionism is the cruel counterfeit of excellence, which flows from a religious spirit."[4] Wow, that is a truth that sets us free! Perfection is not required. Our best is all God is looking for, and then He is happy to top up the rest.

Now, God and I had been going back and forth about sharing this new revelation until finally I had that dream about "insider secrets." I was enthusiastic, but I still didn't do anything about it that day. I didn't act on it by preparing a message to speak about it, nor did I even type up a blog. Nothing. God knew I was not quite "there" yet; I was still not motivated enough to take action. He knew what I didn't know (or would not consciously admit)—that I was scared. So the second night I had another revealing dream.

RUNNING SCARED

DREAM: Leo and I were at a mall with friends when a gang came in and one of the members slit someone's throat. I ran off alone, leaving behind my purse and dress, and hid, naked and safe, until it was over. Nobody else got hurt.

ACTION: Running and hiding

FEELING: Afraid

SETTING: In waking life, I was afraid of messing up my assignment from God so I hadn't even tried to fulfill it.

INTERPRETATION: GOD: *"You got it. That's exactly what this is all about. Here you are, so worried about making it absolutely perfect—that is paralyzing you from even starting. You're 'hiding' in that you're not even trying to begin My work. You're 'afraid' that it won't be perfect, but I'm not concerned; and I'm showing you why you shouldn't be either.*

"Look at your dream. Even in your hiding and fear I protected you. I kept you safe. I made sure Leo and your girlfriends whom you left behind weren't harmed. I kept you all safe and alive. Here you are railing against the counterfeit religious spirit of perfectionism, and you yourself are entertaining debilitating fear because of it?

"This dream is to show you that excellence is all I want from you. Your best is all I'm asking for. I'm not one to require things of you that you cannot give. All that should concern you is your obedience to what I'm asking you to do; the results are up to Me."

ME: "God, I repent. I confess this fear of failure, this fear of imperfection, and I repent of it. I'm sorry for getting sidetracked that way. Thank You for giving me the dream. I say 'yes' and agree with You and Your truth."

GOD: *"Awesome, Char, because as the dream showed, you're feeling vulnerable and exposed* (naked) *and in your fear and hiding you lost your identity* (symbolized by the purse which had the ID in it). *But even then, after all that, it was no matter—you got your clothes back; your purse wasn't stolen by the bad guys. It was all good. Even when you didn't do the right or brave or best thing, I kept you safe and secure and "perfect," in spite of your imperfection.*

"Don't be afraid of messing up. The dream was meant to show you that even in the worst-case scenario (your running and hiding), I take care of everything; I still protect everyone and everything.

"Indeed, I'm showing you the truth—that the only one preventing your voice from being heard and your message from getting out is you. (The dream showed a throat being slit, which is a picture

of a voice being silenced.) *So let's not quench My Spirit in you any longer. Let's get My message out."*

ME: "Yes, Lord. I agree. I repent for restraining Your Spirit. I rely on You to accomplish Your perfect work through me. I love You! Thank You for protecting me and all that concerns me."

That was awesome. I got it. I repented. I said "yes" to God. I really agreed with Him and began to act on it that time (finally). What kind of dream would I have the next night? Again the dream was God's perspective, showing me how He saw my heart. Thankfully, the third night vision was much more positive and better all around.

THE SURFING JESUS

DREAM: A bunch of us were on the beach at night with our surfboards, and Dad said, "C'mon! Let's paddle out into the ocean, and once we see sharks, we'll turn around and ride back to shore!"

I immediately followed without question. Then, in the pitch-black, darker-than-dark night sky, where I could not even see my hand in front of my face, I had the thought flash through my mind that maybe I should just head back to shore right now.

At that moment, I heard Dad's voice. He had been beside me the whole time. "Even though you couldn't see me, I could see you. I have stayed right with you. I kept pace with you and didn't leave you behind. I have always been right here."

Of course I was comforted by this, yet I still felt it necessary to complain a bit about the fact that I hadn't been able to see him. He just laughed and said something about surfing by faith and not by sight. *Great.*

ACTION: Following Dad

FEELING: Unafraid

SETTING: Last two days of dreams and journaling messages from the Lord

INTERPRETATION: I am not scared or worried about moving forward anymore. I'm now jumping in with both feet, regardless of the consequences. All I am concerned about is where my Dad (Heavenly Father) is and that I am staying with Him. He is watching over me. He is leading; I am following, and that works for both of us. Father God is always right beside me, and I feel His pleasure over my obedience and trust in Him.

It was pretty funny, though, because before I received God's full understanding of the dream, the first thought I had as I awoke was: *Let's paddle out until we see the sharks? Wait… what? That's not safe! I mean, how does this sound like a good idea to anyone?*

Holy Spirit immediately reminded me of a C. S. Lewis quote and I realized all over again—while Aslan may not be safe, He is good.[5] And He is the One leading me. Because He is good, I am safe.

Besides, we never did see any sharks.

Chapter 5

PICTURES AND PARABLES: THE LANGUAGE JESUS SPOKE

"Jesus always used stories and illustrations like these when speaking to the crowds. In fact, He never spoke to them without using such parables. This fulfilled what God had spoken through the prophet: 'I will speak to you in parables. I will explain things hidden since the creation of the world.'"
—MATTHEW 13:34-35 NLT

In our culture emphasizing rational understanding with our left-brain minds, we really would prefer a three-point sermon. "Lord, just give us a step-by-step list of instructions in our dream, and we'll wake up and follow it—promise!"

But God has never really been into three-point sermons or to-do lists. He much prefers teaching through narrative theology, using storytelling to reveal life lessons. We learn about faith from the story of Abraham, supernatural victory from the story of David and Goliath, and divine protection and provision from the stories of Noah in the ark and Daniel in the lion's den.

Even when He walked among us as a man, God did not bother to give as many explicit commands as we might have hoped.

"Jesus, how about a set of five principles for a successful life?"

"Actually, let Me just tell you a parable about some talents. See, there was this man going on a journey..."

"Hey Jesus, could You please give us a list of seven keys for an anointed ministry?"

"Well, I really just wanted to tell you about these oil lamps ten virgins had..."

"Jesus, we would love to hear Your three-point sermon on the doctrine of salvation."

"You know, actually, I was just about to tell you a great story about some hidden treasure. So there was this pearl in a field..."

He was clearly not interested in communicating the way we, in our twenty-first-century Western culture, are used to doing. Instead, Jesus spoke in parables that were relevant to the lives of His listeners and incorporated images they would easily recognize. And that is still the way He teaches. Sure, we could complain that God's not speaking a language we understand in our dreams. Or we could realize He's God and we should just learn His language and get on the same page with Him. Pictures, symbols, parables, stories—the Bible is full of them! And so are our dreams.

Dr. Virkler's Dream Key

You can learn the art of communicating symbolically by playing the game Pictionary, or Bible Pictionary.

HOMONYMS

Pictionary, if you've never played it, is a game where you draw a picture to try to get your team members to say a certain word. I happen to love this game, and I especially enjoy winning. So when I play, I am going to be smart. If I need to get you to say "flour," I'm not going to try to draw a mill, or even a bag of flour. That's too hard. Instead, I'm going to draw a flower, and you are going to say "flour"; and we're going to win the point.

That is what God does with us. He gives a dream picture, and He is just trying to get us to say a certain word to help communicate the message to our mind. He might draw a flower in our dream, but we need to play around with it and see what He's actually trying to talk with us about. I love the creativity of dreams. Plus, who wouldn't want to play Pictionary with God? Let me give you an example:

NEW SANTA IN TOWN

SETTING: My husband Leo and I had been asked to lead a Bible study, and we quickly discovered we were the only Charismatics in the group. Though sincere in their faith, no one else was very interested in pursuing the gifts of the Spirit, such as the gift of prophecy, the gift of tongues, etc. This left me seriously questioning if we were the right people to be leading the group.

I went home after one of these meetings wondering how I could authentically live out my supernatural relationship with God in a way that would be relevant and "salty," showing the others how walking in the Spirit enhances the flavor of every part of life.

DREAM: That evening I had a dream. It was like one of those Tim Allen Christmas movies where the old Santa Claus is retiring and needs to christen a newer younger Santa Claus in his place. I was him. I was bestowed with the magical Santa superpowers and commissioned for my new position. Then I woke up.

INTERPRETATION: I immediately understood that this was a picture of God anointing me with His supernatural grace and power for the new leadership position in which I had found myself. I was very much encouraged that He had clearly placed me there and was giving me His wisdom and equipping me to minister effectively for the job He had called me to do. That was great, and at once I was peaceful and optimistic concerning the group and all the Lord wanted to do in and through us there.

However, I did have one small issue regarding the specific symbols used, and I didn't hesitate to let God know about it. I mean, Santa Claus…really? I explained to Him that that was very unspiritual, not to mention entirely extra-biblical. Jesus just laughed and said, *"Aw, come on, Char. Don't you get it? You're bringing My presence/presents to the group. It's all about the gifts!"*

Dr. Virkler's Dream Key

EXAMPLES OF INTERPRETING PARABLES
AND PICTURES

I had two dreams during the night following the day I learned to hear God's voice, see God's visions, and journal (write out what God was speaking to me). The simple act of putting my journal next to my bed and asking God to speak brought me several dreams that first night.

Dream One

I had a new job as caretaker of a house. I was in the house, going up a flight of stairs, and I was riding a horse. After climbing the stairs I entered the bathroom and took out some cleaning supplies.

Interpretation

Question: In what way do I have a new job?

Answer: Just today, I have begun to hear God's voice, see visions, and journal.

Question: In what way do I feel like a horse on the stairwell?

Answer: I feel extremely awkward tuning to the flow of God's Spirit, seeing visions, and journaling. This way of living is an art I will need to practice until I become comfortable with it. Right now, I feel like the proverbial bull in a china closet.

Question: In what way will this path take me up a flight of stairs?

Answer: Hearing the Lord's voice and seeing and recording His vision will take me to a higher place in my walk with Him.

Question: In what way will I be getting out some cleaning supplies?

Answer: Hearing God's voice will clean up some areas of my life.

Dream Two

On the same night I had another dream:

I had pulled my car into a parking lot and turned off the ignition. However, the engine would not stop; it kept backfiring.

Interpretation

Question: What am I trying to turn off that is not turning off?

Answer: My analytical brain, so I can tune in to intuition and thus hear the voice of God.

The above two dreams dealt with issues that were taking place within me. They were counseling and encouraging me, suggesting that even though I felt awkward about the new direction in my life (of hearing God's voice, seeing visions, and journaling), if I kept with it, it would take me to a higher place in God and clean up certain areas in my life. The dreams also confirmed that it was going to be a struggle to shut down the analytical reasoning process that had ruled over me and been a god in my life for many years.

SIMPLE AND UNIVERSAL

Pictures are actually the simplest way to communicate. Go to any library or bookstore, and which section has the picture books? We know it's the children's section, of course. Pictures are easy for kids to comprehend. They can look through a book of pictures and follow the whole story without ever reading a word.

Or take silent movies, for example. It is possible to watch an entire film and hear no dialogue whatsoever yet, by the actions of the characters and the feelings they express, have perfect understanding of the meaning and message of the story. That is how well we intuitively connect with pictures.

Pictures are also universal. When we travel, we don't always speak the language of the country we're visiting. However, if we are driving in Istanbul, we don't need to know the Turkish word for "airport." All we need to do is look for a small picture of an airplane on a street sign and we'll know which road to take.

And let's not forget technology. Our smartphones and laptop screens are full of little icons. We know the picture of sun and clouds represents a weather app, the globe or compass connects us to our online browser, an envelope indicates email, and so on. Suffice it to say, pictures really are worth a thousand words.

PICTURES ARE THE LANGUAGE OF THE HEART

It can seem frustrating that dreams are not more straightforward, which would make them easier to understand. However, as we're learning, the secret to demystifying the interpretation is simply to remember that more than anything else, dreams are allegorical. They are figurative in that the people, objects, and activities they depict are representing something similar in our waking lives. Rarely are they to be viewed literally.

Our logical minds take everything at face value, which is why they generally are confused by the symbolism. We need to change gears when we examine our dreams and realize we must look at everything metaphorically. Let's try to put this into perspective.

$$V(t) = 2\pi\beta(\text{Cos }(\omega t + 2\theta/\pi)) = 2\pi\beta \ (\text{Cos}(\omega t)\text{Cos}(2\theta/\pi) - \text{Sin}(\omega t) \ \text{Sin}(2\theta/\pi))$$

That is just a small portion of a ceiling-to-floor equation my husband had taped up on our dining room wall when he was in grad school. If you have studied electrical engineering, then you know that this gobbledygook of numbers and symbols is actually an equation for sinusoidal voltage. However, to the uninitiated like myself, it might as well be alphabet soup. It doesn't make sense to me. In fact, it doesn't look like anything at all.

Does that make the equation meaningless, just because it doesn't mean anything to me? Of course not. We know that an intelligent mind came up with this brilliant equation, and my lack of understanding is a reflection on me, not the mathematical language.

If I try to take my non-engineering-educated brain and decode those symbols, I would completely misinterpret them. However, that is often what we end up doing when we try to decipher our dreams with our analytical minds. Our minds speak a different language than our hearts. Pictures are the language of the heart and the spirit.

A fascinating verse in the Old Testament affirms, *"It is the glory of God to conceal a matter, but the glory of kings is to search out a matter"* (Prov. 25:2). This Scripture sheds light on an important principle of dream work and helps answer the very common question "Why can't dreams be clearer?"

Jesus constantly spoke in parables, and the dreams we have at night are also in picture and story form. Our dreams take us to the kingdom of the heart, where a different language is spoken. We won't bemoan the fact that we don't understand it. Instead, we will learn to speak it!

We do not want to think of dream interpretation as a "gift" meant only for specially selected people. If you say something to me in Spanish and I understand you, does that then mean I have the gift of Spanish? Or does it mean instead that I took some Spanish classes and actually studied the language in order to learn it? Similarly, the ability to interpret dreams is not a divinely imparted gift bestowed on a few. Rather, it is a skill that we all can learn to cultivate through time and practice.

THAT ROBIN WILLIAMS MOVIE

My husband and I recently watched a good movie again: *August Rush*. There are some great spiritual messages in that film. For instance, the young musical prodigy hears sounds that nobody else hears and writes them down (two of the "4 keys to hearing God's voice" right there).

It is amazing, and everyone is blown away by the incredible symphonies he has captured and put on paper. The little boy says, "The music is all around us" and asks his mentor, "Can everyone hear the music?" His mentor replies, "Not everyone is listening."[6]

That's it. That is the revelation. The spirit realm is all around us. Can everyone hear God's voice? Yes, but not everyone is listening. Can everyone see into the spirit realm through dreams and visions? Yes, but not everyone is looking. The more we listen, the more we'll hear. The more we look, the more we'll see.

GIFT OF SEEING?

After *Charisma* posted an article I wrote on angels, I received an email that said, "Wow, I wish God would give me your gift of seeing. God, are You listening? I just really want that vision imparted to me!" While I appreciate her desire for spiritual gifts, a cultivation of skill is also required to properly unwrap and activate the gifts we've already been given. The Bible says that *"...the mature...because of practice have their senses trained..."* (Heb. 5:14).

Now I know that every good thing comes from above so I'm grateful that He has given me spiritual eyes to see (see James 1:17). But here's the crux of the matter: it takes time to "train the senses" to see God's visions. For example, Michael Phelps swims, and I know how to swim, too. What is the biggest difference between us that accounts for his heightened ability? Granted, he has some natural gifting. But in addition to that—and possibly just as important, if not more so—is *time*. He has basically lived in a swimming pool for the last two decades. He has spent his whole life training, practicing, and developing that gift.

What about Arnold Schwarzenegger? He has the same number of muscles in his body that you and I have. Sure, God has given him some gifting or bent, but he has also lived in the gym. He has invested time into bodybuilding because that is what he values, that is what is important to him.

GIFT OF SNOWBOARDING?

I can't say to God, "Well, if You want me to be an Olympic gold medalist in snowboarding, then tomorrow morning I should wake up and supernaturally have all the right muscles developed and all the important jumps and tricks in my repertoire and skillset."

No, we know it doesn't work that way. We know champions have to practice and they have to fail. They make ten thousand attempts and experience thousands of crashes and falls. Only then—after years of life put into training—do they win the gold medal. Then they are the best they can be.

The same is true with things of the spirit. Looking and listening get easier the more you do it, and it's OK to mess up. I use the snowboarding analogy for good reason: I have fallen while snowboarding because I was trying to stretch myself and do something I wasn't sure I could do. And what happened? I broke my back—literally, a fractured vertebra. So did I give up? Did I never snowboard again? Of course not.

My husband Leo is a perfect example of this. He was born and raised in Zambia. Growing up in South Central Africa didn't afford him many opportunities to play winter sports. Good thing he came to university in the beautiful winter wonderland that is upstate New York! My brother Josh and I introduced him to all kinds of fun things like sledding, ice skating, and best of all, snowboarding.

That is one of the things I love about my husband. It seems like often we are tempted to stop learning new things or cultivating new skills once we've grown up. If we haven't learned something by the time we are adults, many times we don't ever bother trying. Not Leo! He is constantly learning and growing, and he always goes all in.

Well, in case you have never tried snowboarding, I'll enlighten you: it involves falling—a lot of falling. But with Josh's awesome teaching, some lessons on the slopes, a couple instructional DVDs, and a ton of time practicing on the hills, now he is one of the best riders out there. Why? Because he tried and tried and he fell and fell and fell again—just like anyone who learns to snowboard does. He got a bloody face. He suffered bumps and bruises. But he was humble and perseverant and he didn't give up.

And now? Now it is really quite impressive to watch him carve his way down the side of a mountain. He is actually a better rider than I am because he doesn't mind falling. He loves going fast, easily rides switch, and enjoys "black diamonds" (the narrowest, steepest trails). He's amazing!

MULTIPLYING TALENTS

Hopefully it is easy to see how all these examples in the natural translate to our cultivation of spiritual giftedness and the multiplication of the talents God has given us. We might be tempted to say, "Oh, healing? That's Randy Clark's gift. Oh, hearing God? That's Mark Virkler's gift. Oh, interpreting dreams? That's Charity's gift." But the reason any of us have succeeded at anything is because of practice, time, and training.

Just as Leo watched snowboarding tutorials, we have video training on seeing in the spirit and interpreting dreams. Might we make a mistake? Might we be stretched so far we don't quite get it perfectly right the first time? Sure! Is that OK? Yes! A million times, yes.

If we don't try, we will never learn. If we don't take time to practice, it will never get easier. If we don't take the initiative to cultivate the skills necessary to move in the realm of the supernatural, it will forever remain out of reach.

You can do this. Dream interpretation is not just a special gift bestowed on a few. It involves a skillset that can be learned by anyone. You *can* learn the language God speaks while you sleep. You *can* understand His messages in your night visions. You *can* interpret your dreams.

PRACTICING THE ART OF
PROPHETIC DREAMING

I often see my walk in the spirit in general, and my experiences in the supernatural world of dreams specifically, as a wax on/wax off training ground. Remember the movie *The Karate Kid?* The young hero wants to learn the great kicks and punches from the karate master. Instead, the master has him painting his fence and waxing his car, and his student becomes frustrated with what appear to be mundane and unrelated activities that are not moving him toward his goal of becoming a championship fighter.

Finally, the old karate master shows him how the movements he has been practicing in the menial household tasks are actually the same moves he needed to master in order to be a karate champion. It looked like he was just waxing a car, but really he was learning how to block a strike. He thought he was just painting a fence, but really he was practicing how to fight.

God often works with us in similar ways, having us go along in our day-to-day lives not always realizing the importance of what He has us doing. We don't understand that He is preparing and training us through the seemingly "insignificant" things in our lives, like "silly" dreams.

We all know that David had years of private victories, fighting the lion and killing the bear, before he ever had his epic public victory of defeating Goliath. We should not denigrate our small personal victories of understanding "simple" or "inconsequential" messages to us through our visions at night.

We are connecting with the God of the universe while we sleep. He sees dreams as a powerful communicative medium to bring us closer to Him, His way of seeing things, and His heart. We should be grateful for such experiences and appreciate each one, not discounting or despising the day of small beginnings (see Zech. 4:10).

The following is a funny example of what this principle looks like in real life:

A MOUSE IN THE HOUSE

DREAM: A friend is visiting, and there's a creature loose in the workout room. Leo tries to capture it. Then, in the bathroom, another animal climbs up out of the sink drain and grabs hold of Leo's neck! At first I thought the animal was bad, but then I decided it was unique and worth keeping so I was happy.

ACTION: Grabbing; attempting to capture something (Leo tried to trap one animal, and then the other animal tried to capture him.)

FEELING: Weirdness—it's either really horrible or really great.

SETTING: In waking life, my brother was in town and staying with us for a visit. We had set a couple of mousetraps in our home when we first moved in, but in almost two years of living there, they had never caught anything.

INTERPRETATION: This is an example of a dream having meaning on more than one level. It became clear soon after we got up that there was a "prophetic," kind of fun layer, to the dream. During the night, our traps had caught two mice, one in one place and one in another (shown by the two different rooms in the dream). We had never caught any mice before that day, and we've never caught any since. And that night it was not one, but two mice—just like the two creatures in my dream.

It was weird in both a positive and a negative way. We had a guest in our home at the time (just like a friend was visiting in the dream), and who wants people to know you have a mouse in your house? Fortunately, the foreshadowing nature of the dream overruled the unpleasantness of the deceased rodents and we all thought it was cool.

The night vision was not literal because the two creatures I dreamt of in the house were not mice. It was also not literal because neither one of the mice tried to capture Leo in waking life, nor did we end up keeping the mice (as we kept the animal in the dream). Still there were enough similarities that we were able to understand the symbols on this level of interpretation, and doing so strengthened our conviction that all our dreams have meaning. It seemed like one of those "training ground" dreams that don't have great significance except to increase our understanding of our dream language. However, there was also another, more symbolic level of interpretation that we'll come back and explore in a later chapter.

Every time you have a dream and then see it played out in waking life it will encourage your heart. It will make you feel increasingly sure that your interpretations are correct. You will become more confident that what you perceive in the spiritual realm is actually manifesting and becoming a reality in the physical world as well.

Dr. Virkler's Dream Key

DREAMS ABOUT OTHERS

Perhaps only five percent of our dreams are about others— dreams that are not talking about parts of yourself but are about external situations. I have discovered that the more right-brained a person is (i.e., visionary and intuitive), the more likely he or she is to dream farther away from home (away from his or her own self). That means that right-brained people may be more likely to have a greater number of dreams about others.

For example, I have noted that three different women who scored a 7.7 (the highest I have seen) on the "Brain Preference Indicator" test recommended in *4 Keys to Hearing God's Voice* have vivid dreams about others in which they see the murders, rapes, and thefts that are taking place in their communities that night and that are indeed reported in the news the following day. These are literal dreams of real-life events. Obviously, not all dreams about others show such fearsome pictures. These are just given as examples of objective dreams of which I am personally aware.

THE CASE OF THE STOLEN PLATES

Danny Hartwell, one of my graduate students, is a right-brained visionary prophet, and with a name like "Daniel Joseph" it's hard not to be anointed with dreams and visions! Here in his own words is a prophetic dream experience he shared as part of his homework assignment:

One night I had a dream that the license plate on my pickup flew away. I didn't pay any attention to the dream until the next night I had the same dream. When I went out to my truck the next day, I noticed that one of the bolts holding the plate on the truck was missing. I went to get a bolt to fix the plate when I noticed that the plate didn't match the one on the front of the truck.

I took it to the state police, and they informed me that the plate I turned in had been stolen and someone took my plate, replacing it with that one. There was a drug runner in our area that would avoid the police by removing the rear plate of someone's car and replacing it with the one they had stolen. If it hadn't been for my dream, I would have never noticed.

What I appreciate most about this story is the key factor obedience played. What if Danny hadn't paid any attention to the dream? What if, even though it came twice, he chalked it up to an amusing coincidence and didn't take it seriously? What if he treated it as an anecdote to share at the water cooler rather than a prophetic call to action? Then he may never even have found out about the stolen license plate. Who knows what was prevented from happening because he listened to his dream and acted on its message?

WHAT'S THE BIG DEAL?

So these dreams about license plates and mice, are they that big of a deal? Do they really change the world? No, they don't. But they change my world. And Danny's world. Because now we understand God's language in our dreams a little bit more. Now our faith in our ability to receive from the spirit realm and recognize how it relates to "real" life is a little bit stronger. We have connected with God and heard Him speak to us personally in the night. And knowing God more? That changes everything.

We want to trust and obey in all of the little day-to-day messages for practice. Then when the big "important" instructions come, we're ready. We have heard God's voice like this a hundred times before. We know His dream language. We understand what it looks like and how it sounds to us, and it becomes that much easier to live out. We have run the drills, and we know the plays. We are able to receive God's revelation clearly, and we know we won't miss it. We have been practicing day and night, and we are prepared.

Joseph didn't start out by interpreting Pharaoh's dreams. Before that, he was interpreting the dreams of the people around him— the baker and cupbearer. And before that, he was interpreting his own dreams. We just have to start somewhere, and somewhere can start tonight.

THE REST OF THE STORY

I want to share more of Danny's story with you. As I mentioned, he was faithful with the smaller dreams. He learned to pay attention to the "minor" lessons and to act on the truths the Lord spoke to him through his night visions, and by doing so, he proved he could be entrusted with greater revelation. Danny would not let one of the Lord's words fall to the ground so God revealed even more to him. But there was a learning curve.

On September 10, 2001, Danny had visions of planes crashing into buildings as well as into a field. At the time, he was new to hearing from God in this way and didn't know what to do with what he saw. The next day, he saw his visions tragically come to life as they were played over and over again on the news.

Years passed, and Danny pressed more into the prophetic. Granted, he was already gifted in this area, but he took the time to hone his skills. He read books and took courses to develop his ability to understand dreams and visions, so now he knows what to do.

On the night of December 24, 2009, Danny had a dream of an airplane exploding, leaving Christmas gifts strewn all over the ground. In his dream, the plane was about to land in Detroit but never made it. Because Danny understood how God speaks through his dreams, he immediately got up, woke up his wife to share the dream with her, and they prayed into it together. They asked the Lord to intervene. They prayed for mercy and grace and that the plane and all its passengers would be safe. They stood in the gap and interceded for God's protection and presence to be in that situation, for the enemy's plans to be thwarted, and for the Lord to be glorified.

The next morning they watched the news and learned that the now infamous "underwear bomber" had been arrested. He had boarded a plane on its way to Detroit on Christmas Day and attempted to detonate a bomb. It was just like in the dream. But

Danny had listened to God's voice, and God had listened to Danny's prayers; and the rest, as they say, is history.

This incredible story is a powerful illustration of how we can work together with Holy Spirit to accomplish God's purposes on earth. *"Surely the Lord God does nothing unless He reveals His secret counsel to His servants the prophets"* (Amos 3:7). Therefore we will heed Eli's advice to young Samuel: *"Go and lie down, and if He calls you, say, 'Speak, Lord, for Your servant is listening'"* (1 Sam. 3:9 NIV).

May we be ready and expectantly waiting to hear from Heaven all day and all night!

Chapter 6

THE FUN FORM OF DREAMS: PUNS, PARODIES, AND PLAYS ON WORDS

*"I have also spoken by the prophets and I
have multiplied visions, and used similitudes,
by the ministry of the prophets."*
—HOSEA 12:10 KJV

Romans 14:17 tells us that righteousness, peace, and joy are the very Kingdom of God. Peace and joy? They're just emotions, for goodness' sake. Could they really be that important? Jesus showed me through a dream precisely how He feels about them.

There were a few different symbols that illustrated Matthew 11:28-30 (*"Come to Me, all who are weary and heavy-laden, and I will give you rest…"*), but the part I want to explain is about yolks. In the dream I was trying to make eggs, but all the yolks were little stones—they were as hard as rocks! That didn't seem quite right, and it wasn't working at all.

Well, what is the opposite of a hard yolk? That would be an easy yoke—which, incidentally, is the kind Jesus wants me to have. Through my journaling He interpreted the dream's message explaining, *"Hey, I know you're exhausted from all you're doing so come and relax. You're trying to make it work, but you're making it too hard. I have a gentle and humble heart so learn from Me. I'll make your work easy and help you find rest for your soul."*

Rest for what? Not my body. My soul. My emotional equilibrium and inner state of being are what those in the heavenly dimension are most concerned with. First and foremost, they want us to have rest and peace inside. Jesus says He personally is in a healthy place—gentle and humble in heart—and He invites me to join Him there. He showed me, through dreaming about Scripture, *"This is it. This is what I'm talking about. This is for you, for now: a rested soul, an easy yoke, a peaceful heart."*

I love the pun in that dream, and God does, too. He enjoys making us laugh, and that is a big reason He likes to play around with words. These kinds of dreams are like inside jokes between us and God, and they are a lot more fun than if He had just preached a sermon at us.

THE ALMOND STICK

In fact, throughout Scripture God used idioms and colloquialisms to communicate His messages. Unfortunately, His sense of humor has been lost on most of us because we don't speak Greek or Hebrew!

For instance, in the first chapter of Jeremiah we find God in discussion with the prophet about a vision. Jeremiah determines that what he's looking at is the rod of an almond tree, and the Lord confirms his guess by saying, *"You have seen well, for I am watching over My word to perform it"* (Jer. 1:12).

In English, there's nothing there, but if we go back to the original language in which they were conversing, we're able to see the wordplay. Murray Dueck is the President of Samuel's Mantle Prophetic Training School in British Columbia, Canada. In his book *If This Were a Dream, What Would It Mean?*, he discusses the biblical pun in this passage along with several others.[7] His wonderful insights made me curious enough to explore the topic further.

The resources I checked didn't make it clearer, so I was delighted when the Lord brought a new friend into our lives, Aminadav Badichi. Ami is an Israeli whose first language is Hebrew. I asked him about the wordplay in the passage and what it really means. Here is his reply:

> I am not an expert in Jeremiah, but I will do my best. So basically this is the conversation between God and Jeremiah:

> וַיְהִי דְבַר-יְהוָה אֵלַי לֵאמֹר, מָה-אַתָּה רֹאֶה יִרְמְיָהוּ; וָאֹמַר, מַקֵּל שָׁקֵד אֲנִי רֹאֶה. וַיֹּאמֶר יְהוָה אֵלַי, הֵיטַבְתָּ לִרְאוֹת: כִּי-שֹׁקֵד אֲנִי עַל-דְּבָרִי, לַעֲשֹׂתוֹ.

> I will translate freely:

> (Jeremiah speaking): "And the word of God was to me, to say, What do you see Jeremiah; And I said, an almond stick I see." "And God said to me, you have seen well, because I am working on My word to make it done."

> Now for the wordplay: The word for "almond" is *shaked*. The word I translated "I am working" is *shoked*, and it means "to be working and focusing at the moment on something; studying really hard." For example, "I am *shoked* on my Hebrew studies because I want to read the Bible in its original language."

> So yes, God indeed has played with the words, and He shows the *shaked* (almond stick) to make the point that

He is *shoked* (focusing His attention on His word at that moment to make it happen).

Wow, no wonder God chose to have His written Word recorded in such a beautiful, descriptive language. It is so rich and full of meaning!

Another, probably more familiar, example of biblical wordplay is the conversation Jesus had with Simon Peter. When Jesus asked His disciples who they thought He was, Simon answered, *"You are the Christ, the Son of the living God"* (Matt. 16:16). In response, Jesus blessed him and declared, *"You are Peter [Petros], and on this rock [petra] I will build My church"* (Matt. 16:18). Peter's name sounds like the Greek word for "rock" or "stone," and Jesus highlighted that similarity to make His point.

God did the same kind of thing with my friends' names in the following night vision. I dreamt of a guy whose name is Chris, and his last name starts with a "T." Chris T. ended up representing a girlfriend of mine named Christine.

The funny thing is that didn't even occur to me at first. Sometimes we wake up and immediately know the meaning of the dream. Other times we need to keep looking at it and turning it around in our hearts until we see what it is showing us. This dream was one of those times.

SHOWERS OF GRACE

DREAM: I went to a reunion and met my old friend Chris T. I discovered he was blind and his wife had just left him so I wanted to encourage him. When I went to the restroom, I became drenched with water from a shower and ended up dripping wet.

ACTION: "Meeting"—meeting my friend, meeting his needs by leading him as he walked, etc.

FEELING: Compassion and grace

SETTING: In waking life, I was going to a memorial service the next day for a girlfriend's father. Christine was my first close friend to have lost a parent, and I was not sure how to comfort her or what I could do or say to be a support to her.

INTERPRETATION: In the dream, as in waking life, I felt extraordinary compassion, empathy, and concern for my friend. I desperately wanted to help in whatever way I could but didn't know how and felt at a loss.

When I dreamt of a shower, the first thought that came to me as I awoke was "showers of grace." Grace is divine enablement, which is just what I needed. As I searched the Scriptures I remembered Ezekiel 34:26 speaks of *"showers of blessing"*—and that's even better.

The dream showed me that God was going to shower me with His blessings, His strength, and His words of wisdom, comfort, and supernatural love so that I would have something to give my friend. I have nothing to offer in and of my own self but everything to offer in Him. He has drenched me in His compassion. He has soaked me in His grace. I am literally dripping with His presence.

And where was the shower located? In the "restroom," the place of rest. The waterfall of Heaven cascades over me as I find my resting place in Jesus.

This is a powerful picture, and as soon as I received that understanding in my quiet time I was extremely encouraged and ready to meet my friend the next day. I saw myself covered in God's glory, a carrier of His love and presence to her. He would meet her through me. I agreed with this and said "yes" to it.

THE PRACTICE OF PONDERING

Both "Chris T." and "Christine" are friends I have had for most of my life. That was the first thing I recognized, and so right away I understood the person in the dream to represent my friend whose father had just passed away.

However, less than an hour after receiving this great revelation, I was back to being worried about my friend again: *How can I be there for her? I don't know what to say. This is too sad; it's too much.* I let myself get sidetracked with my own thoughts and fears again. So what did I do?

The Latin word *movere* is the root of our English word *emotion* and it literally means "to move."[8] Being aware of this helps us understand how closely related they are, how our emotions are what move us to action. But what moves our emotions? Pictures. Pictures evoke emotion, and emotion, in turn, inspires action.

Recognizing this principle, I decided to pull that dream picture back out and look at it again with the eyes of my heart. I reminded myself of it and kept looking at it whenever my mind was free. As I was folding laundry, I was pondering it (see Luke 2:19). As I was cleaning the kitchen, I was meditating on it (see Josh. 1:8).

I determined to put it in front of my mind and my heart and to keep looking at it until I felt those same emotions. God Emotions are what I want to live out of: compassion that moves me, peace that rules me, and love that controls and compels me. I purpose to see myself this way because that's how He sees me.

A SECOND CHANCE

As I did this, later on in the day I had another breakthrough revelation of the dream message. I had already told my husband at breakfast about my initial understanding of what it meant. However, several hours later, as I was continuing to reflect on the dream, Holy Spirit moved my heart in another way.

He reminded me that years ago, my friend Chris, who was in the dream, had gone through a traumatic health challenge in waking life and I hadn't been there for him. At the time, I didn't know how I could help so I literally just didn't show up for him at all. It was bad, and I repented and had to pray through the guilt of not being a good friend to him at the time. I am grateful that I didn't immediately think of this when I dreamt of him because that showed that the Lord had truly healed my heart over that situation.

God did, however, bring this to my remembrance later that day to show me how I was getting another chance to be a good friend. I definitely didn't want to create any more regret over a missed opportunity to share God's comfort and be a friend when I am needed most. This was my chance to let His love flow through me. It was a do-over, a second opportunity to demonstrate grace and kindness to a hurting friend in her time of need. This was another aspect of the dream that moved me to more confident action.

MATCHING IT UP

As if that wasn't enough, God gave me one more amazing confirmation through the dream that solidified everything He had shown me throughout the day. As I continued meditating on the night vision and replaying it over and over again in my imagination, I realized one of the most obvious connections of all. I couldn't believe I hadn't seen it right away!

It was not until I was brushing my teeth and getting ready for bed that the cleverest piece of the dream puzzle fell into place. As I already mentioned, it was about the names of my friends. The guy I was meeting in the dream, his name is "Chris T.," and in the dream he had just lost a family member he loved (his wife had left him). My friend whom I was meeting in waking life is named "Christine," and she had just lost a family member she loved (her dad passed away). I felt compassion for both of them. So the name, action, situation, and emotion were all the same in the dream and in waking life. They just needed to be matched up.

THE BLIND FACTOR

The reason the symbol of "blindness" came up in the dream is because God was teaching me how even before a need arises, He already has the solution. Even before a prayer is prayed, He has heard it and sent an answer (see Isa. 65:24). Let me explain.

My friend, Tina Luce, is a gifted musician and composer, and she has been blind since birth. We recently had been talking about her father's death several years before, and she had just sent me an MP3 of a song the Lord had given her on the one-year anniversary of her father's passing. "Something After" is an anointed composition about the extraordinary pain of loss but the even more extraordinary and supernatural comfort we find in Jesus and His promise to us of something after this world.

Tina emailed me the song on a Monday. On Wednesday, Christine's father passed away. I sent the song to Christine, who was incredibly touched by the beautiful words and music. She, in turn, shared it with her siblings. Christine has told me several times how much this song encouraged and comforted her and how it ministered deeply to her heart in her most broken moments. Thank You, Jesus.

I had been so worried about how I could be there for Christine, and yet God had already orchestrated everything. I mean, I didn't do anything. I just forwarded an email. It was Tina that received and recorded the revelatory song. God knew Christine would need that encouragement, and He had Tina send it to me, just two days before, so that I could share it with Christine. That's how awesome God is and how much He cares for my friend, her family, and each one of us and about what we're going through.

So I am finally beginning to see more how God sees. I realize how He has showered me with His blessings, drenched me in His presence, and soaked me with His love. I get it now. I see how I can't help but leave drops of grace and footprints of glory wherever I go. Goodness and mercy follow me; they are what I leave behind.

I won't quickly forget this truth because now I have just lived it. The Word became flesh in my life, and God used a dream to do it.

THE TAKEAWAY

The biggest lesson we can learn from this is how important it is to keep pondering our dreams all day long. As with any other issue in life, it is also quite helpful to pray in the Spirit as we consider and contemplate our dreams (see Eph. 6:18). In the same way we prayerfully reflect on Scripture, we should keep meditating on these night visions in our hearts and continue rolling them around in our minds (see Ps. 1:2). Many times I wake up from a dream with one interpretation only to discover that as I continue to pray into it, additional layers of meaning become evident.

Even after our quiet times are over and we are going through the rest of our day, whenever our mind isn't focused on something and is free we can redirect it back to our dreams. *What was that scene again? What did Holy Spirit say about it?* We remember the night vision and ponder His revelation, and those heart pictures cause us to feel God Emotion, which in turn moves us to His plan of action.

LITERALLY SYMBOLIC

One time I had a dream that I was supposed to pray for a certain person. In waking life I had not been thinking about this woman at all, and I did not particularly feel any call to intercede for her. However, the lady in my dream shared the same last name as a good friend who was definitely on my radar. I realized the dream was talking about my friend, an idea that was confirmed by a tremendous compassion that welled up within me and a deep desire to pray for her.

Remember, dreams are rarely one hundred percent literal. We should always look for the symbolic twist in every vision of the night.

Dr. Virkler's Dream Key

When interpreting dreams, look for metaphors, similes, and metonymies. Dreaming about ketchup may be calling you to "catch up" in some area. A fire may be trying to warn you that you are "playing with fire." A dream of being smothered or drowned may indicate that you are feeling "in over your head." A frozen lake, an ice flow, or even ice cubes may be cautioning you that you are only seeing "the tip of the iceberg." Having your glasses broken may be an indication that you are not seeing a situation clearly.

Other examples of expressions that may show up in your dreams include "walking a mile in someone else's shoes," "being born in a barn," "being up the creek without a paddle," "as the crow flies," "throwing the baby out with the bath water," "on a level playing field," "throwing a wrench in the works," "at the eleventh hour," and "speaking with a forked tongue." Your heart may use one of these pictures in your dreams, expecting that you will understand its symbolic meaning. Think outside the box! Be prepared for unexpected and clever ways for your heart to get its point across to your conscious mind. Be open to plays on words and lateral connections.

MUCH ADO ABOUT NOTHING

I had a dream in which my friend, Eunice Adou, was upset because she ran out of milk for her dinner party. I was helping her get ready and told her it didn't matter, as nobody coming to dinner even drank milk!

God used this picture to show me that in waking life, I was getting upset unnecessarily. Instead, I needed to find my peace in Him and not be bothered by minor things. He used my friend's last name as a play on words to tell me that I was making "much *ado* about nothing."

It was also neat because in the dream, I became the voice of God, conveying His perspective to the worried person. In waking life, I was distressed and He was helping me and trying to calm me down. In the dream, it was my friend who was distressed and I was the one helping her and trying to calm her down. I was able to see things the way God sees them, to know that there's nothing to be worried about. I understood that because I had just dreamt it and felt His peace. I experienced His point of view while I slept so it was easy for me to then adopt His perspective in waking life, too.

GET OVER IT

One time I was wondering what I should do in waking life: Should I express my frustration over something that was bothering me? Or should I just let it go and get over it?

That night I had a dream that I was on a pole vaulting team, but I was too sick and weak to participate. So two friends helped nurse me back to health so I had the strength to pole vault, too.

The two friends represented my two guardian angels, who minister to me (see Heb. 1:13-14). The dream showed that I should be "rising above" the situation. A strong and spiritually healthy person should have no trouble "getting over" what was bothering me.

What is a good picture for that? Pole vaulting, of course. I knew then that God wanted me to come to a higher place with His perspective and stay positive, forgive, accept, and, as much as it lies with me, live at peace with all men (see Rom. 12:18).

Dr. Virkler's Dream Key

The most natural interpretation is most likely the correct one.

THE "WRIGHT" GUY

My husband had a dream one night that the famous Hollywood actor Jeffrey Wright came to the open auditions he was holding. He was amazed that such a big-name celebrity would join his small film production team. Leo was surprised, excited, and grateful—both in the dream and when he awoke.

In waking life Leo had been concerned about how many people were going to show up for the auditions he was having that weekend. God was speaking encouragement through the dream by using the actor's name. The Lord was telling Leo that there was no need to be worried about anything because He was going to bring the "right" people for the project.

THE OPPOSITE OF RIGHT

When we dream of turning right in a dream, we can usually feel pretty confident about it. We can often take it as a confirmation that we are headed in the right direction and are on the correct, best path. However, if we dream of going left, that could raise a red flag. We would then definitely want to consider the possibility that we are headed the wrong way in some area of our life, because left is the opposite of right and right is the opposite of wrong.

THE FRENCH CONNECTION

Another dream example of God playing with words featured The Bon-Ton, one of a large chain of department stores in our area. The store carries some of everything so you can always find whatever you need there.

The setting in waking life found my husband and I working on a large project that was too big for us to accomplish on our own. We knew we were pursuing a God-sized dream and we needed Him and His anointing to realize success in the endeavor. Also, at the time we had guests staying in our home, and one of them was originally from France.

That evening, Leo and I prayed together before bed, thanking God for blessing and establishing the work of our hands. Afterwards I fell asleep and had a simple dream. In it, we were enjoying a shopping spree at The Bon-Ton. Then I awoke.

Holy Spirit reminded me of my French lessons from years ago, enabling me to quickly grasp that *bon* can be translated "good." Obviously, a ton is a measurement for a huge amount of something. I was thrilled and encouraged by the interpretation and realized all over again that we had nothing to worry about. The dream message was clear: The Lord has a "ton" of "good" things "in store" for us!

Incredibly, God confirmed this later the same day through a conversation with our French friend. I had not shared the dream with her; we were simply chatting about the best place to find organic produce. Imagine my surprise when she just happened to mention that a Whole Foods supermarket was moving into a former Bon-Ton store nearby. Bon-Ton? God used the same symbol twice, in my dream and in waking life, to make sure I got the message.

PLAYING WITH WORDS

Dreams are precise so we should play around with how we describe the picture until it clicks and the message comes into focus. For example, are we standing "on a street corner" or are we "at a crossroads"? Is the item in our dream a "blanket" or is it a "comforter" (i.e., Holy Spirit)? Are we looking for a "bathroom" or a "restroom" (i.e., a place of rest)?

From the dream examples in this book: Am I making a "small hop" or am I taking a "quantum leap"? Is my friend wearing a "jumpsuit" or "coveralls"? Am I struggling to "pole vault" or am I having trouble "rising above" something and "getting over it"?

Often the meaning doesn't click until we record the dream or share it with someone else. Then as we are recounting it, we end up using slightly different phrases and more specific terms that give us an "Aha!" moment. The accurate wording unlocks the mystery and decodes the message so the interpretation of the dream begins to fall into place.

A NOUN OR A VERB

The next dream illustrates how God used the symbol of my place of "work" to represent how He actively "works" in our lives. I had been pondering Galatians 5:6 on how faith works through love in relation to how Jesus was moved by compassion and healed the sick (see Matt. 14:14). A picture came to me that is analogous in the natural world to what is happening in the spirit realm.

The idea I received from the Lord is how we can see compassion as a "carrier wave" of God's healing power. In telecommunications, a carrier wave is what the message (word, image, music, signal) is carried on. The message is encoded in the carrier wave by modifying the latter's frequency, amplitude, or phase.

SETTING: I wondered if compassion is the divine frequency through which God's grace is carried and released. I went to bed meditating on this and the need for compassion to be present in order to release spiritual power and energy.

DREAM: I was at the office, and my co-worker, Karen, gave me a homeopathic remedy from a lady to whom I was ministering.

SYMBOLS:

The office = Where I work (So, to make healing work...)

Passed through Karen's hands = "Karen" sounds a lot like "caring," and she has the strong character traits of care and compassion. She was the one who "carried" the remedy. (Healing works when moving through the hands of caring; it's carried by compassion.)

Homeopathic remedy = A healing frequency (i.e., God's healing power/energy)

Given from the person to whom I was ministering = Miracles begin with a need. (The person to whom I am ministering has a need and when that is united with care/compassion, then healing occurs.)

INTERPRETATION: Compassion was present in Karen, and it was through her that the energized frequency for healing was transferred and flowed. It was in her presence that the gift was given and received. "Caring Karen" was the "carrier" and connector of the gift of healing.

This dream showed that the divine frequency of compassion must be present for God's healing power to work. Compassion is the "spiritual carrier wave" that conducts God's wisdom, healing, power, and gifts to us and through us to others.

MARRIED AND PREGNANT— LITERAL OR SYMBOLIC?

We are frequently asked, "Is God telling me that I'm going to marry this person just like what happened in my dream?" Maybe, but as demonstrated throughout this book, dreams are most often symbolic and not to be taken literally. We should always try a dream on figuratively first to see how it fits. Usually the symbolic interpretation will click for us and resonate in our hearts as the message God is seeking to communicate. We should never feel the need to try to awkwardly cram it into a literal box.

For example, if you dream you are getting married to the new worship leader at your church, this may be a picture of God calling you to integrate deeper worship into your lifestyle and telling you that will strengthen your covenant relationship with Him.

Or a wedding dream may be speaking to other covenants in your life, such as job opportunities or friendships with your brothers and sisters in Christ. If you have been deepening your relationship with God through two-way journaling and dream interpretation, you may have a dream of marriage because Jesus is responding to your search for Him by showing His strong covenantal commitment to you. As such, He probably would be represented by a spiritually strong person from your church whom you respect and admire.

Of course, if our soul is resistant to the idea that there could be a symbolic interpretation and we *really* want a dream to literally come true, we should examine our hearts to see if there is any idol there that the Spirit may be revealing through the dream. We always want to pray, "Not our will but Yours be done."

Likewise, a dream of being pregnant is usually speaking to a spiritual birthing, not a physical one. It can be showing that you— as a man or a woman—are pregnant with possibility and potential or that you are about to give birth to a new ministry. God may have planted a vision or creative idea within you that He is calling you to incubate for a season until it is fully developed and ready for delivery. Another way this symbol could be interpreted is illustrated in the following example.

GREAT EXPECTATIONS

My friend laughed when telling me about her dream the previous night of being pregnant. Since the main emotion of a dream will help unlock its meaning, I asked her how she felt about being pregnant when she was in the dream. She said she was hysterical.

I knew what was going on in her waking life, and that actually matched up with the main action of the dream, which was that she was "expecting" (pregnant). In waking life she was feeling a huge amount of pressure from the "expectations" of others. She felt the need to "produce" and "deliver" what other people wanted from her, but it really wasn't anything that God was asking of her.

Her emotions in waking life also matched the dream in that she felt stressed and overwhelmed by the expectations of those around her. The Lord was showing her through the dream that she didn't need to be anxious and that if she were still trying to please men, she would no longer be a servant of Christ (see Gal. 1:10). God was saying, "No worries. No need to feel that pressure and let it upset you. You don't have to be 'pregnant': you don't have to carry the weight of these expectations any longer."

She followed the leading of the Lord and ended up acting on the dream. She stepped back from the unnecessary responsibilities she thought others expected her to take on, and as a result, she came into a place of greater peace in her mind and heart.

KEEP YOUR PANTS ON!

Another dream which illustrates the juxtaposition of how I felt about a potentially challenging ministry situation versus how the Lord felt about it can be seen in the following story.

In waking life, I had been asked to be a temporary caregiver for someone who needed twenty-four-hour care and was confined to her bed. Now, just a bit of background on me: I do not have a lot of caregiving experience. I don't have kids. I don't even have a cat.

Regardless of this, I readily accepted the ministry opportunity. Of course I knew that God has not given me a spirit of fear and that perfect love drives out fear (see 2 Tim. 1:7; 1 John 4:18). Besides, *"I can do everything through Christ who gives me strength"* (Phil. 4:13 NLT).

True, true, and true. That is what I told myself all day long and what I declared when I spoke about the situation. However, I had a most telling dream that revealed a state of unrest and uncertainty in my heart.

In the dream, everything was going great until I realized I wasn't wearing any pants. Understandably I found this very disconcerting, so I ran into my friend's house and hurried into her bathroom, hoping she might have a pair of shorts or something I could put on.

Once in the bathroom, I realized that another friend was lying in the bathtub behind the shower curtain. There had been some kind of overdose or trauma that had left her very close to death. I immediately launched into action: I picked her up, carried her outside onto the front lawn, and asked Leo to come pray with me. We started calling Heaven to earth, speaking life over her, and counseling her in profound ways that instantaneously brought her back to health—spirit, soul, and body. Her healing was a supernatural miracle that was awesome in every way.

I woke up very encouraged by the dream. Admittedly, it started out awful, but at least it ended well! God showed me that even though part of me felt unprepared, everything was going to be OK.

WHERE STRENGTH IS PERFECTED

Through the symbol of the missing pants, the dream revealed that I felt like I was lacking something. I didn't have everything I needed; I was uncomfortable, and I tried to conceal my weakness by hiding in the bathroom.

God showed me that in my greatest weakness I find His greatest strength. It was in that place of vulnerability that I discovered the best ministry opportunity of all. It was good for me to have come to that place. It was good for me to realize that I don't have what it takes in my own strength and wisdom. Through the dream God revealed that when I come to the place of recognizing my lack, I am then positioned to receive His abundant grace. I first need to see that I am incomplete on my own in order to truly know how thoroughly complete I am inside of Christ (see Col. 2:10).

We know God's Word, how He promised that His grace is sufficient and that His strength works best in our weakness (see 2 Cor. 12:9-10). That is where His power is made perfect. And while that's all great on paper, what does it actually look like when lived out? And more importantly, what does it *feel* like?

Well, I now know how it feels because I just experienced it. In my dream, I felt the shame of not having what I needed. But then God showed me that my weakness positioned me for His glory to be revealed and His power displayed. *In that place.* In that place, I felt the adrenaline as I saw my friend in need, and then I felt the anointing of God and His presence minister mightily through me. It was powerful. Tangible. I felt all that in my dream, and I awoke changed. I was confident and immovable, steadfast in faith.

Before, I had the Scriptures in my head and I could quote them. But after the dream, I have them in my heart and I can feel them. They are a part of me now. That is how dreams work: they move revelation and truth from our heads down into our spirits, making it a reality that we can that much more easily live into and out of.

In her book *Who Switched Off My Brain?*, cognitive neuroscientist Dr. Caroline Leaf writes: "Even though you can be presented with evidence that something is true, you won't really believe it unless you feel that it is true. It may be reasonable, logical, scientifically proven or just plain common sense, but you won't believe it unless your brain's limbic system (the seat of your emotions) allows you to feel that it is true."[9]

That is what dreams do. They allow us to feel truth in such a way that we can own it. It is not only biblical truth. Now it is our truth, too. In the next chapter, we will continue to explore how God moves His revelation from our heads down deep into our spirits, using dreams to write His Word upon our hearts (see 2 Cor. 3:3).

Chapter 7

Out of Our Minds: How Dreams Get Us out of Our Heads and into Our Hearts

"Guard your heart above all else, for it determines the course of your life."
—Proverbs 4:23 NLT

Most everyone thinks their dreams are wacky and are worried they'll sound crazy and "out of their minds" if they open up about some of the goings-on in their night visions. People often feel so uncomfortable talking about their dreams that they will qualify the strangeness of them with comments like "Well, I'm pregnant so this is a hormonal dream…" or "I was on strong pain meds that day so…"—almost trying to distance themselves from the dream's apparent weirdness.

But dreams are not that weird. We think they are bizarre because we are examining them with our rational minds. In reality, dreams come from our spirits, and when looked at through the lens of our hearts, their messages quickly come into focus.

That is one reason we want to get into our hearts—to understand the origin and language of the dream. The other vital reason to get into our hearts is because that is where God lives (see Eph. 3:17). The Bible is clear that God is, more than anything else, a heart God (see 1 Sam. 16:7).

As we have seen, the Kingdom of God is peace and joy in Him. He is love. He is the Prince of Peace. The abiding realities are faith, hope, and love. The fruit of His Spirit are God Emotions (love, joy, and peace). So God is a God of emotion, and when we dream, we get to connect with His feelings in our heart.

WHY GOD SPEAKS THROUGH DREAMS

Pictures are the language of the heart so they are the language that is spoken where God lives. During the day, we can say, "God loves me" with our mind. But love is not experienced in the mind; it is felt in the heart. In a dream, we get to *experience* being loved. We get to *feel* forgiven. We get to know and walk in these intangible heart realities and actually live them. Dreams are a form of meditation that help move scriptural truth from our heads down into our hearts.

We know that we must guard our hearts with all diligence because from them flows everything else (see Prov. 4:23). We want to connect with our heart and the Holy Spirit who dwells there (see 2 Cor. 1:21-22). It is His perspective we are after. It is His wisdom we need in order to reign in life. It is His compassion we want to move us.

Sometimes we read a passage of Scripture and have no idea what it means. It is easy just to skip over the verses that don't make any sense to us and go on to the more straightforward ones. But the harder ones are often the better ones, in part because they are so enigmatic and inscrutable. If we easily understood everything about God, would He really be that great of a God after all? Mystery is His calling card, and the best way for us to catch glimpses of His glory is through our heart.

He is much too big for our mind; we can't wrap our head around Him. But the awesome thing about our heart is that it is united with His. We are one spirit with Him (see 1 Cor. 6:17). Of all the aspects that form our triune being (body, soul, and spirit) the part that connects most profoundly and intimately with God is our spirit (see 1 Cor. 2:9-12).

HEART UNDERSTANDING

In Luke 12:32, Jesus revealed Father's love when He told us what God wants to do and what brings Him happiness. Jesus said, *"Do not be afraid, little flock, for your Father has chosen gladly to give you the kingdom!"*

The Greek word translated "chosen gladly" is *eudokeo*, which means "ready, willing, determined; prefer to, be well pleased with, take pleasure in, be favorably inclined towards."[10] That sounds good! God actively desires to bless us. We are familiar with this scriptural promise and can quote it. So why do we spend so much time praying for things God has already given us? Asking Him for things that He has already said are ours?

Perhaps it is because we have not yet known these truths deep within our heart and spirit. It is with our heart that we understand (Isa. 6:10). The following story illustrates how God uses dreams to bring heart revelation and heart understanding.

SETTING: After participating in a prayer meeting specifically called to intercede for healing, I was left feeling saddened because some of the prayers had expressed faith that God *could* heal but doubt about whether He really wanted to or *would* do so, even if they begged Him.

This is where dreams come in. Dreams allow us to feel God's heart for us so we can become convinced of and truly know and believe in the love that He has for us (see 1 John 4:16). I wish I could have given this dream to the people in that prayer meeting.

DREAM: I was with my nieces and nephew in a faraway place, and I wanted to get them a souvenir of our time together there. I was suggesting this or that—nice, expensive gifts— while they weren't even that interested; instead, they happily chose colorful magnets and other small trinkets. I was also given a pink toy sword because apparently I had already paid for it. I thought, *Perfect—I'll take it! Because I know the girls will love it and I can give that to them as well.*

ACTION: Actively trying to bless, provide, and give good gifts.

FEELING: Wholehearted desire to express my love through these gifts. In a way, it was almost selfish of me— because I wanted them to have something special and tangible that showed how we had spent time together in this other place. I very much wished for them to have something awesome to serve as a reminder of how much I adore them.

INTERPRETATION: In the dream, I represented God, and my nieces and nephew represented all of God's kids, including me. So often we get caught up in asking for little things (like a fridge magnet), not realizing that our Heavenly Father wants to give us exceeding abundantly more than we can even imagine (see Eph. 3:20).

In the dream we were in a faraway place, which is a picture of when we spend time in God's presence in the heavenlies, living into His Spirit. God wants to give us something to take back with us so we can have a tangible reminder of our time together as well as the extravagant love He lavishes on us (see 1 John 3:1).

So what does God give us? The Kingdom. What is in the Kingdom? Everything we need (see 2 Pet. 1:3). This may be a physical healing, the gift of wisdom for a certain situation, supernatural favor, restoration in a relationship, or any manner of blessing. Every good gift comes from above, and we don't have to twist God's arm to give it to us (see James 1:17). Just as in my dream, the gift has already been paid for! Everything we need was already paid in full through Jesus' death on the cross.

In my dream I wanted to get the kids something special even more than they wanted it. I had been thinking of what they might like. I had been planning to take them shopping and orchestrating how to get the blessing I had in mind for them into their hands. That is exactly what God does for us.

The overwhelming message of this dream was the feeling. It is His *good pleasure* to give us the Kingdom. It is His *great happiness*. It is what He wants to do, and it was His idea in the first place! That is what I felt in my dream: the very heart of God. The deep desire of wanting to share love through giving. "*For God so loved...that He gave...*" (John 3:16).

In my dream I was asking, "Do you want this? Do you want that? What can I get for you? What can I give you?" I wanted it for me. It would bring them joy, sure; but it would bring me just as much joy—more, even—to bless them. *"It is more blessed to give than to receive,"* and I felt that (Acts 20:35).

Dreams guide our heart to the right position, the appropriate feelings, the proper emotions—God Emotions. They take these great big spiritual mysteries and allow us to catch a glimpse of the truth, a snapshot of the spirit. They let us feel the Lord's heart at night so we can live into it and out of it more fully all day long.

GOD'S PERSPECTIVE

Another reason dreams are so helpful is because we get to see our lives from a heavenly perspective, from God's point of view. We may be reading our Bibles and even memorizing passages and praying into them, but how do we know if we've really "gotten" them? We can quote a verse with our mind, but more than anything, we want to feel it in our heart. We want to be changed by it and actually live it.

The truth of the matter is we cannot accomplish this through Bible study alone. The Pharisees tried, and Jesus said, "Sorry guys, you search the Scriptures thinking that in them you have life, but what you really need to do is come to Me, the living Word, to know true life" (see John 5:39-40).

While we are awake during the day, we should meditate on Scripture and ask Holy Spirit to breathe on it, transforming the written *Logos* into revelatory *rhema* spoken by God Himself directly into our hearts. That sets the stage for our night hours, when Father God can give us glimpses of how He sees our progress and growth in the things of the Spirit. How far have we come? What truths have we integrated? What area does He want us to focus on more?

He can easily show us how He views our hearts and our lives through the pictures He paints at night. In fact, dreams are not just a faint representation of our lives, a shadow of the "real" waking life. It is the opposite. The dream is the most real, and our waking lives are but a shadow of the spiritual reality we get to experience through our nightly encounters with Heaven.

We are going to look at several examples to illustrate how God uses dreams to show us His take on our spiritual growth. Where are we missing it? Where have we found victory? We want to be on the same page with Holy Spirit and all He is working on inside of us (see Phil. 2:13). Through dreams, we are able to see what He is up to and where His focus is so we can turn our attention there as well. We agree with all He is doing, actively yield to Him, and lean into His work of grace within.

DREAMING SCRIPTURE: HOW THE WORD IS MADE FLESH IN US

The first four dreams below were part of a series that I had over a week's time. Taken together, they represent what God was teaching me about our "in Christ-ness"—our unity with Him both in the fellowship of death and also the power of resurrection.

The dreams go back and forth between showing the negative results of my own ways and thinking and displaying the positive results of God's ways and thinking. The dreams are not condemnatory in any way; they are simply making two different paths clear. This is how dreams often work. Instead of God just telling us, "Do this!," He lets us experience the consequences of both options through our night visions. He sets before us life and death, and He makes it easy for us to choose well.

O DEATH, WHERE IS YOUR STING?

SETTING: In waking life, I had been reading Dr. Jim Richards' book *Moving Your Invisible Boundaries*, where he discusses how important it is to meditate on our death with Christ on the cross.[11] Well, that was something that had never occurred to me to do before.

But I understand, because Jesus did not just die for us, He died as us (see Rom. 6:3-9). Truly, we have been crucified with Christ (see Gal. 2:20). That is reality. In order to be raised up with Him and to know the power of His resurrection, we must first fellowship with Him in our death together on the cross. In that place of meditation, I had a dream.

DREAM: I was at a movie theater with my brother Josh and my dear friend Becky. They were both dressed to the nines in a suit and gown because it was a significant occasion: my funeral. At the same time it was also an epic, blockbuster movie.

Becky and Josh were excited though; it was a wonderful premiere gala, and they were incredibly enthusiastic about what was about to unfold on screen, which was a film of my life. I entered into the movie itself. It was larger than life—3-D, HD, louder and more tangible and more real than anything I had ever felt before. It was amazing and powerful.

In the film, I ended up in a river with deadly stinging eels, yet when they stung me, it did not hurt a bit.

ACTION: Celebration of death

FEELING: Epic; peaceful and not dark or morbid at all

INTERPRETATION: I realized that as I died to my old life on the physical-world side of the movie screen, I was awakened on the spiritual side of the dimension to a new and more real life than I could have ever imagined.

The river was a picture of the waters of baptism, and my old nature was buried in it. I knew immediately that I had died and been baptized into Christ.

The eels attacking but not harming me left me with vivid memories upon awakening. This dream experience let me actually feel what it is like to know that death has lost its sting. It was incredibly impactful, and the feeling has not left me since. This is an example of how we can live into Scripture and how the Word can be made flesh in our lives (see John 1:14).

BEING FOUND IN CHRIST

SETTING: In waking life, I had been praying into the truths of Philippians 3:8-11, of how I am one with Christ and am supposed to be found inside Him. I also had been struggling with how much time to spend with the Lord each day when there were other pressing needs and ministry responsibilities clamoring for my attention. In this place, I had the following dream.

DREAM: I was invited into a fellowship hall, where I knew Jesus was. There was a craft project ready for each of us to complete, with all the pieces laid out and detailed instructions given.

Instead of staying there, I went back out into the hallway and tried to tape up signs directing others into the fellowship hall, though this was difficult. Also, I ended up judging people in the hallway who were not going the direction I was telling them to go!

In the end, a woman came out wearing a vest/sweater/jacket thing—the new (craft) creation that she had sewn together in that place of fellowship. It would have fit me perfectly! It matched the pants I was wearing, and I loved it. It made me really wish I had stayed in the fellowship hall, where I was supposed to be.

ACTION: Rushed busyness

FEELING: Worry and judgment

INTERPRETATION: "If the devil can't make us bad, he will make us busy." I am worried about "signs" and wonders, helping people and directing them to the Lord, while ignoring my own time with Him in the "fellowship" hall. I am too busy to spend time around that table of communion and intimacy and instead am rushing around, trying to assist others. Really, though, because I have neglected my own quiet time with Jesus I wind up being critical of the very people I am trying to bless.

The symbol of craft instructions speaks to me of Holy Spirit. He is my Teacher who instructs me and leads me into all truth.

The sweater/vest/jacket thing is my favorite symbol in the dream. I kept pondering what in the world it could signify until Holy Spirit finally gave me the revelation: it's not a *what*; it's a *who*. I realized what happens in that fellowship hall/place of intimacy with Jesus: I wear Him! I am literally found in Him and inside of Him, just like a sweater, vest, or jacket.

This may seem like a strange way to picture being found in Christ, but I realized it is actually quite scriptural. The Bible says that we are to *"put on the Lord Jesus Christ"* and *"clothe ourselves with Christ"* (Rom. 13:14; see Gal. 3:27). So the simple outfit symbol in my dream was, in fact, a very accurate way to represent a deep and hard-to-understand spiritual truth.

As soon as I received the awesome revelation, I noticed how fabulous Jesus would look on me. He coordinates well with the rest of my ensemble and is my favorite color. He is a perfect match for me in every way. This dream was a great illustration that contrasted the way I was tempted to prioritize my life with the way God wanted me to prioritize it. I couldn't miss the message; it was too profound and clear.

I immediately committed to giving up my Martha tendencies and instead follow Mary's example (see Luke 10:42). After this dream I happily chose the "only necessary thing" and the "better part": to enter into the fellowship hall of intimacy and sit at Jesus' feet, discovering even more deeply how I have been supernaturally "sewn up" and sealed in Christ through the power of His Holy Spirit (see Eph. 1:13).

In fact, my dream's message was later confirmed when I learned of Billy Graham's revealing interview not long after his 80th birthday. Larry King said: "It must be rewarding to you to look back on your life and not have to live with regrets." Yet Dr. Graham's response was surprising: "I am the greatest failure of all men. I was too much with men and too little with God. I was too busy with business meetings and even conducting services.

I should have been more with God, and people would've sensed God's presence about me when they were with me."[12]

I was grateful for the dream, as well as the waking life confirmation from a hero in the faith. That wasn't the end of the revelation though, as God kept showing me this truth from many different angles.

CIRCUMCISION OF THE HEART

SETTING: In waking life, I had been meditating on Colossians, specifically where it talks about how we have a circumcision made without hands, a circumcision of the heart. In this passage, we learn that the body of flesh is removed by having been buried with Christ in baptism (see Col. 2:11-14). I had also been contemplating unity and fellowship with Christ and how that *koinonia* with Him is supremely important and nothing should take its place. Then I had a dream.

DREAM: I was sitting around a table with several people who were in need of Jesus and some serious ministry. Then I wandered aimlessly around Dick's Sporting Goods, dragging behind me a huge backpack because it was too heavy for me to carry.

ACTION: Burdened by the baggage I was lugging

FEELING: Slowed down, held back

INTERPRETATION: As I mentioned, I had been reading in the Bible about circumcision, so I guess it is no surprise that I end up at a store with that name. I realized that this night vision was saying the same thing as the dream about being found in Christ: that I needed to be fellowshipping with Jesus. I am allowed to be and supposed to be and don't need to feel bad about spending "too much" time with Him.

In the dream, I was spending time with people who needed ministry, which I thought was quite good and noble (sitting around a table can be a natural picture of communing or fellowship). But I was spending too much time focused on them and their various problems, which only dragged me down with burdens I could not carry (hence the heavy backpack). My focus can't be on others; it needs to be on Jesus.

Missionary to Mozambique, Heidi Baker, spends four to six hours a day with the Lord and says the fruit of ministry is only born from a place of intimacy.[13] The deaf hear, the blind see, and the dead are raised to life regularly through her outreach in Pemba so hers is an example worth following. She knows what she is talking about, and she believes that more than anything, we must stay full of "oil"—Holy Spirit's presence.

I thanked God for making it clear through my dream exactly why I would want to have my body of flesh done away with and instead stay in close, continual fellowship with Him. He had shown me that ministry *to* Him is even more important than ministry *for* Him. The dream made that obvious and motivated me to do what I knew I should have been doing all along.

Pictures are the language of the heart and move our emotions, which in turn prompt us to action. Seeing this dream picture helped guide me to the right actions since I was able to view the situation from God's perspective. He doesn't want me dragged down and held back. He wants me to fellowship with Him so that I am strengthened and have something to offer others. The dream unlocked that understanding and showed me how to get there.

THAT I MAY GAIN CHRIST

The next dream is a continuation of the same theme as the previous one, just shown in a different way. In the last dream, I saw the bad results of choosing the wrong thing. In this one, I caught a glimpse of the extraordinary results if I choose the right thing, which is to stay close to Jesus, stay in His presence, and not let Him out of my sight.

DREAM: The actor James Garner was leading an exciting expedition, and I was part of the adventure group. We walked through a charming old mansion, and there was an antique jewel on a dresser that I stopped to take a picture of. Meanwhile the group went on ahead of me.

To get to the luncheon table where Garner and everyone else had begun eating, I had to balance on steppingstones through a body of water, and I got wet. I asked how they managed to make it through the water safe and dry, and he replied matter-of-factly that they walked on it. "What else would we do?" he said.

I knew immediately in my heart that if I had stayed with him and the group, I would have been a part of the water-walking miracle, too, and I was disappointed I had been distracted by the old dusty relic.

ACTION: Getting sidetracked; not being present where I am supposed to be

FEELING: Excited, then disappointed

INTERPRETATION: The dream showed me yet again that being in close fellowship with Jesus and staying at His side is most important. It is where I want to be so that I don't miss out on the good stuff!

The dream also spoke to that bigger issue with which my heart was wrestling: ministry *for* Jesus versus ministry *to* Him. The reason I was taking a picture of that jewel in the first place was that I somehow knew it was a heavenly gem and I wanted to share that miracle with others. I wanted to share the blessing by capturing it so I could show them what God had done way back when, since this was a very timeworn building.

What I came to realize through the dream is that if I am focused on what God did in the past, I am going to miss out on what He is doing right now. May it never be! My motivation was altruistic, but when focusing on others keeps me away from Jesus, I still have missed the revelation.

By the way, James Garner represented Jesus in the dream. That was pretty funny, and I really did not understand why in the world I was dreaming of an old actor I barely recognized. I tried Googling him to see if there was something significant I was missing. I finally realized the symbol's meaning must have something to do with the actor's name, since that is essentially the only thing I knew about him.

Garner—the synonyms for this word are "acquire," "get," "gather," and "gain." Holy Spirit explained to me how I felt the compelling need to go into His presence to acquire, get, and gather blessings for other people. I want to be able to minister effectively so I want to "acquire" His power. I want to "get" His wisdom to counsel others. I want to "gather" His gifts so I can share them with people in need (just like capturing the picture of the heavenly jewel in the dream).

Again, this all seems well and good on the surface. But really, what kind of relationship do I have with God if every time we get together I want something from Him? That is a bit dysfunctional. Even though I want the blessing to give away, that is still not quite right.

I am not concerned with my own feelings so that's admirably selfless. But I am worried about others' feelings and meeting their needs, and God is teaching me that even that is not supposed to be my number one concern and focus.

His feelings should be my main concern. His desires, more than anyone else's, should take first place. God wants me to love

Him for Him. Intimacy without agenda. He has feelings, and I do not want to hurt them.

Here I had been trying to garner, get, gather, and acquire blessings from God to give to others. The dream showed me that the blessing is God Himself. In the dream, He is Garner, so *He* is the One I gain. He is the One I get to have and be with. It is His very presence and glory that I am gathering and garnering. It is He Himself that I am gaining—to be one with, to know intimately, to be found inside of (see Phil. 3:8).

I love what Pastor Bill Johnson teaches: "The problem is we are trying to learn to walk in a greater anointing for ministry, not in relationship. If I want the anointing just for ministry, that's professional intimacy. And you know what we call people who are intimate as a profession…."[14]

The result in my life is that now whenever I remember this dream it makes me want to be with Jesus. I don't want to miss out on what He is doing. I want to be a part of everything He is up to in this moment—the real-time miracles He is performing and the adventures He is having right now. And more than anything, I want to be found in His presence, in *koinonia* with Him. My ending up at the lunch table in the dream was a picture of coming into fellowship with Him. I made it eventually! Better late than never.

GOD'S ANGLE

This dream series gave me God's perspective on what was going on in my heart, mind, and life at the time. First, I was shown the right thing to do in my funeral dream: be buried with Him. Next I saw what not to do at the beginning of the "Being Found in Christ" dream: don't be frustrated with busyness. Then the end of that dream showed me the right thing to do instead: be sewn up and sealed in Jesus, wearing Him.

The dream of lugging the backpack reiterated what not to do and why: put ministry *for* Jesus above ministry *to* Him, otherwise I am too weak to handle it. The last dream of garnering Christ showed once and for all the right thing to do: Stay with Jesus. Stick close by Him. Be united with Him in His resurrection life and not let anything distract me from Him, including His wonderful works. More than I want to know His power I want to know His presence and be found in the place of intimacy and sweet communion with Him.

I think I finally got it.

Dr. Virkler's Dream Key

The four most common topics that your dreams will be about are as follows:

1. your emotional struggles,

2. your sanctification issues,

3. your body and health issues, and

4. your relationships with other people.

SANCTIFIED SPIRIT, SOUL, AND BODY

We often remember more than one dream each night, but usually the various dreams are giving us the same message, just in different ways with different angles. For example, Pharaoh dreamt of fat and thin cows and then full and withered stalks (see Gen. 41:1-32). Joseph told him that his two dreams were one and the same (see Gen. 41:25). And so it is with us.

SETTING: In waking life, my husband and I were praying and fasting, and just before bed, I shared with him some remarkable insights from a book I was reading. In *Fasting to Freedom*, Ron Lagerquist teaches that fasting is healthy and beneficial for the body because it gives our system a chance to get rid of dead tissues, cells, and toxic buildup, cleansing us from the inside out.[15] God designed the body so that it can actually use these sick cells and garbage for fuel while we are fasting, which is how we can go long periods of time without taking in food.

Regarding this miraculous phenomenon, Lagerquist writes, "The butterfly is a magnificent example of catabolism (tearing down) and anabolism (building up). During metamorphosis the butterfly's muscles and organs dissolve into a thick yellow solution. All internal structures are torn down and rebuilt. It emerges from the chrysalis a new creation. During a fast, a metamorphosis occurs. The body undergoes a tearing down and rebuilding of damaged materials."[16]

After learning all this and discussing it with Leo, I fell asleep and had two dreams.

DREAM ONE: My grandmother got up in front of an enormous church, grabbed a microphone, and belted out a song at the top of her lungs before a huge audience.

DREAM TWO: My friend had dyed her hair bright purple and was wearing mechanic's coveralls. She was at a church get-together to help a needy family fix up their home.

Dreams are intensely personal. In this case, you would have to know my grandma and my friend in order to have any idea how these dreams relate to waking life. My grandmother was quiet and conservative and what she did in the dream was completely unlike her. Also, my grandma has passed away. She was old when she left this earth, and because of this, she usually represents to me my fleshly "old nature" or "old man" (or "old woman," as the case may be).

That interpretation did not fit with this dream, though, because the "old nature" part of me does not change and become new or different as happened in the dream. My old fleshly nature is dead and buried, and it stays that way. So this must not be talking about my sinful fleshly nature. Instead, I realized it was talking about my actual flesh-and-blood body.

In waking life, my friend who appeared in the second dream is very trendy, always wearing the latest hairstyles and outfits. She is not known for sporting funky hairdos or masculine work clothes. She does not frequent church so to participate in such an event as she did in the dream would be a big departure from her norm as well—a new, great thing for her, indicating positive spiritual growth.

Now that you understand the symbols, we can talk about what they mean.

ACTION: Change, transformation—in both dreams, the people were drastically transformed from their usual selves.

FEELING: Positive, upbeat—even though everything was different, it was all changing for the better.

INTERPRETATION: Both of these dreams of transformation were set in a church, which speaks of not only a physical transformation, but a spiritual awakening as well. The first dream shows that my body (represented by my grandmother) is being changed and transformed—just like the metamorphosis of the butterfly. (The Greek word in Romans 12:2 that is translated "transformed" is the same word we get the English word *metamorphosis* from.)

The second dream depicted the same thing but in a different way. Not only is my flesh-and-blood body being transformed, purified, and cleansed through this time of fasting, but so is my spirit. My friend's spiritual life is not fervent, but the dream indicated that it was changing as she was now participating in church ministry. So, too, my spirit is being increasingly renewed, changed, and conformed to the likeness of Jesus through this time of fasting.

I have to admit, my friend's outfit confused me for a bit because I kept thinking she was wearing a jumpsuit. But that did not fit with the dream. I wondered, "What is another word for clothes that look like that?" Holy Spirit gave me the revelation: it wasn't a jumpsuit; it was coveralls. My friend's new outfit "covered all" the transgressions and impurity that had been there (just as love covers all our sins [see Prov. 10:12]).

And I love that her hair was purple! Many people see purple as a royal color, so that's great. And for me, when I dream of hair, I often see it referring to "glory" because the Bible says that a woman's hair is her glory (see 1 Cor. 11:15). My friend's "glory" was changed, just like her clothes. As I go into the presence of God (the church in the dream), I am beholding the Lord and *being transformed into the same image from glory to glory* by His Spirit (2 Cor. 3:18).

These two dreams confirmed to me that Leo and I were on the right track with our prayer and fasting. Holy Spirit was sanctifying us through and through—spirit, soul, and body (see 1 Thess. 5:23). He was faithfully going to complete the good work of renewal and transformation that He had begun in us (see Phil. 1:6). Best of all, we could be confident that because the Lord gave me two dreams in the same night, repeating the message twice, it was already "determined by God, and He would quickly bring it to pass" (see Gen. 41:32).

THE VIEW FROM GOD'S HEART

The stories in this chapter illustrate how hearing from God through our dreams is extremely encouraging. Where we might be thinking we are still struggling with our fleshly nature, God shows us another picture. We may feel in our waking life that sin is winning and we are far from where God wants us, but He has a different perspective.

First John 3:2 promises that when we see Jesus as He is, we will be like Him. We get to see Him in dreams. And through our dreams He shows us how He sees us, too: as joined with Him in the fellowship of His suffering so death and sin no longer control us. He shows us how we have gained Christ, and He gives us amazing pictures of what that looks like and how accessible His miraculous lifestyle is to our present reality. He reveals to us how we are united with Him in the power of His resurrection and how we are truly inside of Him. And that changes everything!

We can easily believe what God tells us because we just saw what He meant. We understand what Scripture says more than ever because we just lived it in our dreams. We felt what it was like, and we are confident that we can live into it again on this side of Heaven. In the daytime, we can feel forgiven. In our waking hours, we can be holy. All day long we can revel in knowing how it feels to be the beloved of God because He showed us these truths in our visions of the night.

As we learn to surrender more fully our sleep time to Jesus and dream in the Spirit at night, we are then able to live more fully by His Spirit during the day as well. Finally, the communion is unbroken. We worship in Spirit and walk in His Spirit without ceasing, all day and all night.

Chapter 8

INSPIRATION, INNOVATION, AND INVENTION: RECEIVING GOD'S CREATIVITY THROUGH DREAMS

BY DR. MARK VIRKLER

"I wisdom dwell with prudence, and find
out knowledge of witty inventions."
—PROVERBS 8:12 KJV

Solomon was just stepping into his authority as king over all of Israel. He was probably quite young. He no doubt felt inadequate and unprepared. As he faced the responsibility that had fallen upon him, God came to him in a dream, offering him whatever he wanted. Recognizing his own inability to meet the challenges ahead, he requested, and God granted to him, divine wisdom—in a dream (see 1 Kings 3).

Other people in the Bible who were facing overwhelming problems received divine creativity from God in their dreams, as well. To Jacob the Lord revealed how to provide financially for his family (see Gen. 30:31–31:17). To Pharaoh He revealed how to prepare for a devastating seven-year famine (see Gen. 41). To Joseph He revealed how to escape destruction (see Matt. 1:20–2:23).

There is an extraordinary passage of Scripture in the Old Testament that reveals where creativity originates. In Exodus 31:3-5, the Lord declares, *"I have filled him with the Spirit of God in wisdom, in understanding, in knowledge, and in all kinds of craftsmanship, to make artistic designs for work in gold, in silver, and in bronze, and in the cutting of stones for settings, and in the carving of wood, that he may work in all kinds of craftsmanship."*

The Spirit of God continues to release His creativity nightly into our hearts through the dreams He gives us. Some of the gifts received in dreams touch millions of lives. Others "merely" solve a personal problem for the dreamer. Let me give you a few examples.

The Periodic Table

It is said that Dmitry Mendeleyev was on a three-day work bender when he finally gave in for a few minutes of sleep. He dreamt of an arrangement of elements that would change modern chemistry forever: "I saw in a dream a table where all the elements fell into place as required. Awakening, I immediately wrote it down on a piece of paper.… Only in one place did a correction later seem necessary."[17]

World-Champion Golf Swing

Jack Nicklaus figured out why his swing was off through a dream in which he was playing a masterful game of golf. After analyzing the dream, the six-time Masters champion realized he was gripping the club differently in the dream than he did in waking life: "I tried it the way I did in my dream, and it worked. I feel kind of foolish admitting it, but it really happened in a dream."[18]

The Sewing Machine Needle and Thread

Elias Howe, inventor of the modern sewing machine, had been troubled by how to get the needle to work in his new invention. Having the eye at the base (as in handheld needles) was out of the question. The stories vary, but this is the one that was reported in *Popular Mechanics* in 1905:

> One night, he dreamed that he was building a sewing machine in a strange country for a savage king. The king had given him 24 hours to complete the machine and make it sew, but try as he would he could not make the needle work, and finally gave up in despair.
>
> At sunrise he was taken out to be executed, and with the mechanical action of the mind in times of great crises he noted that the spears carried by the warriors were pierced near the head. Suddenly, he realized that here was the solution of the sewing machine needle. He begged for time—and while still begging, awoke. It was four o'clock. Hastily he dressed and went to his work-shop—at nine o'clock the model of the needle with an eye at the point was finished.[19]

The rest, as they say, is history, as he patented the first sewing machine.

George Washington Carver

Born a slave around July 12, 1864, George Washington Carver became a scientist of international renown. He referred to himself as "*a dreamer who dreams*, sees visions, and listens always to the still small voice. I am the trail-blazer" (emphasis mine).[20]

On January 21, 1921, Carver addressed the United States House Committee on Ways and Means on behalf of the United Peanut Growers Association on the use of peanuts to improve the Southern economy. Initially given ten minutes to speak, Carver so captivated the committee that his time was extended.

Explaining the many products that derived from the peanut, including milk, mock beef, and faux chicken, Carver stated: "If you go to the first chapter of Genesis, we can interpret very clearly, I think, what God intended when he said 'Behold, I have given you every herb that bears seed. To you it shall be meat.' This is what He means about it. It shall be meat. There is everything there to strengthen and nourish and keep the body alive and healthy."

After nearly two hours, the chairman asked: "Dr. Carver, how did you learn all of these things?"

Carver answered: "From an old book."

"What book?" asked the chairman.

Carver replied, "The Bible."

The chairman inquired, "Does the Bible tell about peanuts?"

"No, sir," Dr. Carver replied. "It tells about the God who made the peanut. I asked Him to show me what to do with the peanut and He did."[21]

Benzene Molecule

The discovery of the round formation of the benzene molecular structure came through a dream. After years of studying the nature of carbon-carbon bonds, German chemist Friedrich August Kekulé dreamt of dogs running around in a circle, each one holding the tail of the next dog in its mouth. (Other accounts say it was a snake seizing its own tail.) He realized the benzene molecule was probably circular in shape, and he proved that it was.[22]

DNA

"In 1953, James Watson dreamt of two intertwined snakes (or, some say, a double-sided spiral staircase) that made him picture a double helix. This was pretty key since he—along with input from Francis Crick, Maurice Wilkins, and Rosalind Franklin—went on to prove that DNA is in fact a double helix."[23]

Understanding to Pass Exams

Dr. Ben Carson, retired pediatric neurosurgeon and 2016 presidential candidate, tells the story about struggling to understand a required college chemistry course. He asked the Lord to help him, and the night before a major test, he "picked up his chemistry textbook, determined to learn the whole course overnight. He fell asleep. While he slept, God gave him a prophetic dream:

> I was in this large auditorium.... Just me, and a nebulous figure working out chemistry problems.... When I went to take the test the next morning, it was like *The Twilight Zone*.... I opened that [test] book and I recognized the first problem; it was one of the ones I'd dreamed about. And the next, and the next, and the next.... I aced the exam.[24]

The Messiah

The magnificent "Hallelujah Chorus" of George Frideric Handel's incredible oratorio came to him as a prophetic flow. He said that "he saw all heaven before him" and he heard the music flowing in his mind and wrote feverously for twenty-four days.[25] Handel released the worship that takes place before the throne in Heaven to bless us here on earth.

WHY NOT YOU?

God wants to give the same kind of creativity to you. Whatever your situation, whatever problem you are facing, whatever challenge you are trying to conquer—God wants to intersect your limited knowledge and understanding with a supernatural, creative solution.

You were created in the image of God! The very first thing we learn about God is that He is a Creator. As His twice-born child, His divine creativity is your birthright. And when your conscious mind comes to the end of its abilities, He is there to step in with heavenly wisdom and knowledge. This is an awesome gift that is available to us all.

OUR DAY ACTUALLY BEGINS IN THE EVENING RATHER THAN IN THE MORNING

As God created, He stated over and over, "And the evening and the morning were the (first, second, third, etc.) day" (see Gen. 1:5, 8,13,19,23,31 KJV). That is quite an amazing concept. Let's explore the possible benefits of viewing our day as beginning in the evening.

Since our spirits never sleep, they will work on whatever we ask them to work on as we fall asleep (see Song of Sol. 5:2). It is very significant, in light of the fact that while we are sleeping our mind is at rest, that our heart breaks through with messages from our spirit and God's Spirit, who is one with our spirit (see 1 Cor. 6:17). The ideas received during a night of communing with God can easily set us up for success in our waking hours.

CLOSING OUT THE CURRENT DAY BEFORE FALLING ASLEEP

The Bible is quite clear that we are not to let the sun go down on our anger (see Eph. 4:26). In other words, process your daily stuff and come to peace before drifting off to sleep. You don't want your heart consumed with anger, bitterness, or resentment all night, for if it is, you wake up with poison in your spirit and are toxic for the day. I know. I have done that in the past. I am very careful not to do it anymore.

Research into the effect of traumatic events on the mind indicates that there is a period of time known as the "consolidation window" when fear memories are being established and strengthened in the brain. This window usually lasts about six hours after the experience of a painful event. Left unprocessed and unhealed, such trauma will begin to affect a weak organ or system and eventually will be expressed in disease and pain in the body, in addition to affecting our soul and spirit.

Therefore, God said, "Take care of your emotions before you go to sleep at night. Bring your hurts, frustrations, anger, and pain to Me. Let Me show you My perspective, and let Me touch the brokenness before it can fester and become infected. Don't let the sun go down on an unhealed heart."

In their classic book *Dream Language*, James and Michal Ann Goll discuss our Hebraic inheritance in embracing the visitation of God through our dreams. They explain the traditional Jewish bedside prayers that are designed to prepare the heart and mind to sleep and to be open to Him. Part of that ritual involves reflecting on their day and taking inventory of their soul, looking at what happened, whom they encountered, what feelings they had, what they are proud of, whom they need to forgive, and for what they need God's forgiveness. Finally, they prepare for the next day, considering what their hopes are for tomorrow and where they desire God's blessing.[26]

More than four hundred years ago, St. Ignatius Loyola encouraged looking for God's presence in your life through what has been called the Daily Examen, a technique of prayerful reflection on the events of the day in order to discover what God was doing and to discern His direction for us. The following version of St. Ignatius' prayer is from the *Ignation Spirituality* website:

1. Become aware of God's presence. Look back on the events of the day in the company of the Holy Spirit.

The day may seem confusing to you—a blur, a jumble, a muddle. Ask God to bring clarity and understanding.

2. Review the day with gratitude. Gratitude is the foundation of our relationship with God. Walk through your day in the presence of God and note its joys and delights. Focus on the day's gifts. Look at the work you did, the people you interacted with. What did you receive from these people? What did you give them? Pay attention to small things—the food you ate, the sights you saw, and other seemingly small pleasures. God is in the details.

3. Pay attention to your emotions. One of St. Ignatius' great insights was that we detect the presence of the Spirit of God in the movements of our emotions. Reflect on the feelings you experienced during the day. Boredom? Elation? Resentment? Compassion? Anger? Confidence? What is God saying through these feelings?

God will most likely show you some ways that you fell short. Make note of these sins and faults. But look deeply for other implications. Does a feeling of frustration perhaps mean that God wants you to consider a new direction in some area of your work? Are you concerned about a friend? Perhaps you should reach out to her in some way.

4. Choose one feature of the day and pray from it. Ask the Holy Spirit to direct you to something during the day that God thinks is particularly important. It may involve a feeling—positive or negative. It may be a significant encounter with another person or a vivid moment of pleasure or peace. Or it may be something that seems rather insignificant. Look at it. Pray about it. Allow the prayer to arise spontaneously from your heart—whether intercession, praise, repentance, or gratitude.

5. Look toward tomorrow. Ask God to give you light for tomorrow's challenges. Pay attention to the feelings that surface as you survey what is coming up. Are you doubtful? Cheerful? Apprehensive? Full of delighted anticipation? Allow these feelings to turn into prayer. Seek God's guidance. Ask Him for help and understanding. Pray for hope.

St. Ignatius encouraged people to talk to Jesus like a friend. End the Daily Examen with a conversation with Jesus. Ask forgiveness for your sins. Ask for His protection and help. Ask for His wisdom about the questions you have and the problems you face. Do all this in the spirit of gratitude. Your life is a gift, and it is adorned with gifts from God.[27]

MY NIGHTTIME RITUAL

As I lie in bed, I breathe slowly, saying the name of Jesus over and over again as I breathe in and out. I say, "Je..." as I breathe in and "...sus" as I breathe out. As I breathe in, I see His Spirit as Light, entering me and filling me. As I breathe out, I see my spirit as semi-light going back to Him. If I need something specific such as peace or calm, I may repeat those words as I breathe in and out. I ask for a dream or for insight on an issue that is before me. I drift off to sleep.

PREPARE YOURSELF FOR THE COMING DAY

Notice that both the Judaic and the Ignatius prayers are not complete without offering the next day to the Lord. Presenting ourselves and our upcoming activities to Him at night is an awesome way to get into the spirit and receive supernatural revelation so that the next day is ensured of divine success.

Here is the process I use to make sure this happens regularly in my life: I know that whatever I fill my heart and mind with as I drift off to sleep is what my heart will work on during the night. While my mind is out of the way, my spirit and the Holy Spirit, who is joined to my spirit, are able to sift through all my disjointed thoughts, sort them out, and bring clarity and creativity to them. They then provide revelation, understanding and inspiration to me through dreams as I sleep or as I journal as soon as I awaken. I record and interpret my dreams as soon as I get up, and often they provide a springboard into even greater wisdom and direction from the Lord through my journal.

I receive a lot of creative ideas during these morning journaling times. If there is a dream I remember, I type up a summary of it and then I tune to flow and ask the Lord what it is about. He interprets it as I type. I save the file in my "dreams directory" on my computer.

If I wake up in the middle of the night from a dream, I will sit at my computer for a few minutes and type up a brief summary of the dream, and then I go back to sleep. In the morning, I review the dream, ask God for the interpretation, tune to flow, and record the interpretation in the file.

FILLING THE "HARD DRIVE," THEN USING THE "SOFTWARE" OF THE HOLY SPIRIT

I find revelation comes to those earnestly seeking, exploring, and hungering for it. All the examples of creative solutions seen earlier in this chapter involve people who had immersed themselves in their searches, and their hearts gave them revelation as the reward for their search. When we search with all our hearts, we find Him (see Jer. 29:13).

For example, I spent one year seeking to learn how to "abide in Christ." I had looked up every verse in the New Testament on being in Christ and having Christ in me, and the revelation was ready to pour out of me.

It did so while I was in Singapore, teaching evening classes on how to hear God's voice. I was free during the daytime, and I sat at my laptop and typed for three days with my eyes closed. That became my book *Naturally Supernatural*, which is a world-altering revelation that has blessed many. Three days of flow to write a 150-page book! But, you do see, I had prepared my heart and mind by researching the topic deeply for many months. I was full of insight and revelation, and out they poured.

If you look at many of Charity's dreams that she shares in this book, you will see the same principle at work. She was meditating on a passage of Scripture or a spiritual truth. She had immersed herself in learning everything she could on a subject, such as compassion. And as she was seeking the Lord, He was found by her in a dream, in a vision of the night.

YOU CAN RELEASE DIVINE REVELATION AND CREATIVITY

Now that you know the process, you can release God's creativity through your heart on a regular basis. Hearing His voice makes you the head and not the tail, above and not beneath, a lender and not a borrower (see Deut. 28:1-14 NKJV)! Supernatural ingenuity restored to the Church so that She becomes the innovative leader in tomorrow's world—don't you love it? I sure do. Will you become a part of this visionary army?

Let your answer be "Yes, Lord!"

Chapter 9

DREAM SYMBOLS: PERSONALIZED, UNIQUE, AND ALL YOUR OWN

"…The dream is certain, and its interpretation sure."
—DANIEL 2:45 ESV

As we know by now, the most important thing to understand about dream work is that dreams are symbolic. The second most important thing to realize is that dream symbols are personal. Mine are mine, and yours are yours.

That is why *you* are the best and most qualified person to interpret your dreams. You know what the symbols mean to you, and you know what is going on in your waking life better than anyone. A vital key for dream interpretation is to remember that symbols are specific to your own history and personal experiences; they are not one-size-fits-all. Let me explain.

TWO ARE BETTER THAN ONE

After crisscrossing our third checkpoint along the US-Canadian border in under two hours, an immigration officer asked me, "Are you guys lost?" I smiled sweetly and assured him that was certainly not the case. "Oh no, sir. We're definitely not lost! We just don't know where we are in relation to where we want to be."

So we continued along our "scenic route" and eventually found ourselves where we did want to be. The not knowing where we were simply added to the fun of the experience. I was with my brother Josh, and a friend or two were along for the ride as well. We were laughing and having a great time! We were having an adventure.

However, as much as I love having adventures, if I had been in the exact same situation all by myself, it would not have been nearly as fun. Driving around in the dark, at night, all alone, not knowing where I was going? No thanks. But as it was, with family and friends, it was a blast.

I have traveled by plane, train, and automobile. By camel, parachute, rickshaw, and bicycle-built-for-two. If there is a mode of transportation, I've probably tried it. If there is an inhabited continent, I've definitely visited it. I love exploring new places, and my favorite thing is to go where I've never been.

The best part, though, is sharing the experience, so I like to go *with* someone. Whether it is a girlfriend, a group of friends, my brother, or my husband—together is always much better than going it alone (see Eccl. 4:9-10). Situations like I just described that by myself could be stressful, frustrating, or scary are all at once enjoyable and happy memories in the making. It just all depends on whom I'm with.

A DREAM OF HIGH SCHOOL

Awhile back I had been considering how I could explain the spirit realm as a fun, safe place that is wide open for great adventures. It is not foreign or scary; it's home! In that setting I had a dream.

In the dream, I went to a high school. I did not know my way around and had no idea what to do. But as soon as I arrived, I found four old girlfriends whom I knew from a church I used to attend. They were so excited to see me again! They chatted with me, and when the bell rang, they took it upon themselves to help me get the right textbooks and escort me to the right classroom. They enthusiastically took me under their wing and made sure I was OK, which made all the difference so I wasn't anxious or stressed. It was great.

WHAT'S IT TO YOU?

For most of you reading this, I imagine the idea of high school brings back some memories, fond or otherwise.

That is not the case for me. Having been homeschooled my whole life, I have actually spent more time studying Mandarin at a university in Northeast China than I have ever spent in any high school in the US. Point being, whatever high school may represent to you, I guarantee it doesn't represent that to me. High school is a very foreign place to me. It is a place I have never been, one with which I'm totally unfamiliar. I really only know what to do there based on what I've seen in movies or on television. It is just not part of my world.

So when I dreamt of this, I immediately knew it was an answer to my heart's question about how to present the spirit world as a thoroughly friendly, though admittedly "foreign," place. I understand that people may not have a lot of experience being there, just like I don't have a lot of experience being in high school.

The other reason high school is the perfect picture of the spirit realm is because it is a "school of the spirit." High school is like an "above school." We are supposed to set our minds on things above. And above is up. It is not down low; it's high. So it is *high* school.

OUR HEAVENLY FRIENDS

God's message through the dream was that even if we feel the spirit world is an unfamiliar place where we are not sure what to do, don't worry—we have friends there. The girlfriends I met were from a church I had attended in waking life called Resurrection Life Fellowship. In this dream, the emphasis was definitely on the fellowship, the friendship. It was their relationship with me that made all the difference and that transformed the potentially stressful environment into something that felt altogether navigable and safe.

In waking life, those friends represent my angels (as I told you, they "took me under their wing"). Angels escort us and help us figure out what is going on in the spirit realm. Even though it might be new and unfamiliar to us, they know their way around so we can just stick with them. In like manner, we can stay close to Father God; we are comfortable with Him. We are best friends with Jesus. We work with Holy Spirit all the time. We know these Guys! They are our family, and we can trust them.

The spirit world is their hometown, and they are more than happy to show us around. It is their pleasure to help us get the lay of the land and make sure we get a good feel for the place. They are spirits, and they very much want to share their home, the spirit realm, with us.

MY EYES CHANGED MY DREAMS

Next we want to consider how dream symbols may vary, not only person to person, but also season to season in our lives. For example, when I was a teenager, I would often dream of either my glasses or my contact lenses. I wore both so when I dreamt of them, I knew God was usually talking to me about my vision: His vision for my life and my ability to see it clearly.

However, in my early twenties I had Lasik surgery so I no longer needed to wear glasses or contact lenses. Interestingly enough, I stopped having dreams with those symbols in them.

The fact that even my personal symbols change over time certainly begs the question: Why would God in His infinite creativity limit Himself to one symbol meaning one thing for everyone at all times? He cares enough to make every snowflake unique. Such meticulous attention to frozen cloud droplets certainly confirms our Father's celebration of individuality. He enjoys using different pictures and varied symbols, and He delights in coming up with new ways of communicating His messages to us in our night visions.

Dr. Virkler's Dream Key

Just like the parables Jesus used to illustrate His teaching points, dreams are not meant to be taken entirely literally. Not every symbol is an accurate representation of true reality, otherwise God would be an "unjust" Judge, according to Luke's parable on prayer (see Luke 18:1-8). And of course we know that's not true; He is always just and righteous. So we want to be open to the Lord giving us His meaning for His symbols and allow for flexibility and creativity in the interpretation of our dreams.

AWESOME OR EVIL?

What if we dream of yeast? A biblical dream symbol dictionary may tell us that represents evil—like the *"yeast of the Pharisees, which is hypocrisy"* or the "yeast of malice and wickedness" about which Paul warns (Luke 12:1 NIV; 1 Cor. 5:8). That's pretty clear: yeast is bad!

But then we have another verse over in Matthew: *"Jesus also used this illustration: 'The Kingdom of Heaven is like the yeast...'"* (Matt. 13:33 NLT).

Likewise in the Bible, a lion is used to represent both Christ as the Lion of the Tribe of Judah, as well as the devil that prowls around like a roaring lion (see Rev. 5:5; 1 Pet. 5:8). Therefore, we must maintain our dependence upon Holy Spirit to reveal what symbols represent. Since God used the same symbol to mean different things at different times in Scripture, we can be comfortable expecting that He is going to be flexible with His interpretation of our night visions, as well.

IT'S A BIRD! IT'S A PLANE! IT'S...

It's like those optical illusions where you can see two totally different things depending on how you view the picture. *Is it a duck or is it a rabbit? Is it an old woman or is it a young girl?*

That is how it is with a dream. I see it one way, and you see it another. One picture could mean one thing to me and something entirely different to you. For example, I could dream of a lake, and that would be a picture of a peaceful, relaxing setting to me. But if my grandmother dreamt of the exact same lake, to her that symbol would represent something terrifying because when she was a little girl she almost drowned in a lake.

One online dream dictionary says, "To see a dog in your dream symbolizes intuition, loyalty, generosity, protection, and fidelity."[28] Well, if you are an animal lover and have a dog for a pet, that may very well be an accurate assumption. However, what if at some point in your life you had been viciously attacked by a dog? Do you think you will have the same association with that particular symbol? Of course not. Instead of speaking to friendship, it would speak to fear.

It's a good thing that Friedrich August Kekulé didn't have access to the dream dictionary that states: "To see a dog chasing its tail or running around in circles in your dream implies that you are not handling a situation in an effective way. You are spending too much time on fruitless labor."[29] He would never have recognized the creative revelation he was being given, and a scientific breakthrough would not have occurred!

We see, therefore, how the meanings of symbols absolutely change depending on who is dreaming them. We must ask the right question. It is not, "What does this symbol mean?" The question to the dreamer is always, "What does this symbol mean to you?" The interpretation must resonate within the dreamer. It should bear witness in the heart. Therefore, it is always the dreamer's responsibility to say, "That's it! That clicks with me." That is when we know we have the correct understanding and we have captured God's message through the dream.

Dr. Virkler's Dream Key

The people in your dreams may represent characteristics within you. You can determine what facet of yourself they represent by simply asking, "What is the dominant personality trait of this person as I know him?" The answer will tell you what aspect of yourself you are dreaming about.

For example, your heart may want to show you the entrepreneur, the hospitable host, the administrator, the class clown, the spiritual leader, the laid-back one, the workaholic, etc., that is within you by the appearance in your dream of an individual who epitomizes that kind of person to you. Your pastor may be the spiritual part of you; a president or king may symbolize other leadership qualities within you; a policeman, judge, or dictator may be the authority figure in you; people in uniform (nurses, waiters, choir members) may represent your desire to conform. It is also possible that the person's name may be the point that the dream is trying to bring out, especially if that name is spoken within the dream. Dreaming of a friend named Joy or Grace or Joshua or David may be your heart's way of calling your attention to the qualities that are seen in the meaning of the name. Or the name may actually sound like the message the dream is trying to convey. It is also possible that the Lord Himself or one of His angels may meet you in the dream.

Driven by Compassion

As mentioned, names of people are an easy symbol to identify and understand, and we have already looked at one dream involving my co-worker, Karen, that illustrates this. Because her name and her dominant personality trait (as I see it) completely match, she makes the perfect recurring symbol whenever the Lord wants to teach me more about His compassion.

For example, in waking life Holy Spirit had been showing me in Scripture what motivated Jesus for ministry. He healed the sick out of compassion (see Matt. 14:14). He ministered deliverance out of compassion (see Mark 9:22). He fed the hungry out of compassion (see Matt. 15:32). He even spoke and taught the multitudes out of compassion (see Mark 6:34). That's what moved Jesus. Compassion is what drove Him.

It was in this setting that I had a dream about my friend: compassionate, caring Karen. I dreamt that all the people from our ministry offices were caravanning together and Karen was in the lead car. She ended up on the side of the road, and I followed her. However, the people behind us weren't paying attention and ended up slamming into the back of my car, which in turn propelled my car into Karen's, making all of us plunge down the embankment. It was pretty scary!

By looking at the main action of the dream, we see the message is that all ministry needs to flow out of, or follow, compassion. Love and compassion need to lead the charge. It is dangerous to lose sight of caring, to let that pure heart motive be relegated off to the side. Just like compassion was driving our lead ministry vehicle in the dream, everything was going great until compassion was marginalized and sidelined off to the edge of the road. Through the dream God warned me that if we don't keep compassion front and center as our guiding force, we'll crash and burn, and burn out on ministry.

Deliverance, teaching, healing—the different gifts represented by the various ministry staff members following in their cars—they all need to be born in the heart of God. It is His compassion that must move our ministry. It is His love that must compel us and His caring that must lead us (see 2 Cor. 5:14). Otherwise, even our best intentions and Kingdom work can become derailed and end up a train wreck—or a car wreck, as the case may be.

COMPASSION AND HER SON

The third and final Caring Karen dream we will look at is very simple and builds on the truth of the last one. In regards to the setting, in waking life God had been teaching me about *splanka*, the Greek word that is translated "compassion" in the New Testament. Remarkably, the Gospel writers felt the need to coin a new word form to describe the emotion they saw come upon Jesus. "Splanka" is the term they used to convey what moved Him to action, and significantly, that motivation was uniquely His. No other person in the Bible is described as feeling *splanka*; only Jesus, the God-Man Himself.

I was beginning to see how emotions like pity are just a shadow in the natural realm of true compassion from Heaven. Human sympathy pales in comparison to divinely inspired compassion. We might feel sorry for people and pity them without necessarily doing anything to alleviate their suffering. But compassion can't. It is a God Emotion flowing out of the spirit realm straight from Father's heart, and it always moves us to do something: to help, to heal, to serve, to bless.

In the previous dream we saw how important it is for God's compassion to lead us. It has to come first, and all ministry should follow that divine emotion. In this next dream, we get to see the other side of that same truth. In it I discovered that Karen and her son shared a birthday not only on the same day, but also in the same year.

Since we have established Karen represents "compassion" to me, we then want to ask, "What does it mean if compassion and its fruit have the same genesis?" Normally, fruit comes after a tree is fully grown. Usually, a child is born after a woman has become an adult. But somehow—in a surprisingly matter-of-fact way—this dream showed something different.

God revealed how the fruit of compassion, which is ministry, cannot be separated from compassion itself. As we just saw, scripturally speaking, it should move us to action. Jesus felt compassion and healed, fed, taught, and delivered. He didn't just feel compassion and walk away; His ministry immediately followed that God Emotion.

The dream illuminated yet another facet of the truth that if it is genuine compassion from Heaven, it will always move us to action, without a long time lapse between feeling and doing. There isn't a distance or break between connecting with God's emotions and releasing His power to meet the need at hand. While it is very important for compassion to be what inspires our actions, it is just as important that action immediately follow. Exactly as depicted in the dream, compassion was born and so was her fruit—all at the same time, with no distance and no delay.

DIALECTS OF DREAMS

Hindi and English are the official languages of the government of India. However, within that one nation there are several hundred different dialects spoken. While there are two common languages in which official business is conducted, there are also many more diverse and individualized "heart" languages that are spoken in homes throughout that country.

The same is true with dreams. Pictures are the official language of dreams; however, there are as many different dialects as there are dreamers. This fact does not make dream interpretation more difficult. Instead, it actually makes it easier for each of us to interpret our own dreams. Let me explain.

Shortly after we were married, my husband and I discovered we both enjoy traveling by cruise ship. It is relaxing for us, and a great way to see the world. When I was single, my vacations were different, but also ocean-related. Years ago, my brother Josh and I would go on surfing trips, and even now when we get together, we still like to hit the beach whenever we can. That is why when I dream, surfboards and cruise ships are regular symbols. They are familiar to me and are part of my waking world.

I have a friend who is not into surfing at all but instead is an avid bicyclist. She loves watching the Tour de France and logs miles and miles on her own long-distance rides. Biking is her exercise and recreation of choice. When God speaks through her dreams, He does not speak my dialect of waves; He speaks her dialect of wheels. She will dream that she is part of a bike-racing team because Holy Spirit knows that is a meaningful symbol for her, one to which she can immediately relate. God knows us more intimately than we know ourselves, and He is fluent in the dialect of each of our hearts.

SOME PERSONAL SYMBOLS
AND EXPLANATIONS

I already shared how being on a mission trip in my dreams is confirmation that I am where I am supposed to be. Similarly, I have an amazing girlfriend, Becky, who is a powerhouse for the Kingdom. She and her husband shine brightly as they labor among an unreached people group giving their lives in extravagant love and service to "the least of these" (see Matt. 25:34-40). When she shows up in my dreams and I am interacting with her, I'm always encouraged that I am identifying with and integrating the best spiritual parts of me.

Remember the dream of my funeral in Chapter 7? Becky attended the epic celebration of my death in Christ. Her being in the dream was very significant, for it served as another affirmative symbol that burial with Jesus was definitely what I wanted. Becky's presence confirmed the experience was positive and happening in order that I may be raised from the dead through glory and walk in resurrection power as a new creation in Christ (see Rom. 6:4).

Another consistent dream symbol for me is packing. I have traveled quite a bit and always like to make sure I'm ready with plenty of time to spare so as not to forget anything. Often if I don't feel ready for something in waking life, I dream of trying to pack my luggage but not being able to get everything I need. For instance, it will be time to leave for the airport, but I haven't gotten my clothes together yet and I can't find my passport; and as a result, I'm frantic.

When I wake up from that dream, I have to ask, "In what area of my life am I feeling unprepared? Where do I feel like I don't have it together, and what is causing me to panic?" The action is unpreparedness and the feeling is stress so those are what I need to correlate with my waking life. God wants to get my attention so I can confess my worry and anxiety to Him, invite His presence and grace into the situation, and once again live into His peace and joy.

My favorite packing dream occurred when I was concerned over meeting a deadline in waking life. In the dream I thought I still needed to organize and fill my suitcase but was relieved to discover that everything was already packed and my bags were sitting in the hotel lobby. I ended up having all kinds of time and wasn't hurried a bit. This dream was an encouragement that God was helping me prioritize my responsibilities in waking life and anointing me to get the job done on time—no rush or stress required.

The members of my family are also common dream symbols for me. My family is constant, like God. My parents have always been my parents since the day I was born. My brother has always been my brother since the day he was born. In this way, they are like God, who is the same yesterday, today, and forever (see Heb. 13:8). Therefore, many times, my father symbolizes my Heavenly Father in my dreams. My mother is a gentle comforter so she often represents Holy Spirit. My brother is Joshua so of course he represents *Yeshua*—Jesus, my elder Brother.

It is helpful to recognize what this may actually end up looking like at night. For instance, when I dream of my parents visiting us and staying in our home, that is a simple yet meaningful picture of our hosting the presence of God. Of course, if someone else has the same dream but different life experiences—for example, an absent father or an abusive mother—the message of the dream will be completely different. Even with identical symbols and actions, the meaning will vary based on what those represent to the individual dreamer.

My parents don't always symbolize members of the Trinity, though. Sometimes my dad might represent my mind, where my mom would represent my heart. Or Dad might represent the Word of God and Mom the Spirit of God. My father is a theologian and my mother is a prophetic visionary, and they would both be very happy to represent these things. It just fits.

Having said that, there is actually someone else who even more consistently represents God in my dreams. He is the leader of a Christian organization, and his ministry has impacted me more than anyone else's, other than my parents'. Because I have so much respect for his spirituality and because he has had such a tremendous influence on my walk with the Lord, he makes an ideal God symbol for me. His name is Ron, and below is a dream I had about him and his bride.

GOD'S NEW BRIDE

DREAM: Ron had just married a very young bride, maybe eighteen years old—young enough to be his daughter. This was rather shocking, and even he admitted to me that his staff had a problem with it.

The thing I loved about this particular dream was how I saw Ron/God in it. He looked so much younger with his new bride. He was so relaxed and comfortable and didn't have his guard up in any way. She was such a good influence on him!

The only reason I was surprised by the arrangement was her age. She really wasn't immature; she was just...young. And playful. And carefree. I noticed how that made Ron more playful and joyful, too. In that moment I was reminded again of the influence we can have on our Beloved. The Lord, as represented in the Song of Solomon, even says, *"Turn your eyes away from me, for they have confused me"* (Song of Sol. 6:5).

Really? Can our actions confuse God? If we have such "power" over God's heart and He has allowed us to get close enough that we even affect how He feels, we can do that for good. *"You have made my heart beat faster, my sister, my bride; you have made my heart beat faster with a single glance of your eyes"*

(Song of Sol. 4:9). He is enamored with us. Captivated by us! And that is what I saw in my dream.

I saw that even though God is "older" (i.e., more knowledgeable, more powerful, more everything than we are), He still chooses us, the young bride. He doesn't mind, and in fact, our youth is a delight to Him. He takes great pleasure in our company. That is the feeling the dream gave: that God wants to be comfortable in our presence. He wants to let His guard down and share His heart with us. He was wearing sweatpants in my dream! He just wants to hang out and do life together with us.

Now, that may sound a little strange somehow, to picture God having feelings and them being affected in that way by us. It is hard for us to imagine the Creator could be so moved by His creation, and the dream even hinted at our incredulity when Ron/God mentioned his staff and leadership team questioning his choices.

I love what author and Bible teacher Dutch Sheets shares on this topic in his book *The Pleasure of His Company*. He does a word study about the meaning of *rejoicing* and writes:

> There's a new description of heaven for most of us—a happy, playful, skipping God with His happy, frolicking angels!
>
> Some will think I'm insulting God's dignity by ascribing to Him human emotion and celebrative actions. Let me assure you that this is not my intention. I don't for a moment believe He acts like us—I believe we act like Him! We were created in God's image and likeness. That means we have emotions because He has emotions: We love because He loves, laugh because He laughs, cry because He cries, and dance because He dances.... God is fun, cool, "real," and will be the life of heaven's party.[30]

That makes it clear: God cares. What we do and don't do influences His emotions. He wants to be pursued and sought after for no other reason than that we're crazy in love with Him. How do I know? Because He calls us His children. He calls us His bride. Are there any other relationships on earth He could use to more persuasively communicate intimacy and closeness and extravagant love?

As a young man marries a young woman and a bridegroom rejoices over his bride, so our God rejoices over us (see Isa. 62:5). My dream illustrated this truth in an awesome way—how He glories over His Bride, the Church; how He is so taken and moved by her and fond of her; and how, even though she is still young, He is so very, very pleased with her.

Dr. Virkler's Dream Key

The meaning of the dream must be drawn from the dreamer. Realize you know nothing about the dream, but through dependence upon Holy Spirit and the skillful use of questions, you can draw the meaning of the dream out from the heart of the dreamer.

As for these four children, God gave them knowledge and skill in all learning and wisdom: and Daniel had understanding in all visions and dreams (Daniel 1:17 KJV).

Counsel in the heart of man is like deep water; but a man of understanding will draw it out (Proverbs 20:5 KJV).

The dreamer's heart will leap and say, "Aha!" when it hears the right interpretation, so never accept an explanation that does not bear witness in the dreamer's heart.

DEPENDENCE ON HOLY SPIRIT IS THE GOAL

Rather than refer to lists in dream dictionaries that have no knowledge of us or understanding of our personal histories, unique perceptions, or waking lives, it is easiest and best simply to ask Holy Spirit Himself what the symbols in our dreams represent. *"Do not interpretations belong to God?"* (Gen. 40:8).

A dream symbol dictionary might seem like a good idea to begin with, but what began in the Spirit are we now going to try and complete in the flesh (see Gal. 3:2-3)? Now that someone else has received anointed revelation from the Lord about their dreams, do we really just want to let their personal and inspired walk with God be a substitute for our own unfolding journey with Him?

Generally speaking, God prefers to skip the rules and laws and just sit down and have a conversation with us. *Hey Jesus, what was up with that funny dream last night?* He laughs and says, "Yeah, We knew you were gonna get a kick out of that! Well, you see…"

Every key we have offered in this book is flexible. Every principle is a suggested guideline. Your dreams will often work like this, but sometimes they may not because of God's infinitely creative nature. And that's fine. What we have presented here are ideas and concepts to get you started. The rest is up to you and Holy Spirit. We should let Him interpret our dreams for us. That is usually what the "interpretation" portion of my dream records are: first-person translations and explanations straight from the Giver of the dream Himself.

In fact, if we want to follow scriptural example in our Christian dream interpretation, angels actually did quite a bit of translating of the messages in dreams and visions. When Zechariah didn't understand what he was seeing, he asked the angel with whom he was speaking, "What is this? What is that?" and the angel broke it down for him (see Zech. 4).

Similarly, in the Book of Daniel, we see how God sent the angel Gabriel to help Daniel understand the vision He had given him (see Dan. 8:15-17). Another time when Daniel didn't understand his dream, he asked the angel in it to enlighten him (see Dan. 7:13-16). So we have biblical precedents for angelic assistance as well.

WE ARE GOD'S HAPPY THOUGHT

In closing this chapter we will look at a final set of dreams to illustrate the reason we do not recommend dream symbol dictionaries. From my experience of working with dreams over the last twenty years I have learned something profound: any symbol can mean anything. God is God, and He gets to do whatever He wants. And He will, just for fun! The following is an example of this principle.

In Chapter 4, I shared a dream in which I was naked. Often that might signify feeling exposed or vulnerable in some way. We could easily interpret that as a negative and something we would not want to have happen, which was true for the "Running Scared" dream.

But there was another time I had a dream series—a few different dreams over the course of a week—and in every single one of them I wasn't wearing any clothes. Yikes. That must indicate some serious transparency issues. *What in the world was wrong with me? How uncomfortable was I feeling, and in what area? Obviously, this couldn't be good!*

NAKED AND NOT ASHAMED

Remember, setting is everything. So what would happen if I told you that during that same week in waking life I had been prayerfully meditating on Genesis? I love the beginning of that book because it gives a clear picture of God's ideal, what His initial intention was when He created everything. Looking around now at the world we're in—this is not God's original plan. Creation has been subjected to futility, and it is a slave to corruption. This is a people and a planet afflicted by sin eagerly longing and waiting for the revealing of the mature sons of God (see Rom. 8:19-21).

But what was it like at first, in Eden? Genesis tells us that the Lord walked in the Garden in the cool of the day (see Gen. 3:8). Adam and Eve were so aware of their relationship with Him and were so focused on His realm of the spirit that their eyes were not yet looking at their humanity in the natural. They were in the best place with God: close fellowship with no sin, sickness, or death separating them. It was perfect. And in the Garden, they were naked and unashamed (see Gen. 2:25). It was a good thing!

When I had this dream series in which I was not wearing any clothes, it was in that context. God was showing me how He was restoring fellowship to my soul like He had with Adam and Eve—an intimate relationship without anything between us. This was a marvelous picture. I was excited to have these dreams! It was a wonderful confirmation of the progress in my walk with the Lord, and I was so happy that He saw our relationship in such a positive way. It was bright, light and beautiful!

Toward the end of that same week I had another no-clothes dream, but it was not as bright as the other dreams. Worse yet, I had something in my hands—some type of clothing. I couldn't figure out what it was, but it seemed like a sheet or cloth of some kind. Whatever it was, I instinctively knew that it was something to cover myself with.

"But I'm not supposed to be covering myself. This is the Garden of Eden. They only tried to wear something after they messed up! Oh man, is this some type of fig leaf? Here it is getting dark in my dream *and* I'm trying to cover myself. God, what gives?"

"Well, Char. I thought we were hanging out. You want to live Scripture, right? The Word made flesh in your life? We've been hanging out

together in the Garden all day long, and now the sun is setting. It's the crepuscular time of day. You know, later in the evening, like dusk?

*"It's not a bad thing. You're walking and talking with Me in the cool of the day. Why does it get cool? Because the sun goes down. What happens when the sun goes down? It gets **darker**. Don't get all bent out of shape, girl!"*

He was fairly amused at my jumping to conclusions, but I still wasn't satisfied.

"God, that's all well and good. But seriously, what's up with that, that…thing? The cloth/sheet/whatever deal? I thought I was naked and unashamed before You and that that was a good thing. Why would I want this to cover me up?"

I was sure it was a bad omen of some kind. What had I done now?

"Charity, Charity, Charity. You are worried and troubled by so many things," He says with a twinkle in His eye. Jesus can no longer hide the huge grin spreading across His face as He explains, *"Charity, I gave you a shawl. You know, like a wrap? For your shoulders? Ladies sometimes like to wear them in the evenings to take the chill off… I told you this was a dream about walking with Me in the **cool** of the day, remember?"*

Oh brother! "Jesus, are You kidding me?"

I wanted to snap that shawl at Him like a dishtowel as He doubled over with laughter, barely able to catch His breath. I tried to get Him, but He took off running, and just like that we were at it again, playing, joking around, and just sharing life together in the Garden.

John the Beloved revealed to us a secret mystery of the ages: God created all things and it was *"for His pleasure"* they were created (Rev. 4:11 KJV). As extraordinary as it may seem, communion with Him is what we were designed for. It's what life is all about (see John 17:3).

God is for us and not against us. He is in a good mood! And spending time with His kids is what He likes best. He wants to have a relationship with us; it's why we are here. Intimacy is the desire of God's heart, and we were made for His pleasure. We were created that He might enjoy the pleasure of our company.

Chapter 10

Why All Bad Dreams Aren't: The Blessing of Nightmares and Other Surprising Revelations

"Indeed God speaks once, or twice, yet no one notices it. In a dream, a vision of the night, when sound sleep falls on men while they slumber in their beds, then He opens the ears of men and seals their instruction, that He may turn man aside from his conduct, and keep man from pride; He keeps back his soul from the pit and his life from passing over into Sheol.... Behold, God does all these oftentimes with men, to bring back his soul from the pit, that he may be enlightened with the light of life."
—Job 33:14-18;29-30

At times God has repeatedly warned me that something is danger-ous, but I've been a little rebellious and didn't believe Him. I think, *I've got this.* I decide that maybe I can actually play with fire and not get burned. So even though God keeps telling me, "Hey, don't spend too much time getting involved with this person! This path leads where you don't want to go," somehow in my pride and selfishness I think I know better and that I might be able to handle it just this one time.

In addition to many spoken warnings during the day, God also gives me picture warnings at night through my dreams. Dreams are much harder for me to ignore, escape, or deny—especially intense dreams, like nightmares. Can God speak through them? Sure He can. God will give me the same message: "Hey, danger. Watch out." But the difference is, I'm living it. I am not just hearing Him say, "Going any farther down this road will lead to trouble and pain." Instead, I'm dreaming it. I am actually going down that road—or in my case, it was a river.

WHITEWATER TERROR

In my dream, I'm being carried quickly down a violent river. I was not in a raft; I was all by myself, and I was being tossed about the whitewater from rapid to rapid. I was totally out of control and could do nothing about it. It was scary and dangerous, and I was terrified. My heart was pounding; my hands were shaking, and I knew it was going to end very badly.

I wake up. God says, *"See, told you."* I'm clearly distraught, and He calmly explains, *"Well, if you would have listened to Me the first ten times I told you in waking life, I wouldn't have had to scream it in your heart at night."* Point taken.

As we have seen, dreams are pictures that we live. We feel them. We can't tell the difference between something we are dreaming and something that happens in waking life. That is why we sometimes wake up with sweaty palms and racing hearts. For all our bodies know, we really did just live that experience.

Not only are our physical bodies influenced by dreams; our emotions are also fully engaged. God can even fast-forward and let us experience during our night visions the future consequences of the path we're considering taking. He does this as a blessing for us, to help make the message palpable so that we don't miss it and disobey. He wants us to get on His best path and stay on it, following His perfect plans.

Pictures evoke emotion, and emotion moves us to action. Experiencing emotion is an extraordinary benefit of dreams, and we should always be mindful of the feelings we have in them. Dreams exaggerate to get our attention. They will also reoccur if we ignore their messages to us.

AMPLIFICATION AND EXAGGERATION

God looks at things differently than we do, and if how we view life is not lining up with how God sees it, we should reevaluate the lens through which we are looking. That is what dreams help us do: look through His eyes and see a person, situation, or issue the way He does.

For example, perhaps there is someone in our waking life who is frustrating us. We are just a bit upset, a little impatient, or slightly unhappy with them. Then we fall asleep and dream that we are beating that person up! We are yelling at and hitting him. When we wake up, we are so relieved to discover it was not in waking life that the fight broke out. Wow, where did that come from? Should we feel guilty that we obviously have so much pent-up hostility?

No. The dream, like Holy Spirit Himself, reveals but does not condemn. As we have mentioned, dreams amplify actions and exaggerate feelings so that we won't continue to overlook them. In waking life, we may be tempted to dismiss a small grievance as unimportant, but ignoring it doesn't make it go away.

Through our dreams, the Lord calls us to address these "minor" heart issues of frustration or impatience. We may consider these attitudes inconsequential, but in reality, since they are opposites of the fruit of His Spirit—joy, patience, and self-control—they are not insignificant at all.

Dr. Virkler's Dream Key

DREAMS THAT TELL OF THE FUTURE

In a sense, many dreams are foretelling the future. Some dreams may simply be showing what will happen in the near future if one does not repent and change his or her ways. Other dreams seem to tell of the very distant future, as some of the Bible dreams appear to do. Perhaps more prophetic people may find that they dream further into the future and farther away from themselves, while people who are not as prophetic may tend to dream closer to home (i.e., have dreams that deal with issues concerning their own heart's struggles).

As with prophecy, the messages and warnings in dreams are conditioned upon man's response (see Ezek. 33:13-16). A dream can call you to act or change so that some calamity does not befall you. If you respond appropriately, the hardship will not come.

God wants us to live inside of His Spirit, to live in peace and joy. He always wants what's best for us. Also, our heart is His home, and any invasion of these ungodly emotions fails to provide a pleasant, hospitable environment in which His Spirit may rest.

Therefore, when frustrations arise in our waking life, the Lord will give a dream that highlights any leftover issues we have not fully processed with Him before going to bed. God does not want us to give the devil any opportunity by letting the sun go down on our anger (see Eph. 4:26-27). If we go to bed upset, we will often have dreams of rage or aggression to get our attention. They are simply a red flag from the Spirit of God, letting us know we have some prayer work that needs to be done.

We will then confess our wrong emotions to the Lord, agree with His truth about the person and situation, and walk in forgiveness. We can even ask God to give us a dream showing us how He feels about the person with whom we are struggling. Often, experiencing His point of view and His affection for that person through our dream helps us live into His kind intention toward him or her that much more freely upon awakening.

KEEP LOOKING

We discussed objective dreams in Chapter 3, and the next story about my friend is another example. Objective dreams are rare and mean the dream is about someone other than the dreamer. The clue to help us discern that it is not a subjective dream about one's own heart issues is the fact that the dreamer is not an active participant. Instead, the dreamer simply is watching the scenes as a spectator.

DREAM ONE: I saw a little girl in the cab of a pickup truck that was on fire. I didn't see how she could escape and thought she and the man in it were going to die so I turned away.

DREAM TWO: God took me back to the same scene and told me that I had turned off the movie too soon. If there is not a good ending, His story isn't over yet. Like the eminent dream interpreter Daniel, I must look and keep on looking (see Dan. 7:2,9,13).

I obediently kept watching the dream play out. I saw the man use the power locks on the passenger side where he was seated to roll down the window and unlock the driver's side door, where the little girl had been sitting. Because the man unlocked the door in time, she was able to open the door and escape to safety.

ACTION: Escaping disaster

FEELING: Grateful surprise

SETTING: The day I had this dream it was my friend's birthday. My heart was heavy because I felt like she had trapped herself in a dangerous place through unwise life choices, and I didn't want to watch what was going to happen next. I did not want to witness the outcome of her poor decisions.

INTERPRETATION: GOD: *"In the dream, just as in waking life, you didn't see your friend's decisions turning out well for her and were tempted to give up on her. But I'm showing you the story isn't over yet! Yes, she has been in the driver's seat of her life, which, as the dream clearly shows, is not the best place for her.* (Remember, she was pictured as a seven-year-old child.) *That's My place. But because she insisted on being in control she crashed and now feels trapped yet again.*

"You didn't have to save her, though. Nobody on the outside came to her rescue. She got out herself. Actually, it was the guy in the truck with her who unlocked the door and rolled down the window so she didn't inhale the smoke—He is the one who actually made it possible for her to escape.

"Who do you suppose that would represent? Me, of course! I have not left her alone. Even when she tries to shut out you or her family, she can't shut Me out. I'm not only with her; I'm in her. I never leave her or forsake her. Although she may try to leave Me, I am not leaving her. And the dream shows that when she insists on being in charge, steering her own life, and she has an accident, I'm still right

there with her. Right beside her. So when she is ready and wants to get out, I help her escape. I always make a way."

ME: "God, that's awesome. Thank You! Can You please explain the power locks and power windows? You unlocked them for her."

GOD: *"It's a picture of My Holy Spirit's 'power' in her life. As soon as she's ready, I have already provided a way of escape. My power is working to unlock the situation in which she's found herself trapped, and I have supernaturally rolled down the window so she can breathe in the fresh wind of My Spirit. Whereas you see her suffocating in a bad situation, I see an opportunity for My salvation and redemption. Where sin abounds, grace abounds more. Remember, it's in weakness that My strength is made perfect.*

"She then crawled over and pulled the door open, and really, she saved herself. It was her decision, her choice. It is I who answer your prayers by moving in her heart. The only way this works is if it's an inside job. It's got to come from within—within the situation, within the mess, within her heart.

"I'm right there in the middle of it with her, and I'm not giving up on her. She is Mine, and she knows it. My love is a strong river that will sweep her off her feet. My goodness will overwhelm her, and My kindness will bring her to repentance. My compassion and grace cannot be overestimated. I am determined to win back her heart with My love."

ME: "In the dream, the door opened inward so she needed to move over to the passenger side in order for the driver's side door to open far enough for her to squeeze out. Why?"

GOD: *"Because I was the Passenger on the other side, and the dream was showing that in order for her to get out and be saved from the situation, she needs to get closer to Me. She needs to move back over to where I am to be in a position to escape."*

ME: "OK, that makes sense. But why is she in a pickup truck? That's not her type of vehicle."

GOD: *"That symbol is showing that as soon as she makes her move toward Me, we're going to 'pick up' right where we left off. I know you feel like she's wasting time, but I live outside of time. I'll redeem the time. I will take what the enemy meant for evil and turn it not only for her good, but for My glory. She won't have to be in a remedial class with Me! We'll make up for the lost time, and I will see to it that we pick up right where we left off and keep moving forward. Not in reverse or at a standstill, but moving ahead."*

Essentially, this dream played out Romans 8:28 for me in a personal way. I saw how God causes all things to work together for good for those who love Him and are called according to His purpose. If there is not a good ending, His story isn't over. No matter the situation, He always provides a way of escape. His Spirit's power is unlocking the doors and setting my friend free from the place in which she has found herself trapped. It is an inside job, and as soon as she moves closer to God she will pick up with Him right where they left off. Amen!

Dr. Virkler's Dream Key

Dreams reveal but do not condemn. Their goal is to preserve life, not to destroy it (see Job 33:13-18).

NIGHTMARES: DISTRESSING OR DIRECTIONAL?

The next four dreams come from one of our Christian Leadership University students who took the online course, "Wisdom Through Dream Interpretation." Karyn Pearson shares some disturbing night visions along with the powerful messages God gave her through them.

STRINGS ATTACHED

DREAM ONE: "I was walking somewhere when I noticed a thread in my mouth that annoyed me. I felt for the thread, which ended up being more like a string, and started to pull it out. As I continued to walk, I kept pulling out the string; however, it seemed to have no end. I came to the end of my journey, and a person who seemed faceless asked me if I wanted help getting to the end of the string. I accepted his help. He pulled on the string and out came a miniature grey clay object of a perfectly formed wolf.

"I looked up into the sky and somehow knew there were people up there watching down on this scene. I asked a man if he knew what this could mean. He replied that perhaps it represented unbelief. I said, 'Maybe'—but knew in my heart that answer didn't witness with my spirit. I had a sensing or knowing in my heart that the wolf represented the muscle relaxants that I was taking and that it would be dangerous to continue to take them for a long period of time."

SETTING: "At that time in my waking life, I was suffering from muscle knots that caused inflammation and pain throughout my body. I was becoming dependent on muscle relaxants as a quick fix even though I was aware of other physical treatments that also brought relief."

ACTION: "Walking and pulling on a string."

FEELING: "In the dream, I had an attitude of really wanting to know the truth about my situation."

INTERPRETATION: "This dream was about my walk—physically and spiritually. The wolf represented the muscle relaxants that had become an idol in my heart. I was becoming more and more dependent on them for relief instead of turning to the Lord. The strings spoke of having 'strings attached,' meaning having this idol would cost me something.

"The faceless man who helped pull the string out represented the Holy Spirit, as He is our Helper. The people in the sky who offered me support and counsel were the great cloud of witnesses in Hebrews 12:1. The 'unbelief' of which they spoke was the denial my heart was in. Hebrews 3:8 and 3:15 tell us not to harden our hearts when we hear God speak.

"I hardened my heart when I made a conscious choice to ignore the dream upon awaking, even though I knew this dream was from God. I justified it to myself by saying that I was too busy to worry about it at the time. As a result, the next night I had a nightmare."

Dr. Virkler's Dream Key

Repeated dreams occur because we did not hear and act on the message of the dream when it spoke to us the first time.

WHEN DISOBEDIENCE BRINGS A NIGHTMARE

DREAM TWO: "I was at a woman's house, and we were trying to lock the back door. We then proceeded to walk through the living room to the front door. I stood facing the open front door, and before the woman could return, I saw something travel underground—underneath the dirt—at an extremely fast pace. A man popped up and started choking me. It happened so fast I didn't have a chance to scream for help. I woke up terrified!"

INTERPRETATION: "This nightmare was a clear result of disobeying the voice of God in the previous dream (see Job 33:14-18). I now had an open door in my life that gave the enemy access to my soul.

"I repented for ignoring the voice of God through my dreams and received His forgiveness and instruction."

LIONS AND TIGERS AND BEARS, OH MY!

DREAM: "I was driving in a car with my husband, Doug. We were going up a mountain that had become too steep to continue driving on. Therefore, we got out of the car and started to push it. Out of nowhere a bear jumped out and started chasing us.

"My husband was running in front of me so I jumped on his back. I could feel the paw of the angry bear brush my shoulder very lightly. Then I woke up."

SETTING: "In waking life it was a very busy time for me."

ACTION & FEELING: "I was frustrated by having to push the car as I was in a hurry to get somewhere."

INTERPRETATION: "The Lord showed me through this dream that I was frustrated and was taking it out on my husband. The message of the dream read: 'Get off his back and quit acting like a bear!'"

Dr. Virkler's Dream Key

Nightmares are often the scream of an unhealed heart asking you to apply the prayer ministries of inner healing and deliverance to the areas of need within you.

FACE THE FEAR

PRE-MINISTRY DREAM: "I had a frightening reoccurring dream for over thirty years. The dream was always about me running and hiding from a man. Sometimes it would be someone else who was running and trying to hide; however, by the time I woke up, the person running would have morphed into me."

SETTING: "The dream changed for me after receiving prayer in waking life during a revival meeting at my church. The Lord ministered to me powerfully, and upon leaving the church, I knew I had been delivered from a spirit but didn't know which one—until my dream that night."

POST-MINISTRY DREAM: "It started out the same way with someone chasing me; however, this time I turned around to face him and pointed to him, saying, 'No! I rebuke you in the name of Jesus.' I have not had that dream since!"

ACTION: "Running"

FEELING: "Intense fear"

INTERPRETATION: "The dream was revealing the scream of my heart. I grew up in an alcoholic home with lots of fighting and violence. My father would physically beat my mother while he screamed at her. The Lord showed me that when the beatings would start, I would run for cover to get away from him. This traumatic time opened a door in my life to the spirit of fear, which was often played out in this nightmare. However, after the Lord delivered me from fear the dreams completely stopped!"

SPIDERS AND SUCH

I appreciate Karyn's dream of deliverance, and also the following one from another CLU student, Kathy Keicher. Both beautifully illustrate how our dreams are calling us to face our fears and realize that with Jesus at our side, there is nothing to be scared of.

These "bad" dreams are bringing to our consciousness unhealed parts of ourselves that we need to let Holy Spirit touch. In the sense that they are summoning us into the Lord's presence, they are in fact "good." And once we've invited God into those broken places, we are ready to face the fear or temptation head on, sometimes realizing it was nothing to be upset over after all. Kathy's dream is a great example of this.

DREAM: "A spider landed on my pillow and was ready to pounce on my face. I quickly turned my head away and woke up, frightened. I wanted to switch the lights on and see if it was gone. Instead, I decided to face my fear by turning my head back toward it, but it was gone."

INTERPRETATION: "There are things in my life right now that are bothering me, and some are actually frightening me. I believed that I had turned the corner this morning on this depression and that I was going to move on up emotionally. This dream confirmed that I had indeed had a turnaround and faced my fears and that I would continue to face them."

Dr. Virkler's Dream Key

Animals often represent your emotions. Ask, "What emotion might this animal signify to me?" This will depend on your geographical location, your personal experiences, your knowledge of the Bible, and your own culture. For example, a bull might represent anger (an angry bull); a fox, craftiness; a dove, peace; an eagle, freedom; a snake, subtlety; a lion, royalty; and so on.

CURIOSITY KILLED THE CAT

Animals may represent various things in our dreams as demonstrated in the stories above. One possible way to interpret them is by viewing them as representative of an emotion within us. Whatever the dominant characteristic of an animal is, that might be the part of us to which the animal is speaking. An example of this principle can be seen in the following dream my mom, Patti, had.

> **SETTING:** "I was mad when I went to bed. I don't remember why but someone had wronged me. I had a right to be angry, and I was!"
>
> **DREAM:** "I opened the door to my house, and a bull was right outside. He somehow knocked off my glasses, then stepped on them and crushed them."
>
> **QUESTIONS:**
>
> - "What emotion does a bull represent to me? What adjective would I normally use to describe a bull? Answer: 'an angry bull'—so a bull means anger to me."
> - "What is the main action of the dream? Answer: Knocking off my glasses and crushing them."
> - "What does this action symbolize? Answer: Destroying my ability to see clearly."
>
> **INTERPRETATION:** "When I open the door to anger, I lose my ability to see things clearly."

TRIP TO THE ZOO

A fun way God confirmed to me that I should go with what I was feeling about a situation in waking life was when I dreamt of a zoo. In my dream, everyone had plans to go somewhere else, but

I wanted to go to the zoo instead and was headed there by myself. Once the others found out, they all wanted to come, too, and that turned out great! We all had a good time together.

Obviously, a zoo is full of animals. In this dream, the animals signified my emotions so I was following, or going after, my feelings. That message is actually spoken twice: by my going after the animals at the zoo and, even more literally, simply by doing what I wanted to do.

In the dream I acted on what I felt regardless of others' opinions, and it turned out for the best. This picture encouraged me to move confidently forward in what I was feeling led to do in waking life, knowing that it was the right decision and direction.

IF ANIMALS REPRESENT EMOTIONS...

What would a veterinarian represent? After having an intense emotional roller coaster of a day, Leo and I watched a movie with an elderly horse trainer in it. That night I dreamt of that actor, and he was a veterinarian. In my dream, I was going to him for counsel and advice—not for a pet, but for myself.

Since we know that animals in dreams can represent emotions and because my emotions had been all over the place, it actually made perfect sense. I woke up realizing I needed to spend some time in the Wonderful Counselor's presence dealing with the unruly feelings from the day before.

WHY WE DREAM OF THINGS FROM OUR DAYS

The previous dream illustrates another important principle, too. Often we dream of the same things—movie actors, specific locations, certain people, food, or activities—that just happened or were part of our waking life earlier in the day. Because of this, we may be tempted to think that the dream is actually about those things, that our hearts are just working through the day's events and our minds are processing any unfinished business. While that's a reasonable assumption, there is a better explanation that we are going to explore next.

TABOO

Besides playing Pictionary at night in our dreams, God is also a big fan of Taboo and Password. For both games, the idea is that you have a word you want to get your teammate to guess, but you have to be strategic with the limited number of words you're allowed to use as clues.

For example, say you and I just caught up on each other's lives over dinner, and now we're playing Taboo together. The phrase I'm supposed to get you to say is "Hawaiian Islands." There are several ways I can go about doing this: I could try to describe the climate there, or maybe the local cuisine. I could possibly attempt to give you the geographical coordinates, hoping you'd guess the right location. Those are a few ways not to do it.

In order to win we have to play strategically, which means all I need to do is refer back to our dinner conversation. I can simply say, "This is where you said you want to go on your next vacation," and you'll know exactly what I'm talking about because we just discussed it right before we played the game.

And so it is with dreams. God wants to use symbols that are fresh in our minds, often referring to things that happened right before we fell asleep. It wasn't that I wanted to discuss your vacation plans in the middle of our game. I wanted to get you on the same page with me so we could win the point.

God uses the same methodology. He is not necessarily speaking about the places or people we saw that day as much as He is simply using a symbol that is immediately familiar to us. We saw this principle play out with the actor in the movie who worked with animals and the veterinarian in my dream. The night vision wasn't really about the actor; he was just a symbol from the setting of my day that was easy for me to recall and identify. Let's look at one more example to demonstrate how this works.

A DAY AT THE DEALERSHIP

I remember one sister in Christ who, more than any of my other Bible school students, was really struggling to connect with God. It was such a challenge for her to learn to hear the Lord's voice, to quiet herself in His presence, and to believe in and receive His love. In every way, all "the good stuff" came hard for her.

My heart went out to her. I prayed with her and for her and kept encouraging her to connect with Jesus. Holy Spirit is her Wonderful Counselor, and I knew that He was the only One who could truly comfort her and minister deeply to the broken places in her soul. Only a supernatural revelation of Father's heart for her could set her free and bring her the joy unspeakable and peace unexplainable that were absolutely her birthright as a child of God. But was I doing enough? Was it working? This was the general setting of the dream.

The specific setting of that very day was that my husband and I had just spent our evening at a car dealership looking for a new vehicle and talking with the salesman about our options. That night I had a dream that I was at a car dealership. A customer was there who needed a salesman but couldn't find one. I remembered that my cousin is a salesman there, and I had his cell phone number so I texted him and was able to get them connected.

Well, in waking life I do have a cousin who was a salesman at a car dealership. And like I said, that's where Leo and I had just been earlier that day. Is the dream about my cousin? Is it about our new car? Turns out it wasn't about either one. Those were just symbols from the "dinner conversation" immediately before the dream game of Taboo, and the whole night vision ended up being a bit prophetic, too.

We know that we first need to look at the action of the dream, which in this case was my connecting someone in need to an invisible helper. Initially the feelings in the dream were of concern, but they shifted to feelings of relief that I was actually related to the person who was needed and gratitude that even though he is unseen, we can still talk with him and receive his help.

THE MIRACLE

I trust you see where I'm going with this, but it gets even better. The dream was about someone needing help whom I couldn't help—but I knew the person who could. Upon awakening from this dream, I went to work and found an email from this same woman who very much needed help and about whom I had been wondering how much assistance I was actually offering. Her note to me had a different tone than any message she had ever sent. She was over-the-moon excited about what God had just done and was writing to share the praise report.

She wanted to let me know that she had received a powerful prophetic word for a sick child to whom she was ministering. She saw Jesus with the baby, and she watched Him touch and heal her. She agreed with the vision and prayed into it, declaring the life of Jesus to be within the little girl, and she noted the time.

The very next day, the baby's parents told her how at the exact same hour she was with Jesus and the little girl in the spirit in prayer, that was the precise time the baby began improving dramatically. God showed up big and showed off, and my student was overjoyed at seeing her prayers immediately answered and feeling so connected with the Lord. She was thrilled to have heard from Heaven, seen Jesus, and partnered with Him in helping someone in need. She didn't have what was needed, but she knew the Guy who did.

And I was just as thrilled for her! I was excited, relieved, and grateful—all the same emotions I had in the dream—because I, too, had the privilege of helping connect her to our Heavenly Father through the "Communion With God" course, encouraging her to press into her visions and not give up. It all came to pass just as it had in my dream: I knew I didn't have what she needed, but thankfully I was related to the Guy who did.

WHEN SEX ISN'T REALLY SEX

One area that is particularly troubling to Christians is sexual dreams. They want to know why they have such "sinful" dreams. The ones that are romantic in nature may be fine, but then there are the ones where they can see themselves having relations with someone other than their spouse. Other times they might not see themselves, but they know that it is them in the dream. They don't go around throughout the day thinking about sex or fantasizing in that way, so why would they have such erotic dreams at night? It makes them feel that they are not pure in God's sight.

Dr. Virkler's Dream Key

THE POTENTIAL ROOTS OF A SEXUAL DREAM

First possible cause: I'm allowing and entertaining sin in my life.

If I am reading or viewing pornography or otherwise fantasizing about illicit sex, then the dream is coming from a perverted heart and is showing sin in my life of which I need to repent. I think we all agree that dreams can reflect evil within and call us to repentance. So fine, I repent and stop sinning!

A related subject about which I have been asked is the so-called incubus and succubus dreams. Down through Church history we have records of demons sexually molesting both men and women in their dreams.

Incubus—a demon in male form that lies upon sleepers, especially women, in order to have intercourse with them. St. Augustine touched on this topic when he stated, "There were too many attacks by incubi to deny them."[31]

Succubus—a demon in female form, appearing in dreams, seeking to seduce men through sexual intercourse.

My counsel to those who have experienced such dreams is that they see them as a warning that their spiritual defenses have been breached. Pornography, drug use, immorality, sadomasochistic movies or video games, and abuse are among the activities that could leave you open to such satanic attacks. Ask the Holy Spirit to reveal the place where you allowed your shields to be weakened, then repent, stop sinning, and ask Him to rebuild the walls. As you continue to grow in holiness and relationship with the Lord, such attacks will diminish and disappear.

Second possible cause: Normal sexual rhythms within our bodies.

Sometimes our bodily needs show up in our dreams.

If you have a dream where you need to go to the bathroom, it may be symbolic: you're feeling under pressure in some way, or needing to release unnecessary waste from your life (e.g., unforgiveness, worry). Sometimes, though, it can be literal as well as symbolic, so you may wake up and say, "Oh my goodness! I actually really do need to go to the bathroom right now!"

Similarly, a sexual dream could be the natural call of your body. God has built sexual rhythms into our bodies (both male and female), and there are certain times of a week or month when we experience stronger sexual urges. So if there is sexual tension in your body, it may show up in your dream. I don't consider that evil because I am not the one who built sexual rhythms—or any kind of rhythm—into my body. God did! Therefore, I don't consider that an evil dream. It's just a dream showing the condition of my body.

Third, and I believe the most important and frequent, cause of a sexual dream: It is symbolic, just as most all dreams are.

Sexual intercourse is a symbol of union, so ask the question, "In what way is there a union or joining taking place within me?"

I have a strong workaholic nature within me. I just love working. And when I used to take vacations, I found I couldn't take more than one or two days without feeling guilty, like I ought to be working. If I ever come to a point in my life where I can take a week-long vacation with no guilt, that would mean two warring parts of me had worked out their disagreement—the part that wants to kick back and have fun, and the workaholic part within me.

A dream to symbolize such a spiritual maturation taking place within me might involve images of me having sexual intercourse, since that is a picture of joining and coming together. And because I'm the workaholic, I'd probably be having intercourse with a woman who is not a workaholic, a woman who can easily have fun in life. This would symbolically show me that two parts of my personality had come together and united.

People have asked me, "Why would God use an evil picture (e.g., adultery) to communicate a spiritual truth?" My answer is, "It is only an evil picture if you assume it is literal rather than symbolic." And God has clearly shown us in the Bible that dreams are to be viewed symbolically. Therefore, it is not an evil picture.

So how do I protect my dream life?

First, you pray for a covering of Christ's blood over you and the room. You bind all attack of the enemy and command him to leave. I suggest we focus on Jesus as we fall asleep. I simply repeat the name "Jesus" and breathe slowly as I am falling asleep. Since abiding in Christ is to be my focus during the day, why would it not also be my focus as I drift off to sleep?

Of course, if you are aware of unconfessed sin in your life, repent, ask for the cleansing blood of Jesus to wash over you, and put on His robe of righteousness. This will give you a positive, protected dream life. And if you wake up and are under spiritual attack, call upon the name of Jesus to protect and defend you. Bind and cast away any demonic attack in the name of the Lord Jesus Christ.

HEAVENLY TERROR?

We want to remember, though, that just because a dream brings terror doesn't mean it's not from God. When the Lord established His covenant with Abram, the Bible says that as deep sleep came upon the patriarch, *"terror and great darkness fell upon him"* as well

(Gen. 15:12). Likewise, when Jacob awoke from his dream of the heavenly ladder, he, too, was afraid (see Gen. 28:17). Obviously those dream encounters, scary as they may have been, were most certainly from God.

Dr. Virkler's Dream Key

Dreams are reliable messengers. They reveal the condition of one's heart as well as the voice of God within one's heart (see Dan. 2:30; Acts 2:17). They may, from time to time, reveal direct attacks of satan or demons upon the heart. (Job 4:12-21 may be an example of a demon speaking accusation that leads toward hopelessness and death. This is the only biblical example of a demon speaking through a dream.) In my own life, I have had only one dream that the Lord has told me to ignore because it was satanic. Thus, because of the biblical evidence and because of my own personal experience, I do not attribute many dreams to satan or to demons.

HOLY DAYS BRING HOLY NIGHTS

I definitely don't give the devil credit for my dreams because I do not allow him any place in my waking life. I don't remember ever having a dream I would consider demonic. However, I will say that if you habitually engage in sinful behavior or violate Philippians 4:8—for example, looking at porn or watching horror movies—then it would come as no surprise if you end up having bad dreams.

Because I trust we are all living as right as we know how to live and pursuing holiness spirit, soul, and body, that means there is no place for satan to gain any foothold and no way he can influence our dream life. We are covered with the blood of Jesus, dressed in the armor of God, and anointed by the Holy Ghost. Like Jesus, we can say that the enemy has found nothing in us and therefore has no claim on us or power over us (see John 14:30).

We are protected and hidden with Christ *in God* (see Col. 3:3). How is an unemployed cherub going to reach us inside there? Especially if we repent of any sin and pray through any negative issues before we go to sleep. Because we commit our nights to the Lord and ask to connect with His Spirit in our dreams, we can be confident that He hears us and that we already possess what we have requested of Him (see 1 John 5:14-15).

Chapter 11

Scary Sleep: Darth Vader, Dragons, and the Dreams Children Dream

"Jesus said, 'Let the children come to Me. Don't stop them! For the Kingdom of Heaven belongs to those who are like these children.'"
—Matthew 19:14 NLT

We have learned that our dreams at night have much to do with the emotions we experience during the day. Whether we are actively expressing them or unconsciously repressing them, our true feelings come to light through the messages our hearts communicate in the night.

And so it is with children.

TOO MANY NIGHTMARES

One reason kids have such intense dreams at night is because they have such intense feelings during the day. Who hasn't seen a four-year-old move from the throes of bitter disappointment to the heights of delighted exhilaration in a matter of moments? If there is one thing children do exceedingly well, it is expressing their emotions. The good, the bad, the ugly—they know how to connect with their emotions and don't bother trying to suppress how they feel.

That is, until we, the "mature" adults, step in. How often have we overheard a parent dismiss their child's tears, saying, "If you don't stop that right now, I'll really give you something to cry about!" Or what about the "irrational" fears little ones have that can be so easily misunderstood or trivialized: "It was just a movie; it's nothing to be scared of" or "You're too old to be afraid of the dark."

Hopefully most of us don't come across quite this insensitively in our dealings with children. We must be aware of how delicate their hearts are. Their spirits are impressionable, and what they absorb in their early years shapes their perceptions for the rest of their lives. Studies have shown that the input children receive up until age seven literally defines them in ways that nothing later in life ever will.

That is why it is so important to guard the special time when they are young. This requires honoring their spirits, their hearts, and their feelings. Instead of demeaning their fears and belittling their worries and wonderings, we need to listen to and respect them. Feelings—good or bad, right or "wrong"—must be acknowledged. While we don't condone temper tantrums or meltdowns, we also realize there is an underlying reason for their reactions, and that's what we need to address.

HOW DREAMS HELP

This is where dreams come in. If children have not been permitted to adequately express themselves during the day—for example, to openly demonstrate their fear or sadness—this will result in those same feelings being amplified and exaggerated in their visions of the night.

Therefore, we must create a safe space for kids to share their hearts and express and confess any negative emotions to the Lord. At night before bed we can help our children work through their days energetically and emotionally, to process the highs and lows and prepare their minds and hearts for rest. Have them recount the day's events, thanking God for the good things, and allow them to share the bad situations that upset them as well.

Encourage them to talk about anything that made them sad or mad or afraid—whether it was a scene on television or something that was said to or about them. Then teach them how to see Jesus as present with them even in the scary times: What was He doing? What was He saying? Once they receive God's perspective they will be able to prayerfully exchange their sadness for His smiles and their fear for His fun.

TAPPING INTO GOD'S JOY AND PEACE

Another useful skill to successfully process negativity and achieve emotional equilibrium is taught by retired nurse Sherrie Rice Smith in her excellent book *EFT for Christians*. She writes:

> Emotional Freedom Techniques is a God-created physi-ological technique whereby tapping gently on acupressure points of the face and upper body can release, via the neurological system, pent up emotional stress of both daily and long-term events and memories. Hundreds of university research projects now show why EFT works so well in releasing various trauma, including PTSD, anxiety, fears, and depression.[32]

I use EFT tapping myself and have had the privilege of teaching it to my nieces as well. We have found this tool to be easy to learn, fun to practice, and effective in quickly producing healthy, positive shifts in our emotional states.

Regardless of the methods we use, we want to teach our kids that just as David did in the Psalms, they can tell Jesus all about their bad feelings. He wants to hear about them, and He wants to heal them. But He can only do that once they've allowed Him in by sharing how they really feel.

Just as the Jews processed their days before retiring at night, we want to get our children in this habit when they are very young. Once negative feelings are given to the Lord before going to sleep, they will no longer need to scream for attention through terrors in the night.

Lastly, it helps to understand that emotions are basically one size. Love is massive. Fear is huge. And when you take these large emotions and put them inside tiny people, they overflow easily. There is no "kid-sized" sadness. They experience it just as fully as adults do, and without us encouraging them to pray through the feeling, they can easily be overwhelmed by it. If not acknowledged during the day, these emotions unfortunately will get their due consideration at night.

INTERPRETING CHILDREN'S VISIONS OF THE NIGHT

As with all dreams, we must first start by looking at the setting: What was going on in their waking life before they had the dream or nightmare? What kind of movies have they been watching? What kind of games have they been playing? Who has been influencing them and their thoughts and feelings during the day? Have they been feeling bullied at school? Struggling with learning a specific subject? Embarrassed by a music recital? Any or all of these things may be going on, and their heart will communicate these messages in pictures, often much more clearly than they can even put into words or consciously describe themselves.

Just as with our own dreams, we want to isolate the main feelings and actions of our children's dreams. We must understand, though, that kids often do not yet have the vocabulary to articulate the nuances of complex feelings. Most three-year-olds don't have words like *insecurity, inferiority, anticipation,* or *contentedness* in their verbal repertoire so it can be challenging for them to explain exactly how they felt in the dream. They may just be able to say they felt "yucky," and that's fine. They need to know it is OK to feel that way; they just need to invite Jesus into those bad places.

We always want to be patient and never minimize children's feelings. We don't make light of the emotions they experience during the day, and we don't want to do it with emotions they experience at night. Just because something isn't "real" doesn't mean it's not real to them. It is their current reality, and we need to acknowledge those feelings in order to help them move to a brighter, truer reality of God's peace and presence with them.

PEACEFUL SLEEP 101

As we have said, nightmares are often the cry of an unhealed heart so we want to be sure to lead our little ones into a personal relationship with Jesus Christ at an early age. He is the One who brings ultimate healing and restoration.

As a parent, grandparent, or concerned loved one, we can also exercise our spiritual authority in Christ and bind any unclean spirits that are seeking to disturb the children for whom we care.

Anointing their room with oil, playing soft worship music at bedtime, reading Bible stories together, and welcoming Holy Spirit's presence into the bedroom are also atmosphere changers. As we encourage children to look into the spiritual realm and see the Lord and His mighty angelic protectors watching over them as they fall asleep, they will find rest comes more easily and dreams more peacefully.

BRAINWAVES AND BIBLICAL PRINCIPLES

In the Gospel of Matthew, we find the disciples of Jesus asking Him who is the greatest in the Kingdom of Heaven. "He called a little child to Him, and placed the child among them. And He said: 'Truly I tell you, unless you change and become like little children, you will never enter the kingdom of heaven.'" (Matt. 18:2-3 NIV).

While this revealing Scripture can speak to various aspects of childlikeness, the one we will explore for our purposes is the brainwave state of children. Scientists use electroencephalography (EEG) monitoring to record electrical activity in the brain, and what they have learned about the various frequencies is not only fascinating, but also extremely relevant to dream work.

God has created us so that we all cycle naturally through four basic brainwave states throughout a twenty-four-hour period. As we learned in Chapter 1, sleep laboratories have proven that everyone dreams for one to two hours each night during a certain type of sleep known as alpha level, which is light sleep. Alpha level refers to a slowed-down brainwave state. Theta is slower than alpha, and delta is the slowest level, where we are in deep sleep.

When we are wide awake during the day and thinking logically with our minds, we are not in alpha state but rather the faster, conscious beta state. As we fall asleep at night and begin to wake up in the morning, we experience the meditative, prayerful state of alpha brainwaves. In this state, we're not quite sure if we are awake or asleep; however, we are very peaceful and relaxed. It is in this quiet state that the veil between the physical and spiritual becomes very thin and our minds connect most easily with our hearts.

CHILDREN LIVE IN A CONTINUAL "DREAM" STATE

One amazing discovery that science has made in recent years is that children live almost constantly in the meditative alpha and theta brainwave states, day and night, until approximately seven years of age. It is in this brainwave state that the inner world is more real than the outer world, an idea that is remarkably similar to that expressed in the fourth chapter of Second Corinthians:

> *We fix our eyes not on what is seen, but on what is unseen, since what is seen is temporary, but what is unseen is eternal* (2 Corinthians 4:18).

That's what children do naturally. They live out this Scripture innately, intuitively, and happily. Children fully engage in the present moment, and in their own version of it. Their focus is on the picture they're drawing, the story they're telling, the silent music they are dancing to or conducting. They play with invisible friends in a "make-believe" land. They instinctively live from an unseen world within.

Given that children live in a state of lower-frequency brainwave activity, it makes sense why they have such active imaginations and often have trouble distinguishing between what is "real" and what isn't. For example, scary movies can terrify small children because they do not yet have the state of mind to clearly differentiate an animated threat from an actual danger.

Children have extremely sensitive spirits and perceive the supernatural world surrounding them much more easily than adults. This is God's original intention and design. Life started that way in the Garden of Eden, and each new life born begins that way as well.

As we have said, everything we learned in the last chapter regarding nightmares applies equally well to children and their bad dreams, too. Even though the dreamer is younger, the principles remain the same. We ask the same key questions about the main feeling, action, and setting of the dream.

However, one difference we recognize is that many children tend to have nightmares and night terrors more often than adults. Again, this is because of their sensitive spirits. Young children are thoroughly impressionable because for the first several years of their lives they are little alpha sponges, literally soaking up every single thing in their environment—for better or worse—and becoming defined by it. What they see and hear becomes their truth. What they absorb in that early window of ages zero to seven becomes their hard-wired identity, through which every other experience for the rest of their lives is perceived. The following dream illustrates this concept.

HEART TATTOOS

One night, after meditating on what to include in this chapter, I had a dream about tattoos. In the dream, I went to my chiropractor, Dr. Insinna, who was going to tattoo little hearts all over my skin. Even in the dream I realized that wasn't a good idea. What does a chiropractor know about tattoos anyway?

This was a dream picture of how the influences of our early years are forever etched on our hearts, and even our skin. Our very cells are stained and colored by the "tattoos" of experiences and emotions we have when we are young, when we have "little hearts."

Well, in waking life I have no tattoos. However, I did have a chiropractor named Dr. "Insinna," which translates easily to "in sin." I knew the chiropractor had no idea how to give me a tattoo, and that concept of ignorance or lack of knowledge was the main message of the dream.

We are often completely unaware of the sinfulness that is tattooing our children's hearts. We don't even realize the influence that the music we expose them to has, or the impression a broken promise can leave. We're not trying to hurt our kids; we probably just don't recognize that there is a spirit behind the music that affects them, as well as us.

Or perhaps it hasn't occurred to us that if we speak empty threats or we don't keep our word to our children, we are inadvertently instilling the seeds of mistrust and doubt in an otherwise faith-filled, wholly believing heart. When an earthly father doesn't watch over his word to perform it and do what he said he would do, it makes it that much harder for a son or daughter to believe their Heavenly Father's word and trust that He always keeps His promises. May we be an accurate representation of Father God to the little ones in our lives!

AN EXAMPLE OF WHAT *NOT* TO DO

It goes without saying that we want to protect our kids from negative and demonic influences, which can come through many mediums: music, video games, movies, television programs, or questionable friends. Obviously, we wouldn't take a ten-year-old to a horror show, but anything that evokes fear in the heart of a child must be suspect. I've had little ones climb in my lap and turn away from the screen during Disney movies. It doesn't matter if it's "just" a movie and is designated as appropriate for all ages. Children have ultra-sensitive spirits, and we need to honor their feelings.

Another subtle and not-as-easily recognized influence can simply be sad possibilities. To illustrate, I'll share the personal example of a recurring nightmare I had when I was around five years old.

In the dream, I was on a little ride. I was sitting on a special chair, and it made a loop, bringing me back to where I started. My seatbelt wasn't fastened as I sat on the ride, so when I got back to the starting point the ride operator yelled at me. Much worse than that, though, was that once the ride was over, I realized my parents were gone. I'd been left all alone, and I was terrified.

Now, in waking life, my parents had not abandoned me, either emotionally or physically. They were very present and loving, and they couldn't figure out why I was struggling with such a fear of abandonment. It took a long time for us to realize where this seemingly "unreasonable" fear originated. Thankfully, because of prayer, the nightmares stopped even before we were able to discover why they had begun.

Eventually, the connection was made: I had watched a made-for-television movie about a group of siblings who were deserted at a gas station by their parents. In retrospect, this was not ideal viewing for a young child, but the point is that it was not explicitly evil, with witches or sorcerers. It wasn't full of violence or profanity, things from which you would normally be careful to shield your child. No, it was just a story, albeit a very sad one.

The reality is, though, that small things have big effects on little hearts. This tragic story played out in my dream over and over again. I identified with the kids in the movie: they were on a cross-country road trip, and I was on an amusement park ride, something that should have been fun. But it turned out not to be safe (I wasn't wearing my safety belt), and I was in trouble (being reprimanded by the ride operator). I felt all alone, just like the children I had seen on television. And just like what happened with them, my parents had disappeared.

Children have a wonderful sense of compassion and empathy, easily relating to others. And kids, especially as young as I was, don't really understand that what is on television did not necessarily happen. Those kids I saw crying weren't really sad; they were just acting. Adults often assume children automatically differentiate reality from movies and television, and sometimes they can. But I had now been introduced to a heartbreaking "reality" that had never before entered my suggestible little consciousness. Parents leaving their kids? This was a horrific possibility, and it now became a terrifying potential that I experienced repeatedly in my dreams at night.

SIDEWALK OF OUR HEARTS

This is just one example, but it cannot be emphasized too strongly: what children are exposed to, hear, and see when they are young goes deep. It enters their soft hearts, and it stays there. What happens to them and around them during their formative years affects them for the rest of their lives.

Imagine this supernatural window of time early in life when our spirits are so impressionable as the constructing of a sidewalk. Once the liquid mixture has been poured, you have a very limited amount of time to imprint anything on the cement. However, if you can draw your initials in the concrete before it hardens, it is permanently etched forever. Whatever else makes contact with that cement later on does not have the same impact or long-standing effect as those original markings.

And so it is with our hearts. This is why it is imperative that we write the Word of God upon our children's hearts while they are young, while the cement of their spirits is still pliable. We know we are to guard and watch over our hearts with all diligence, and how much more so the young hearts entrusted to our protection (see Prov. 4:23).

While there are variations, the following quote is most often attributed to St. Ignatius and the Jesuits: "Give me a child until age seven, and we will have him for life." They understood that whatever influences a child influences him for life.

We want to forever imprint the soft cement of our children's hearts with God's initials, His handprints, His words of truth and life. We want to teach our children as early as possible about their identity in Christ, that they are "King's kids" and that they have the gifts of God and resources of Heaven available to them. They are called, anointed, and destined for greatness, and they don't need to wait until they grow up to experience God's intimate love and extraordinary power. He loves kids! And He loves doing life together with them.

YOUNG SEERS

Another reason children have scary dreams is because they are naturally prophetic. They can easily sense the supernatural world around them and discern spiritual attacks from the enemy. I have had mothers share how their children's nightmares gave warnings about warfare taking place and insight about demonic activity. These wise women acted on the revelation and knew how to pray strategically and win these battles in the heavenlies because they honored their children's prophetic visions of the night.

Thirteen-year-old Isabel in Malaysia has been receiving messages from Heaven on the spiritual climate around her family for years. I appreciate the way her mom, Shekinah, helps her make sense of some otherwise strange and scary dreams.

For instance, when Isabel dreamt of "many mummies rising up in the shopping mall," they prayed about it together and received an encouraging message through it. God helped them identify this as a picture of the dead being raised to newness of life, speaking to the promise of revival. They acted on the dream by saying "yes" to God's intentions, agreeing with His vision, and interceding for His presence and life to invade their city.

FAMILY DREAMING

Families can also dream together. A friend of ours, John, had almost the same dream as his adult daughter on the same night. A few weeks later, his wife, Lynn, also dreamt a similar dream as their daughter on the same night. God knows this is a great way to get our attention!

Six-year-old Steven dreamt of Jesus saving him from a green monster/man the same night his four-year-old brother, Phillip, did. Their mother, Karyn, shares the amazing story in their own words:

> Steven said, "I was being chased by a green man, who I think was a monster. I was afraid at first, but then I turned around and Jesus was standing there. He had His arms outstretched, and power was coming from His

hands. The power started to shrink the green man until he was a vapor on the ground. And then I went up to him and stomped all over him."

Later that afternoon, my second oldest son, Phillip, came to tell me he had a dream. He said, "I was being chased by a green man so I started running away." I asked him, "Where did you run?" He said, "Up to Heaven, where Jesus was." Phillip reported that he and Jesus then ate a snack and played together in Heaven because, as he explained, "The green man couldn't chase me up there."

Hallelujah! These are powerful experiences with God written forever on little hearts. They saw Jesus rescue them. They experienced His salvation and felt His presence. They know His love and protection intimately because they lived it in their dreams.

Karyn also demonstrates how environmental factors can influence our dreams in the following dramatic example:

Once when we took the boys on a mission trip to Quebec, my son and I both had terrible nightmares of brutal killings with axes and so much blood. The thing is, we stayed in different houses while we were there but had the same nightmare more than one night. Later we found out about the bloodshed that had taken place in the Campbell River area. We used those dreams in our intercession time for the Church and community and repented on behalf of those involved in the massacres. The nightmares stopped.

Leo and I have also had complementary dreams, which we were able to piece together in the morning to form a more complete picture of the dream puzzle. Other couples have also testified about receiving revelation together like this, and it certainly gives wonderful confirmation to these dream messages from the Lord.

BLUE MONSTERS AND BIG APOLOGIES

As we have seen throughout this book, God gives profound spiritual revelation to us through our dreams—and children's dreams are no exception. Dreams received through little hearts are not only meaningful; they are also fun to work with because they're filled with symbolism from their young world. Superheroes, fairy-tale princesses, and other exciting characters often make an appearance in their action-packed movies of the night.

Six-year-old Anjelica has had many such dreams, which her mother, Erica, has graciously allowed us to share. Sometimes Anjelica dreams of blue monsters, other times giant dragons, but always God's protection from the enemy can be found. Anjelica will pray and angels will come and put the bad guys in jail or take her into Heaven safely out of reach. In her dreams she has seen *dragons* on the earth; however, when she visits Heaven in the dream, there she sees *dragonflies*.

I love the juxtaposition and how the Lord shows her that what may seem scary to us on earth is harmless in His presence. As we see ourselves with God, our enemies appear as grasshoppers in our sight, instead of vice versa, and we realize there is nothing to be afraid of (see Num. 13:33).

My favorite dream story that the Lord gave to Anjelica was when the monsters tried to come after her and some other children, but God provided a way of escape: "The monsters chased us and kept trying to scare us and we ran into a bubble and we started praying. The bubble floated into Heaven and then the monsters had to tell us 'sorry.'"

Beautiful! Colossians 2:15 tells us how Jesus "...*disarmed the powers and authorities, [and] made a public spectacle of them, triumphing over them by the cross.*" How could God make that weighty scriptural truth a living reality in His six-year-old daughter's heart? Monsters needing to say they are sorry is a perfectly apt and relevant dream picture for Anjelica, and one she will not soon forget. God is so good.

DO ASK, DO TELL!

We must encourage our children from the time they can begin communicating with us to share their dreams. No matter how fantastic and far-fetched their night visions may seem at first, know that God is speaking through them. There is no "Junior Holy Spirit," and they experience His voice, vision, and revelation just as adults do—in fact, often more easily than adults do.

When I was growing up, we would discuss what we had dreamt the night before around the breakfast table. We should find a good time to ask our kids what they saw in their night visions. If they don't remember, we can just ask how they felt when they awoke. Were they excited? Wonderful! What are they excited about in waking life? Were they nervous? What in waking life can we pray with them about to relieve that fear and stress?

We should teach by example and share our dreams with them, being vulnerable and demonstrating how God gives us messages through our dreams at night, too. Nothing is more powerful than truth modeled. Let them imitate us as we imitate Christ and exemplify living and walking by the Spirit by interpreting our visions of the night and, upon awakening, acting on them.

Because we want to protect our children's hearts, we want to listen to their dreams. We want to teach them at a very young age how to remember their dreams, understand them, and live out of them. As we have seen, this is quite instinctive for a child, as the line between the physical "real" world and the less tangible dimensions of the spirit realm is still blurry. That blurred line is a gift. Children can easily step into the spirit world because they so easily live from their hearts. We know the Kingdom of Heaven is within, and children are blessed to live into that realm intuitively, living naturally supernatural.

LUCID DREAMING

We understand now how children can effortlessly move in and out of physical and spiritual states of awareness because of the way God designed their brainwaves. In fact, children dream lucidly more often than adults. *Dream lucidity* is awareness that you are dreaming while you are dreaming. It makes perfect sense that children would have more lucid dreams since they live in the alpha/theta brainwave states, out of their hearts. As we have discussed, kids essentially live in that "dream state" until they're seven years old. So awake or asleep would be similar—hence their ability to dream lucidly more easily. Fascinating how God created us!

A wonderful aspect of lucid dreaming is that children can learn how to exercise spiritual authority in Christ and call on Him in the midst of their nightmares. Karyn has taught her sons how to become active in their dreams by using the name of Jesus against the enemy. She reports that once her boys started to understand this, they began to see tremendous results. A dream might have started out as an attack, but as they engaged it, it would end in victory. Most remarkable is that upon awakening from these dreams, her children would then experience great breakthroughs in the natural for whatever they were facing in waking life as well.

My niece, Jasmine, has dreamed lucidly. Next we're going to explore one of her exciting, involved, frightening, and ultimately prophetic dream stories.

A CASE STUDY: DARTH VADER AND THE STORMTROOPERS

We have spent some time looking at what not to do and how not to expose our kids to unnecessary evils in life, thereby contributing to negative dream experiences in the night. Now we are going to turn this around and end on a positive note. What does it look like if we do the opposite? What happens when we seize the opportunity of a lifetime and mark young hearts with truth, impressing upon them the love of God and the amazing plans He has for their lives?

Albert Schweitzer famously said, "Example is not the main thing in influencing others. It's the only thing."[33] With that in mind, I will close this chapter by sharing a detailed dream my niece had when she was eight years old. I'll demonstrate by example exactly how she and I talked about the setting, broke down what the pictures represented to her, and translated the message from her movie in the night. I'm leaving it in the same vocabulary used as we discussed the dream. God used her language to speak at night, and I endeavored to do the same.

Below is the dream in Jasmine's own words as told to her mother, followed by a copy of the letter I sent interpreting God's message to her.

> I was in church. There were a few kids. All of a sudden, the bad guys from *Star Wars* came up!
>
> Then I went to the back to close my eyes (because I wanted to find a way out of this dream. I knew it was a dream). Pastor Robert came over and asked, "What are you doing over here?" And I knew that I could say it and not get in trouble or anything. I said, "I'm trying to get out of this dream."
>
> And then, I prayed. And he gave me a key! I didn't know what to do with it so I put it on the ground.
>
> And then, all the bad guys shrunk! I went over, and they were rocks—big rocks! Little Stormtroopers were all over them! Then I went over to the other side, and there was little Darth Vader in a cave. I accidentally picked him up and then dropped him, and then he got big again.
>
> I went to the back again and prayed. Once again, he gave me another key! So I tried to use it, but it didn't work. So Mommy (only Mommy!) came.

And then we went to the sound booth because I saw something. One of the ladies was showing people something: a big spotted dog, and a spotted fish. They were both the same color, and they looked like they had the same feeling. I asked, "What are these?" The lady said, "This dog you see here can turn into a fish by going in water! It gets a bruise and then turns into a fish."

Mommy went back, and I tried to find a seat. There was a girl sitting exactly where a good friend was sitting on Sunday. I asked what her name was, and it was a name I'd never heard because I didn't see her nametag. And then I closed my eyes once more and woke up.

Key action: Getting the keys. (Get it?!)

Key emotion: Confused

Symbol of church: Where we learn and have fun

Symbol of key: Something that unlocks something to get somewhere else. (We're reading *The Secret Garden*.)

Setting: A girl at church had been mean to me (and other kids), and I was upset about it.

My Letter to Jasmine—The Interpretation

Wow, Jasmine! What an amazing dream!! I LOVE it. God is definitely giving you a huge and important message, and I'm so proud of you for listening to Him and hearing what He has to say to you and show you in your dream. Good girl!!

And you knew you were dreaming while you were dreaming?! That's so cool, and very unusual. God is showing you that you have a gift, and that you are special. You are able to see things the way they really are. You can see things how God sees them!! Wow! That is

AWESOME. So, let's see what mysteries we can unlock from your dream...

> *I was in church. There were a few kids. All of a sudden, the bad guys from Star Wars came up! Then I went to the back to close my eyes (because I wanted to find a way out of this dream. I knew it was a dream). Pastor Robert came over and asked, "What are you doing over here?" And I knew that I could say it and not get in trouble or anything. I said, "I'm trying to get out of this dream."*

I love this part of your dream because I imagine that Pastor Robert might be, like, a picture or symbol of God since he's the one who teaches at church about God and the Bible, right? And, how did you feel when you talked to God/Pastor Robert? You weren't afraid! You knew that you could be honest with him about how you were feeling and you wouldn't get in any trouble. So that is a picture from God showing that you can always tell Him exactly how you're feeling. If you're mad or sad or scared or anything—He'll never get mad at you about that! He'll never get upset with you, and you don't have to be embarrassed or afraid. He is right there with you and cares about you and loves you.

> *And then, I prayed. And he gave me a key! I didn't know what to do with it so I put it on the ground.*

This is so good, Jasmine. You prayed? Beautiful! This is again showing how you know the right thing to do, and you are doing it! When you're in trouble or confused you talk with God about it...and what does God do? He answers you! He gives you the key that unlocks the door from where you are to where you want to go to. Cool, huh?

But you know the other cool thing? It's OK if we don't know everything, or even what to do with the key that

He gives us. He is still with us and helps us even when we don't understand and just "put the key on the ground." That's OK too! And how do I know that it's OK? Because of the next thing that happened in your dream:

And then, all the bad guys shrunk! I went over, and they were rocks—big rocks! Little Stormtroopers were all over them!

All the bad guys shrunk?! Woohoo! YAY GOD!! I love that picture, Jasmine. Always remember it! Whenever there is something that seems big or hard or scary—you can pray, and then the problem will shrink and get small and not be scary anymore at all! Isn't God so awesome?! I love that!

And you know what? I think I might even have an idea of what the two keys are that God gave you in the dream. Have you figured them out yet? I know that Mommy and Daddy helped give you some good keys and advice about the girl at church. And we also know that Grandpa always teaches about the "4 keys to hearing God's voice" too, right? But I think that of all four of those keys, TWO of them are most important of all. And you talked about those two in your dream! One of them is "Looking" and the other key is "Listening"—so we can see and hear what God is saying to us. Because, see, that's what happened in your dream.

The *Star Wars* guys were big and bad, right? But then you talked to Pastor Robert/God, and you prayed. After you prayed and received your key, *you looked again* at the situation and realized that they were actually small! From our perspective, bad things might seem really BIG, but when we SEE things from God's point of view, then they are small (because everything is shrunk and tiny compared to the bigness of God, right?!). Like the girl at church who's been mean to you…maybe that seems like a big bad thing, but when we talk to God about it, then He shows us that it's not as bad as we thought. She's only a tiny little Stormtrooper now so she can't hurt you at all!! The Bible says that God is bigger inside you than any bad thing in the world, and that's what you got to see in your dream. You lived a picture of that verse!!

Then I went over to the other side, and there was little Darth Vader in a cave. I accidentally picked him up and then dropped him, and then he got big again.

This is a pretty interesting part of your dream, and I think it's a hint and clue and kind of just a warning for us of what we shouldn't do. I don't think you have done this; God is just showing you what could happen if you DO do it. So don't be sad or anything…it's just a good teaching lesson for us all, actually. Do you want to know what the little Darth Vader in the cave taught me? It taught me so much!

Well, we'd been doing great in the dream, praying and getting our keys and everything. But then, we crossed over to the dark side. Oh no! We "went over to the other side" where Darth Vader was. Yikes! And where was this "other side"? It was in a cave. You know, I checked online for the actual definition of a cave, and they say it's a "natural, underground space." And, caves are kind of dark and secret and private. Wouldn't you agree? You can't really see a cave, or inside of it, very easily from the outside, can you?

So, I was thinking maybe the cave is a picture of our minds and of our hearts (since those are places "underneath the surface" of our body). They are the secret places in us that you can't really see, and it's in THOSE hidden places in our thoughts and in our feelings that we actually fight our enemies. That's where we touched little Darth Vader, our enemy!

The Bible says that we actually do our fighting against satan in our hearts and in our minds. We don't actually have a gun in our hands and shoot bullets at him, do we?! No way. That's so silly! So, if we don't fight him with guns in our hands, how do you think we fight? God actually gave us a clue in Second Corinthians 10:3-5. It says that we should always make sure that every thought we have is obeying Jesus. So we want to make sure to think things that God wants us to think (whatever is true and right and pure and lovely and excellent).

So what does all that have to do with the little Darth Vader?? Well, I know for me, sometimes if somebody is mean to me, I'm tempted to think mean thoughts about them. Sometimes—and this is so bad (!)—but if I let myself go to "the other dark side," in the secret cave of my mind I think to myself, "Man, that person hurt me so much! Well, I hope they get hurt then, too! That would serve them right for being so mean to me!" And, I might even imagine a picture inside my heart of me hurting them and getting back at them for how they hurt me. Oh no! Is that the kind of lovely and pure thoughts and feelings Jesus said I should have? Not at all!

And then what happens if I engage that little Darth Vader and pick him up, if I let myself go there and get close to the bad thoughts and let myself feel those bad feelings inside my heart? It makes the little Darth Vader get big again! Oh no! It makes the bad thing even worse! That's a really perfect picture of what we DON'T want to do, right? Right! And now that you've had this awesome dream, we can both remember to keep our thoughts and feelings holy so we don't let little Darth Vader grow bigger in our lives. Awesome picture, Jasmine! Thank you for that great reminder of how God wants me to think and live!!

I went to the back again and prayed. Once again, he gave me another key! So I tried to use it, but it didn't work. So Mommy (only Mommy!) came.

Ooh, and this part is sooo good too! Your whole dream is blockbuster from beginning to end! SO, this is showing us again God's graciousness and His goodness. God is showing us that even if we DO make a mistake or even sin and are disobedient (and make little Darth big in our lives), all we have to do is go back to Jesus again! All we have to do is pray again! You did the exact right, perfect thing, Jasmine! You knew what to do, and you did it!! GOOD GIRL.

And, what did God show us in the dream? Even though we may have been bad for a second, when we prayed to Him and said we were sorry, was He mad at us? Did He yell at you in the dream? Was He upset at all?! No way! Not a bit!! No matter what we do, God will never stop loving us. He'll never love us any less! Isn't that awesome? So yeah, instead of getting mad at you, what did God do? Instead of being angry, He was the exact opposite. He didn't care about what we'd done. Instead, He gave you another key! A second one?! Woohoo!! God's keys and gifts are always amazing, and He is giving them to you!

But then, you tried to use the key, and it didn't work. Oh no! I'm sorry. I know it's so frustrating when we don't understand and can't get things to work, right? Well, I was thinking...maybe the reason you couldn't get that key to work is because you didn't quite know what the key was yet. Do you think that could be part of the reason? Because I have an idea of what that second key might be. Do you want to hear my idea?

Remember I said that God was teaching us about the two keys of Looking and Listening? And then right after He gave you the first key, then you were able to look and see the bad guys shrunk down tiny, the way God sees them. So we want to look and see life the way God sees life, number one.

And then number two, the second key I believe He's giving us is that we should listen to hear what He's saying to us about life. He can give us a picture of how He sees things and sees people, and then He can also talk to us about His opinions and perspective, too. Just like you're doing with this dream, Jasmine! You're already doing it! You're looking and listening to know God's message to you from the dream, and God is so excited about that!! He is grateful and thanks you for listening to Him and watching the movies He's making for you in the night!

Do you want to know WHY I think the other key is listening to God?? Because of the next scene that happened in your dream, right after you received your second key...

And then we went to the **sound** *booth because I* **saw** *something. One of the ladies was* **showing** *people something: a big spotted dog and a spotted fish. They were both the same color, and they looked like they had the same feeling. I asked, "What are these?" The lady* **said**, *"This dog you see here can turn into a fish by going in water! It gets a bruise and then turns into a fish."*

Usually a sound booth has to do with things you hear, right? Talking and music and voices? The sound booth helps get the message from the speaker out to you loudly and clearly enough so that you can hear and understand what he's saying, right? So I think God is showing you a picture that He's taking you to the sound booth, where you're able listen to His voice and hear what He's telling you loud and clear. Wow! That's an awesome picture, isn't it? I love it!

So, we've got listening to God at the sound booth, and again we've got our looking and seeing mentioned because you went to the sound booth after you SAW something. So Looking and Listening go together—again! Wow, God must really want us to remember this since He keeps saying it over and over, huh? That's nice of Him to remind us so many times so we will not forget it!

So you are being SHOWN something; you're SEE-ING the spotted animals (at the sound booth). But yeah, since it doesn't always make much sense when we just see something, it's nice to know that we can ask God questions and be like, "Hey God, what's up with these funny animals?!" and then He'll answer us! Just like the lady in the dream explained what was going on, God, too, will give us understanding and help things to make more sense if we just ask Him questions about what He's showing us, and He will teach us and make it clearer.

Anyway, the COOLEST part about those spotted animals is…I think you are one of them!! Oh yes, I do! Does that sound funny? I know, it does, but there is a story in the Bible about spotted animals, and I bet you've read it and know it. It's in Genesis 30, and it's actually talking about sheep.

Do you remember what was so cool about the spotted sheep? They were the chosen ones. They were the special ones that were set apart and taken away from all the other regular sheep. The spotted ones were the best ones! They ended up being the strongest animals and the ones that were most prized of all. Just like your most favorite dress that you keep set aside for only special occasions, YOU are the special dress, Jasmine. You are the chosen, cherished one!

I was wondering why the animal was a dog, though. And the thought came to me that they are great companions. They say that a dog is a man's best friend, so I got to thinking: maybe it's because YOU, Jasmine, are a great companion of God. You hang out with Him and are best friends. Jesus is your BFF!! That's an awesome idea, isn't it? Because you (just like a good dog) are LOYAL. You are loyal to God, and you are His friend. And He is so pleased and blessed by you. He loves to be friends with you, Jasmine!! *You* are a blessing to *Him*!

And you are chosen and set apart, separate—because of your spots. Hmm...spots? What do you think the spots might be a picture of? I have the idea that you are spotted with the anointing of God. Oil makes spots, doesn't it? Oil spots on the road. Oil splashing from a pan, getting a spot on your clothes—it sticks and stains and stays on you, which normally isn't a very good thing...BUT if it's the Oil of Joy and Gladness from the Lord, then that oil we want to permanently stay on us forever and ever and never wash off!

Your dream is like a picture of Psalm 45—God is saying to you that "because you've loved what's right and not loved evil, now God is anointing you, pouring out the oil of joy on you more than on anyone else!" Wow, thank You, Jesus!

So if you're that spotted dog—the loyal, anointed friend of God—then what do you do? What happened next in the dream?

The lady said, "This dog you see here can turn into a fish by going in water! It gets a bruise and then turns into a fish."

Really? Whoa. I've never seen that before, haha! I was wondering why God would give you that picture, and I felt He gave me an idea about it. We have a saying, "like a fish out of water," and that means that someone is uncomfortable and not doing well because they're not really in the environment that they're used to being in. A fish does not do well outside of water, but he does GREAT in the water, right? Kind of the same thing with a dog, but in reverse. A dog does great outside of the water, but IN the water, a dog doesn't do as well, does he? I mean, he can sort of swim a little bit—but not like the fish! Compared to a fish, a dog can't swim well at all, right?

So the idea is, if I were a dog and I went into the water, it would actually be really awesome for me if I turned into a fish, wouldn't it? Then I would be just as quick and agile and awesome in the water as I am on the land. That would be perfect!

Sooo maybe God is showing you that even when you go into uncomfortable situations—like with the girl at church, and even other stuff in life that seems hard or scary—God is saying, "You might feel for a second like you're a dog in water" (a quick bruise, a tiny bit uncomfortable for a minute but nothing serious), but then—THEN—God will turn you into a fish! He'll make it so that you ARE comfortable and you CAN "swim well," meaning He will give you strength and cleverness and confidence to do whatever you need to! In ANY situation! Wow! What an incredible picture that is!

And would you believe, there is a verse that even kind of talks about this in the Bible? No way, right?! Now, it doesn't talk specifically about dogs turning into fish, BUT it does say that when the Spirit of the Lord came powerfully on Saul that he was changed into a different person (1 Samuel 10:6)!! He got so spotted with God's anointing oil that his friends couldn't hardly even recognize him anymore. It was like he was a totally different person because God blessed him so much and made him so strong and bold and confident and wise!

Holy cow, right? Your dream is a perfect picture for us to always remember that verse, and that because the Holy Spirit has anointed you with the spots of Joyful Oil and Gladness, now you have the power to do whatever you need to do. You can easily change and grow and become all that God wants you to be! If you are confused, He will help you understand and make you clever. If you're scared or embarrassed, He will give you peace and confidence. If you're sad, He'll give you hope and happiness. If you're weak, then He will make you strong and powerful. And if you ever don't know what to do, He will show you and tell you and help you—with everything. Just like He's doing through this dream! WOW. I love it, Jasmine! And I'm so excited for you!!

Mommy went back, and I tried to find a seat. There was a girl sitting exactly where a good friend was sitting on Sunday. I asked what her name was, and it was

a name I'd never heard because I didn't see her nametag.
And then I closed my eyes once more and woke up.

You know what I see in this scene of your dream, right? I see the same thing as when you were being "*shown* something in the *sound* booth." It's all about Looking and Listening—again! Do you see it? I know the biggest emotion you had in the dream was being confused, but I feel like God is saying that, if you look at Him and listen to His voice when you're confused (just like you're doing right now with understanding your dream), that those are the keys that will unlock the answers and the cleverness and the smartness that you need.

I mean, I totally get what you meant about seeing someone's nametag and how that helps you hear and understand better when they say their name to you, right? Seeing it helps you listen to it better somehow, doesn't it? And I think that's how it is with God sometimes, too… maybe He can tell us something, but it's easier if we can SEE it too, right? And then it makes more sense. That's why He gives us dreams, just like this! Not only are we hearing Him say something to us, but we're seeing it; and even more than that, we're feeling it, too. That's the best of all three!!

I actually really, really like this part of the dream too, Jasmine. Because you know why? It reminds me of another verse in the Bible. Can you believe it? You're just dreaming Scriptures from beginning to end in this dream! Wow. The verse that God made me think of is one of my most favorite verses in the whole entire Bible. It says that "eye has not seen and ear has not heard all the marvelous things that God has prepared for us who love Him—BUT God shows us these things *by His Holy Spirit!*"

That's like you in the dream, Jasmine! Your eyes couldn't see her nametag, and your ears couldn't hear what she said her name was, but...BUT you still were friendly with her. You did the RIGHT thing and you talked with her and asked her name and tried to be friends with her and get to know her.

I think she represents the wonderful wisdom and revelation and cleverness that God wants to give you, things you are learning from God Himself as He teaches you through your dreams—just like you're doing right now. "You say to wisdom, 'You are my sister,' and you call understanding your best friend" (Proverbs 7:4).

And how do I know for sure that you are becoming friends with God's wisdom? Because that's what your dream showed! That girl, whom you didn't know before, you started to get to know her and talk with her a little bit, right? AND she "was sitting exactly where a good friend was sitting on Sunday." So all this wisdom and revelation from God are becoming your friends! YAY, Jasmine!

And, after all these amazing, incredible adventures in your dream, God shows you the end result. After you've spent the whole entire dream listening to everything He's said to you, looking at everything He shows you the way He sees it, and obeying Him...then what??

You got what you wanted!! You "closed your eyes once more and woke up," which is what you said you wanted to do at the very beginning! You wanted to get out of this dream, right? God didn't forget. He knows what you care about! And He gives you what you want and ask Him for. You want to wake up and get out of the dream? God answered your prayer, and you did! (Matthew 6:33)

Wow!! What a happy ending, Jasmine! It's perfect. I love it!

I am so thrilled for you and all that God is saying to you and showing you in your dreams. Watching God's movies in the night while I sleep is one of my most favorite ways to hear from Him! So I think it's absolutely fabulous and incredibly exciting and totally wonderful to see the awesome dreams He's giving to you, too. You are such a good and wise girl to be listening to God in your dreams. He is always speaking to you!! All day long, and all night long.

Jesus and I are so proud of you and love you so much, Jasmine!

XOXOXO,
Auntie Charity

SO WHAT DID SHE THINK?

I typed out the dream's message for Jasmine in a bright purple print, and she kept it in a special place on her dresser for a long time. She was grateful, and it made her very happy because as she said, "God is basically saying, 'Jasmine, you're awesome!'"

Indeed, He is. And that is the message He is continually endeavoring to communicate to all His children, young and old, every night through their dreams: "You are awesome. I love you so much. I'm so proud of you, and I love being your Dad."

This is the heart of our Father, who tenderly chose us before the foundation of the world to be in His family, according to His good pleasure and the kind intention of His will (see Eph. 1:4-5). Translation: He's crazy about us!

We are now nearing the end of our journey together so as we turn to the final chapter, we will summarize our findings and pull together everything we've learned thus far. There are just a few more tips, ideas, and answers to share, and then it will be your turn to do the interpreting!

Chapter 12

PUTTING IT ALL TOGETHER: PRACTICAL TIPS FOR DREAM WORK

"And He said, 'Hear now My words: If there is a prophet among you, I the Lord will make Myself known to him in a vision, and will speak to him in a dream.'"
—NUMBERS 12:6 WBT

We find a most helpful principle for dream work in the Book of James: we have not because we ask not (see James 4:2). The best place to start is by asking the Lord to speak His messages to us through our visions of the night. If we have discounted dreams in the past, let's repent and let God know we are now restoring dreams to their rightful place of honor as a precious gift from Him.

Next, we must expect Him to speak. We know according to our faith it is done to us, therefore we trust that as we seek His

Spirit through dreams, He will not disappoint (see Matt. 9:29; Luke 11:9-13). God wants to connect with us even more than we want to connect with Him, so as we lay our head on our pillow, let's turn our heart and affection toward Him.

Dr. Virkler's Dream Key

Say to yourself, "I believe dreams contain a valid message." This is a signal to your heart that you are taking dreams seriously and want to hear what they have to tell you. You are giving your heart permission— and even asking it—to awaken you after each dream. And it will do exactly that. You see, if you do not wake up within five minutes of the dream ending, you will not recall it. If you tell your heart that dreams are undigested leftover pizza, then it will let you sleep through the dream and won't awaken you after it is over, and thus you will not recall it.

SHORT AND SWEET

Daniel kept brief summaries of his dreams, and we should also keep ours short (see Dan. 7:1). The "*Reader's Digest*" version of our dreams is the easiest way to cut to the heart of their messages.

We can keep a journal or tablet beside our bed and leave it open to a blank page with a pen sitting on top of it. We want to lay these items out before we go to sleep for a couple of reasons. First, it is a signal to our heart and mind that we value our dreams and believe they have significance. Once we have made that clear and set our intention to recall them, we will more easily wake up and remember them. Secondly, in the middle of the night, we don't want to be fumbling around, trying to arrange pen and paper in the dark. If we set them out beforehand, we won't need to turn on a light; we will just need to feel around for them, and then write.

It is amazing how a dream in the middle of the night can be so powerful that we are positive we could never forget it. And then we do. If we don't write it down, the chances of our remembering a dream when we get up for the day are too close to zero for us to chance it. Usually, jotting it down is all we need to do. We don't have to write out the entire dream, and in the night, we don't always have to write down a summary of it either. Sometimes just recording a few key ideas—a main character, characteristic, feeling, or place—is all it takes to unlock the memory and have the entire night vision come flooding back to our consciousness.

Another way to help us remember our dreams is to pray in the Spirit as we begin to wake up. This is extremely effective, as it maintains our connection with the flow of the Spirit and makes it much easier for us to recall and bring back to the surface those dreams we just had. Continuing to pray in tongues as we reflect on the dream also helps us "combine spiritual thoughts with spiritual words" and more easily discern the interpretation of the night vision (see 1 Cor. 2:12-13).

Some people use a cell phone or voice recorder to help them remember their dreams. If you live alone and it doesn't matter if you make a little noise in the middle of the night, then that can be great. Find whatever is best for you. We just have to make sure we can somehow retrieve and record our dream content in order to have something to interpret.

Dr. Virkler's Dream Key

If the name of someone or something is spoken, or you read something that is written down in your dream, it's especially significant.

One time I dreamt I was riding in a truck and a weather report came on. Two different times in the dream the weatherman said the same thing. That was a key to unlocking the meaning of the dream. We definitely want to pay attention to any spoken phrases we hear or any written letters, business cards, or signs we read in our dreams. If there is a song or specific type of music playing, take note of it. Many times important clues are hidden in these seemingly insignificant details.

FRAGMENTS OF REVELATION

Sometimes we wake up and don't remember our whole dream. We know it seemed quite long and involved, but all we can recollect is the very last scene or just one conversation. It may not seem like much, but that is definitely enough. We do not worry about what we can't recall; we trust Holy Spirit to bring to our remembrance what He wants us to focus on (see John 14:26).

In fact, I have often received much encouragement and wonderful insight through one simple scene in a dream. Therefore, if it doesn't all come back to us, we shouldn't lose sleep over it! We work with what we have, and God will make sure He gets His message through to us.

INTRUSIVE AND INVASIVE

We should always try to wake up naturally, if at all possible. Alarm clocks shatter dream recall. Personally, I find them somewhat disrespectful to the spiritual experience we are having with God through our dreams. We are resting with Him and then are violently jarred back into a conscious state. We have just sent a message loud and clear to our heart, saying, "Sorry, but whatever's going on down there is not nearly as important to me as this waking life I need to hurry up and get on with."

Granted, in our modern culture, it seems somewhat unrealistic not to use an alarm clock. Of course I have an alarm clock, and every night I set it. However, I almost never wake up to it. Not waking up to an alarm clock is not about when we wake up as much as it is about when we go to bed, which, for most of us, is something we are able to adjust and control.

If we view sleep as a waste of time and something that is keeping us from getting on with our "real" lives, we have not yet known as we ought to know. If we instead understand sleep and dream time as connecting us with the supernatural realm of the spirit where God lives, then we will actually want to spend as much time there as we can.

THE RESEARCH IS IN

We know that eight hours of sleep has been proven ideal for almost everyone to stay physically strong. Interestingly, studies have also shown that eight hours of sleep is optimal for dream work, as essentially our last sixty to ninety minutes of sleep is REM dream time. Therefore, if we discipline ourselves to get to bed by 10:00 or 11:00 P.M., then by 6:00 or 7:00 A.M. the next morning we will have successfully clocked our eight hours and secured optimal dreamtime sleep.

Sometimes, though, we may wake up at 5:00 A.M. and think if we get up now, we will have such a great jump on the day. That is not necessarily the best idea. We should remember that we are fellowshipping with God in our dreams, so we don't want to miss a thing. Deny the rush and hurry; roll over and fall back asleep. It is then that we will have the most impactful dreams because that last hour is generally entirely light REM sleep, the kind of sleep during which dreams occur.

SACRED SLEEP

We were created to connect with God so we should endeavor to structure our whole lives around that one thing. Dreams help accomplish this goal by allowing us to experience life in the spirit, outside the four-dimensional walls of our physical world. They demonstrate to us that there is more than just this space-time matrix.

We want to live into "the heavenlies" of which Scripture speaks, and dreams are a fast track to getting us there. They are a bridge we can cross to journey into the realm of the spirit, the very Kingdom of God, every single night. What a gift. What an adventure!

God created evenings and mornings and sanctioned a day of rest. We don't need to fight against the way He designed us. We want to live in agreement with the rhythms of Heaven, which is why sleep can be one of the most "spiritual" activities we do. Dreaming with God opens up the supernatural to us in ways that are different from waking life, when our conscious, natural minds find the need to scrutinize and analyze things of the spirit. With dreams, we get a pure flow of revelation directly from God's heart to ours.

Obviously, we discern spiritual matters with our spirit. We know we have the mind of Christ (see 1 Cor. 2:16). No one knows the thoughts of a man except the spirit of the man that is in him. Likewise, no one knows the thoughts of God except the Spirit of God, whom we have received in order that we might know these things (see 1 Cor. 2:11-12). It is through His Spirit that we know; it is Holy Spirit who reveals to us the very depths of God (see 1 Cor. 2:10).

Daniel 2:30 is an amazing verse. It tells us that once we receive the interpretation of our dream, we understand the thoughts of our heart. Jesus lives in our heart, and His Spirit is joined to our spirit (see 2 Cor. 1:22; 1 Cor. 6:17). So through dream work we understand the thoughts of His heart, too.

Out of our innermost being flow the rivers of His Spirit (John 7:38-39). So we want to go deep and connect with our heart, where the Spirit of Christ dwells (see Gal. 4:6). Then, as we begin to live more and more out of our heart union with God, we are able to use

Holy Spirit-taught words to explain the hidden mysteries of His spirit realm (see 1 Cor. 2:7,13).

Dr. Virkler's Dream Key

Do not pose as an expert on interpreting others' dreams until you have been interpreting your own for five years. You can offer ideas and advice to others concerning their dreams, but don't claim more skill or authority than you actually possess. Remember that you bear responsibility for the counsel you give.

GETTING THE BIG PICTURE

It is also important not to be so consumed with all the details of a dream that we miss the overall "big-picture" message. This can be a tricky balance because there is meaning to be found in the nuances and smaller details of dreams.

I have very vivid dreams that I remember almost every single night. I have left out a lot of details in the dream examples in this book because it is too easy for us to get bogged down in the minutiae. I recommend keeping it simple at first. Look at dreams from the most elemental level possible when beginning to work with them.

When we learn a language, we don't start out writing sonnets. We start out learning the ABCs. We begin with small words and phrases, and we develop our understanding of how all these things fit together. In the same way, we begin with the simple "Key Question Approach" to dream interpretation and build from there.

For example, in the "Running Scared" dream from Chapter 4, I could have included much more information describing the rest of the dream: the mall we were in, the other people I encountered, the specific color and style of the dress I was wearing, etc. And yes, there is meaning in those components, but there are a couple reasons why I chose not to get into such details here.

For one, it's distracting. In the prophetic dream about capturing animals that foreshadowed the discovery of a mouse in our house, you might have thought, "Wow, that's a really literal dream. There wasn't any symbolism there."

Actually, there was; I just didn't want to confuse the story at the time. I'll let you know now though what the "unique animal" was that crawled out of our sink drain. It was a snake at first, and then that snake turned into a baby dinosaur. No, I'm not kidding.

If I would have told you that, we all would have gotten lost in the weirdness. We would have gotten hung up on those details and missed the general cool idea that the dream was about capturing animals and that's what was happening in my house.

The other reason I did not get into a lot of detail is simply because if I did, then I would need to explain my personal feelings and past experiences about every single aspect of the dream in order for you to understand its meaning and message the way I do. It is just a lot of words and time for comparatively little pay off. It means a lot to me because I'm dreaming it. And once you get comfortable with your own dream language from God, the details in your night visions will mean a lot to you, too. Until then, don't worry about the details.

THE FOREST FOR THE TREES

Similarly, in the "Insider Secrets" dream, there was another brief scene that conveyed an important idea to me, and then another entirely separate dream later that same night that confirmed and clarified the message. I purposefully did not get into all these details, or "trees," because I wanted to ensure that we didn't miss the "forest." We can always go back and pray into the finer points later. It is the overall meaning that is most important. More than anything, we want to make certain we identify the general idea of the dream so as not to miss out on the main message God is speaking through it.

Another way to look at this principle for simplifying dream work is summed up in the following quote often attributed to Albert Einstein: "If you can't explain it to a six-year-old, you don't understand it yourself." In the Gospels, Jesus said you can't enter the Kingdom of Heaven unless you become like a little child (see Matt. 18:3). If any aspect of our spirituality is too complex for a child to appreciate, then it's too hard, and we probably don't need to be doing it.

To illustrate the potential effortlessness of dream interpretation, let's take that nightmare from Chapter 4 about fear paralyzing me. I could share it with my five-year-old nephew, and he could explain it to me. I would say, "Buddy, what am I doing in that dream?"

"You're running! And hiding!"

"You're right! And why am I running and hiding?"

"Because you're scared!"

And there we have it. That's what the dream is about. All we have to do is ask ourselves (or ideally, ask the Lord), "In what area of my life am I running away from something? How am I hiding? Of what am I afraid?" We need to look for how the main action and emotion of the dream match up to similar actions and emotions in waking life. Once we establish a correlation, we will understand exactly the area of our life to which God is speaking.

DREAMING TOGETHER

Another fun way we have honed our skill of dream interpretation is by doing it together in a group. Growing up, my family was my "group" where we shared our dreams and what God was saying to us through them. When my father was teaching in a Bible school, one of his classes was on Christian dream interpretation. Each week students brought in their recent dreams and they worked together to interpret and understand them. When the semester ended, the class members requested another term together in a Dreams Lab where they could continue to sharpen their skills. I encourage you to find at least one other person who shares your passion to hear from God 24/7 who will grow together with you.

Next we'll look at some helpful principles to use in a group setting.

Dr. Virkler's Dream Key

GUIDELINES FOR INTERPRETING DREAMS IN A GROUP

1. Have group members keep journals beside their beds, and ask God to give them dreams, which they will immediately record upon awakening. Dreams shared in class time are to be recent ones so that the dreamer knows the setting of the dream; that is, the issues on his or her heart when he or she went to bed. Also, it is best in group dream work to interpret shorter dreams rather than longer ones.

2. In a group setting, never go further in interpreting a person's dream than the dreamer is willing to go. As the meaning of the dream is being drawn out, the dreamer may suddenly realize it is speaking about something he or she is not ready to discuss in front of the group. Preserve the right of the dreamer to say, "That is as far as I want to go in interpreting this dream."

A METHOD FOR INTERPRETING DREAMS IN A GROUP

(Adjust and apply to interpret your own dreams, as well.)

1. With the group leader presiding over the interaction, interpret two or three dreams using the following approach.

The Key Question Approach Leading to Heart Revelation (Guided Self-Discovery):

   a. Write the dreamer's name on the top right corner of a blackboard or whiteboard so everyone can address him or her by name. Have the dreamer stand or sit in the front of the room, available to answer questions from the group.

   b. Have the dreamer read the dream aloud twice. While the dream is being read, have someone write on the board the key elements and events of the dream, leaving space between each. If no blackboard is present, each member of the group should create a list on a paper for their own reference.

   c. Ask the dreamer:

   - What was the key feeling in the dream?

   - What was the key action in the dream?

   - In what area of your life are you experiencing this feeling and action?

This will give the dreamer and the group a reference point as to the setting of the dream and what issue is likely being discussed. The answers to these questions can be listed across the top of the blackboard after the phrases "Key Feeling" and "Key Action."

   d. Beginning with the first event or element of the dream and continuing to the last one, have the listeners ask questions like the following:

   - What is the dominant trait of that person?

- What emotion does that animal represent to you?

- In what way are you experiencing (the event described in the dream) in your life at this time?

e. If the dreamer cannot come up with an answer to any of the above questions:

- Remind him to relax and tune to flowing thoughts, rather than analytical thoughts, thus moving from the mind to the heart.

- Have the group brainstorm (heart storm), offering suggestions of what an item in the dream might mean. These should be listed on the board.

- Then have the dreamer go to the board and draw a line through the ones that definitely do not ring true in his or her heart and circle the ones to which his or her heart leaps, offering any interpretation God is revealing in the process.

2. If time permits, break the class into groups of four to six and have them work for two to three hours on dreams of individuals within their groups. Follow the guidelines for interpreting dreams in a group given above. Instruct the groups to use The Key Question Approach. If they need help, they should raise their hand to attract the attention of the classroom leader to work with their group.

When the seminar/classroom leader is not assisting a specific group, he or she should rotate from group to group, making sure things are progressing well in each.

CAN YOU HEAR ME NOW?

Sometimes I dream of trying to call my mom without being able to get through. There is a bad connection or not enough bars on my cell phone. The sound keeps breaking up or my phone keeps dropping the call, and it is just a struggle to communicate. As I've mentioned, Mom typically represents Holy Spirit to me, so I will often have dreams like this when I am struggling to hear clearly from God on a matter. Not that He is being unclear; usually it's just that I am not receiving the message well!

There might be a lot of other things going on in the background of the dream, but our conversational challenges are the key action. That is also what gives me the strongest emotion (e.g., exasperation). This is the essential symbol to focus in on without getting distracted by all the less significant activities and details surrounding this main event.

Phone calls are an ideal picture of connecting with the spirit world. On a phone, we communicate with someone who is not really "here." We can't see them or touch them, but we are still connected to them. Though not entirely perfect in its correlation (since the spirit realm *is* right here), it is still a useful picture in the natural for what is happening in the spirit.

Dreaming about a dropped call, a bad connection, static, or interference is a signal we need to examine our hearts, our "receiver." God is always "transmitting" so there must be something we are doing that we shouldn't be, or something we are not doing that we should be. Maybe we are simply hanging up too quickly when we have an idea as to what He is going to say but don't want to hear it. If we have such a dream, we will want to consider prayerfully if there is any area of our life where we are not obeying God.

Dr. Mike Murdock is Senior Pastor of the Wisdom Center in Fort Worth, Texas. One of his "Wisdom Keys" is that "God will never give advance instruction beyond your last act of disobedience."[34] If we haven't acted on the last dream God gave us, or if we haven't applied His previous words to our life, why would He give any further direction? If we decide to skip a right turn on our road trip and instead jump ahead to the next instruction on the map, we will not arrive at the intended destination. In His mercy, He waits for us.

Most of the time, we don't do that anyway. We are not purposefully living in habitual sin. No, we are willing and obedient and are usually in sync with all God wants to do in our lives. Therefore, if we dream of a bad phone connection or a dropped call, it is most likely a simple reminder to make sure we are still in the best position to receive all the Lord is speaking to us.

Dr. Virkler's Dream Key

The dream calls the dreamer to action. In the Bible, when people woke up, they acted on their dreams. Act on your dreams, too!

DRIVING IN CIRCLES

One night I had two dreams. In the first one, I was totally lost, driving around in circles and getting really upset. I was on the phone with my mom, but I couldn't even tell her where I was so she wasn't able to help give me directions. It was extremely frustrating.

The setting of the dream was that in waking life, I was in a rather strange, unhappy mood that night, and instead of processing those negative emotions and giving them to God, unwisely, I just went to sleep. I awoke in the middle of the night from that driving-in-circles dream and immediately knew what God was saying: *"I can't help you unless you let Me! You have to acknowledge where you are now in order for Me to bring you to a better place."*

The dream was calling me to confession and repentance. Biblically speaking, confession simply means "to say the same thing as." When we confess our sin, we are saying the same thing about our sin that God says, acknowledging that it's not His best for us or where we should be.

Often we think of repentance as turning around and changing direction, as I was attempting to do in my dream. The Greek word that is translated "repent" enlightens us as to what we need to do before we can even change direction, for it literally means "to change our thinking." When we repent, we are changing our thoughts so that they align with God's.

My experience through this dream and its effects are similar to what David described in Psalm 19:

> *Who can discern his errors? Acquit me of hidden faults. Also keep back Your servant from presumptuous sins; Let them not rule over me; Then I will be blameless, And I shall be acquitted of great transgression. Let the words of my mouth and the meditation of my heart Be acceptable in Your sight, O Lord, my Rock and my Redeemer. (Psalm 19:12-14)*

As a result of this dream, I aligned the words of my mouth and the meditation of my heart with the Lord's. I acknowledged that I was in a bad place, emotionally speaking, and I agreed with Him that my heart is His home and, as such, is certainly no place to host negative feelings. This was the setting for my second dream that night.

A FUNKY FEELING

As I mentioned, I had been in a weird mood, in a bit of a funk, that evening before going to bed. I couldn't put my figure on what my problem was. Then I had the driving-in-circles dream. I woke up, acted on the dream through confession and repentance, and fell back asleep.

Next I dreamt of an odd little animal that basically looked like a cucumber with legs running around, terrorizing everyone in the house. I first called for help, but then I just faced the fear and took matters into my own hands. I grabbed hold of that strange animal, but I knew I still needed assistance. I called my mom, and she brought over a banana, of all things. I was quite certain that it was not going to kill the unwelcome creature, but sure enough, she crushed him with it and saved the day.

By this point you may be able to track the symbols and thus may have already figured out the interpretation of this dream. If it's still a bit confusing, here is the breakdown:

The weird-couldn't-identify-funky animal represented the weird-couldn't-identify-funky feeling. The dream made it clear that the animal was wreaking havoc in my house so it needed to be dealt with, revealing in turn how unchecked negativity wreaks havoc within me (God's house); it must be given to the Lord.

As in the previous dream, I tried to call for help, but really I needed to do something on my own first. This showed how I must acknowledge my indulgence in wrong thoughts and feelings (anxiety, stress) that got me into this mess.

Catching the animal with my bare hands indicated that I was finally able to "put my finger on," or identify, what my problem was. Because Mom represented Holy Spirit in this dream, my presenting the creature to her to deal with showed how I was surrendering the problem to the Lord. I had confessed my sin of worry and doubt, which was like catching that sin and laying it on the altar before God.

The final symbol was a banana from my mom that crushed the evil one. This showed how the fruit of the Holy Spirit puts to death the deeds of the flesh (see Rom. 8:13). I just needed to present my negative feelings to the Lord and let Him take care of them. By acting on the dream, emotional equilibrium was restored and I was once again able to live inside God's holy feelings of peace, joy, and love.

Crazy dream? Maybe. Encouraging interpretation that blessed me? Definitely.

Dr. Virkler's Dream Key

Usually we will receive one main message in our dreams at night. There may be several different dream scenes or segments, and we may even wake up and then receive another dream or two after we fall back asleep, but the key messages are the same. They are speaking to a single heart issue. God is communicating one revelation to us using various pictures and symbols.

SAME ACTION, DIFFERENT PEOPLE

To illustrate this dream key, let's look at a final dream scene series that involved several seemingly random and varied images that did not appear to go together at all. However, we know an easy way to focus in on the main message is to see if there is any common thread that runs through the scenes, or through two or more dreams in one night.

For example, I had a dream about abuse. First, a pastor I love was being gossiped about (spiritual/verbal abuse). Next, there was a scene showing the abuse of alcohol. Third, my cousin was overdosing on pain pills (abusing medication).

Now, the dream did not have anything to do with the pastor, my cousin, or alcohol. Instead, the common factor was abuse: abusing a person, abusing alcohol, and abusing prescription drugs. Because I was able to see the abuse clearly for what it was, I was able to react to a situation in waking life with understanding and patience. Where I had assumed belligerence, God revealed brokenness. Through the dream He showed me what was really going on so I could respond the way He was calling me to: with His compassion and grace.

TOP TWELVE TAKEAWAYS

In summary, below is a review of several core principles for dream work. Once we filter our dream through the lens of these understandings, the interpretation will quickly come into focus.

1. Most dreams are symbolic and full of figurative language; they are not literal.

2. Most dreams are about the dreamer and the issues his or her heart is facing, not about others.

3. The setting of a dream is like the legend of a treasure map; we don't understand one without the other.

4. The main action and feeling of the dream usually correlate with a similar action and emotion in waking life.

5. Once we match the dream's action and feeling with the corresponding action and feeling in waking life, we understand to which area of our life the dream is speaking.

6. Dreams, like Holy Spirit Himself, reveal but do not condemn.

7. Dream pictures evoke emotion, and emotion moves us to action.

8. Dreams amplify and exaggerate to get our attention.

9. If we ignore a dream's message it will reoccur, often more dramatically (i.e., in a nightmare).

10. Nightmares are often the scream of an unhealed heart revealing broken places into which we must invite Jesus to touch and restore.

11. Dreams are a form of meditation that move scriptural truth from our heads to our hearts.

12. Dreams are God's contingency plan, ensuring He always has a way to connect with us.

Dr. Virkler's Dream Key

A lady came to me with the following dream:

She entered her house and smelled smoke. She went upstairs looking for the fire, but she couldn't find it. Then she looked downstairs but could not find it. She went into the kitchen, and the smoke smell was stronger. She opened the upper kitchen cabinets and could not locate the fire. She opened the lower kitchen cabinets, flames leapt out, and she awoke.

At the time, we could not understand what the dream was saying. Two months later, she went to the doctor with an intestinal ailment that was diagnosed as inflammation of the intestines. It was a stress-related disease, and the doctor put her on medication that took care of the inflammation.

Do you see that her dream was warning us of this physical ailment two months before the doctor diagnosed it? Her dream showed that in her house, there was a fire. Her house was the place where she lived—her body. The fire was in the kitchen.

The kitchen is the place we eat; it thus symbolized her digestive tract. The fire was not in the upper cabinets, which would have symbolized her upper digestive region, or her stomach. It was in the lower kitchen cabinets, which symbolized her lower digestive region—her intestines. The dream revealed that there was a fire in her intestines two months before the doctor diagnosed it.

A year later, the dream returned. She realized immediately that if she did not relax, the stress she was experiencing would bring another visit to the doctor's office. She did relax and was able to offset another attack. Awesome guidance worth listening to and acting upon! The dream provided her with God's counsel, warning her of the calamity to come if she did not mend her ways. Wow!

NIGHT VISION

Night vision is the ability to see clearly at night. As we have discovered through both the biblical and contemporary examples in this book—that is a perfect picture of what dreams help us do. We see life more clearly and more from God's perspective through His visions of the night. Through night vision.

Dreams help us access God's vantage point. Once we have His point of view—His take on the world in general and our lives specifically—we have a glimpse into the mind of Christ. We understand His thinking more. Our ambition is not just to be like the Israelites who saw God's works. Our goal is to be like Moses and understand God's ways (see Ps. 103:7). Dreams help us do that. As we have demonstrated again and again, dreams allow us to see through God's eyes.

This is especially significant when we recall the principle of observation we learned from quantum physics: when we observe something, we affect it. Once we see God's truth in the spiritual realm, we "change" it so that it is no longer just supernatural truth in Heaven; it is our truth manifested in a tangible dimension.

We release the resources of the Kingdom into our atmosphere through vision, by seeing what God sees through our dreams. By agreeing with these snapshots of the spirit, we become a bridge for the supernatural to invade the natural, for His glory to be revealed in our world, and for Heaven to come to earth.

WHERE DO YOU GO FROM HERE?

To sleep! My prayer is that you, like Daniel, will receive knowledge and wisdom from God and insight and understanding into all kinds of dreams and visions (see Dan. 1:17,20). I hope you feel more equipped and empowered to understand the language God speaks at night.

Now you see how *you* are the very best one to work with your dreams. You understand why you are the most qualified person to interpret your night visions. You know the setting and what was going on in your waking life. You know what you were thinking about when you went to bed that night. You know how the dream made you feel and what each symbol means to you personally.

Your spirit is one with the Holy Spirit (see 1 Cor. 6:17). You have His anointing, which teaches you all things, and He is leading you into all truth (see 1 John 2:20,27; John 16:13). It is your heart that received the night vision as your own personalized gift from Heaven. That makes *you* the absolute authority and expert on the interpretation of your dreams.

I hope, too, that after reading this book you have been encouraged to see how incredibly meaningful your dreams are and how much the Lord longs to meet you through them. God is in relentless pursuit of your heart! He does not give up on you.

As you press into learning God's picture language you will find yourself growing ever more confident in His messages to you. He will anoint you with His wisdom while you sleep. He will guide you with His instruction and protection in your night visions. He will shower you with His grace and goodness through your dreams.

This is what you were made for—intimacy with God. Step into a supernatural encounter with the Lover of your soul each and every night. Dreams are God's contingency plan. He would not risk losing His connection with you, His most personal and cherished creation, so He fashioned you with a spirit just like His—one that never sleeps.

While your body rests, your heart is awake so that you may commune with your Heavenly Father. You are the apple of His eye. Through your visions of the night you are safely embraced in His strong love, experiencing who you are meant to be: the favored child of His kind affection.

The atmosphere of Heaven is peace and joy, and God invites you to dwell with Him there. Live into His Kingdom and live out of it. You are going to spend forever in eternity basking in the glorious presence of Jesus. Seeing the compassion in His eyes. Hearing the laughter in His voice. Heaven is too amazing to wait until after you have left earth to experience it. By living into the spirit realm now through your dreams, forever can start tonight.

Every blessing on your journey!

How to Hear God's Voice

By Dr. Mark Virkler

She had done it again! Instead of coming straight home from school like she was supposed to, she had gone to her friend's house—without permission, without our knowledge, without doing her chores.

With a ministering household that included remnants of three struggling families plus our own toddler and newborn, my wife simply couldn't handle all the work on her own. All members of the household had to pull their own weight. All had age-appropriate tasks they were expected to complete. Fourteen-year-old Rachel and her younger brother were living with us while her parents tried to overcome lifestyle patterns that had resulted in the children running away to escape the dysfunction. I felt sorry for Rachel, but honestly, my wife was my greatest concern.

Now Rachel had ditched her chores to spend time with her friends. It wasn't the first time, but if I had anything to say about it, it would be the last. I intended to lay down the law when she got home and make it very clear that if she were going to live under my roof, she would have to obey my rules.

But…she wasn't home yet. And I had recently been learning to hear God's voice more clearly. I thought, *Maybe I should try to see if I could hear anything from Him about the situation. Maybe He could give me a way to get her to do what she was supposed to (i.e., what I wanted her to do).* So I went to my office and reviewed what the Lord had been teaching me from Habakkuk 2:1-2: *"I will stand on my guard post and station myself on the rampart; and I will keep watch to see what He will speak to me…Then the Lord answered me and said, 'Record the vision…'"*

Habakkuk said, *"I will stand on my guard post…"* (Hab. 2:1). **The first key to hearing God's voice is to go to a quiet place and still our own thoughts and emotions.** Psalm 46:10 encourages us to be still, let go, cease striving, and know that He is God. In Psalm 37:7 we are called to *"be still before the Lord and wait patiently for Him…."* There is a deep inner knowing in our spirits that each of us can experience when we quiet our flesh and our minds. Practicing the art of biblical meditation helps silence the outer noise and distractions clamoring for our attention.

I didn't have a guard post, but I did have an office so I went there to quiet my temper and my mind. Loving God through a quiet worship song is one very effective way to become still. In Second Kings 3, Elisha needed a word from the Lord so he said, *"Bring me a minstrel,"* and as the minstrel played, the Lord spoke (2 Kings 3:15). I have found that playing a worship song on my autoharp is the quickest way for me to come to stillness. I need to choose my song carefully: boisterous songs of praise do not bring me to stillness; rather, gentle songs that express my love and worship do. And it isn't enough just to sing the song into the cosmos—I come into the Lord's presence most quickly and easily when I use my godly imagination to see the truth that He is right here with me and sing my songs to Him, personally.

"I will keep watch to see...," said the prophet (Hab. 2:1). To receive the pure word of God, it is very important that my heart be properly focused as I become still because my focus is the source of the intuitive flow. If I fix my eyes upon Jesus, the intuitive flow comes from Jesus (see Heb. 12:2). But if I fix my gaze upon some desire of my heart, the intuitive flow comes out of that desire. To have a pure flow I must become still and carefully focus my eyes upon Jesus. Quietly worshiping the King and receiving out of the stillness that follows quite easily accomplishes this.

So I used **the second key to hearing God's voice: as you pray, fix the eyes of your heart on Jesus, seeing in the spirit the dreams and visions of Almighty God.** Habakkuk was actually looking for vision as he prayed. He opened the eyes of his heart and looked into the spirit world to see what God wanted to show him.

God has always spoken through dreams and visions, and He specifically said that they would come to those upon whom the Holy Spirit is poured out (see Acts 2:1-4,17).

Being a logical, rational person, observable facts that could be verified by my physical senses were the foundations of my life, including my spiritual life. I had never thought of opening the eyes of my heart and looking for vision. However, I have come to believe that this is exactly what God wants me to do. He gave me eyes in my heart to see in the spirit the vision and movement of Almighty God. There is an active spirit world all around us, full of angels, demons, the Holy Spirit, the omnipresent Father, and His omnipresent Son, Jesus. The only reasons for me not to see this reality are unbelief and lack of knowledge.

In his sermon in Acts 2:25, Peter refers to King David's statement: *"I saw the Lord always in my presence; for He is at my right hand, so that I will not be shaken."* The original psalm makes it clear that this was a decision of David's, not a constant supernatural visitation: *"I have set* [literally, "I have placed"] *the Lord continually before me;*

because He is at my right hand, I will not be shaken" (Ps.16:8). Because David knew that the Lord was always with him, he determined in his spirit to *see* that truth with the eyes of his heart as he went through life, knowing that this would keep his faith strong.

In order to see, we must look. Daniel saw a vision in his mind and said, *"I was looking.... I kept looking.... I kept looking..."* (Dan. 7:2,9,13). As I pray, I look for Jesus, and I watch as He speaks to me, doing and saying the things that are on His heart. Many Christians will find that if they will only look, they will see. Jesus is Emmanuel, God with us (see Matt. 1:23). It is as simple as that. You can see Christ present with you because Christ *is* present with you. In fact, the vision may come so easily that you will be tempted to reject it, thinking that it is just you. But if you persist in recording these visions, your doubt will soon be overcome by faith as you recognize that the content of them could only be birthed in Almighty God.

Jesus demonstrated the ability of living out of constant contact with God, declaring that He did nothing on His own initiative, but only what He saw the Father doing and heard the Father saying (see John 5:19-20,30). What an incredible way to live!

Is it possible for us to live out of divine initiative as Jesus did? Yes! We must simply fix our eyes on Jesus. The veil has been torn, giving access to the immediate presence of God, and He calls us to draw near (see Luke 23:45; Heb. 10:19-22). *"I pray that the eyes of your heart may be enlightened..."* (Eph. 1:18)

When I had quieted my heart enough that I could picture Jesus without the distractions of my own ideas and plans, I was able to *"keep watch to see what He will speak to me"* (Hab. 2:1). I wrote down my question: "Lord, what should I do about Rachel?"

Immediately the thought came to me: "She is insecure." Well, that certainly wasn't my thought! Her behavior looked like rebellion to me, not insecurity.

But like Habakkuk, I was coming to know the sound of God speaking to me (see Hab. 2:2). Elijah described it as a still, small voice (see 1 Kings 19:12). I had previously listened for an inner audible voice, and God does speak that way at times. However, I have found that usually, God's voice comes as spontaneous thoughts, visions, feelings, or impressions.

For example, haven't you been driving down the road and had a thought come to you to pray for a certain person? Didn't you believe it was God telling you to pray? What did God's voice sound like? Was it an audible voice or was it a spontaneous thought that lit upon your mind?

Experience indicates that we perceive spirit-level communication as spontaneous thoughts, impressions, and visions, and Scripture confirms this in many ways. For example, one definition of *paga*, a Hebrew word for "intercession," is "a chance encounter or an accidental intersecting." When God lays people on our hearts, He does it through *paga*, a chance-encounter thought "accidentally" intersecting our minds.

So **the third key to hearing God's voice is recognizing that God's voice in your heart often sounds like a flow of spontaneous thoughts.** Therefore, when I want to hear from God, I tune in to chance-encounter or spontaneous thoughts.

Finally, God told Habakkuk to record the vision (see Hab. 2:2). This was not an isolated command. The Scriptures record many examples of individuals' prayers and God's replies, such as the Psalms, many of the books of the prophets, and Revelation. I have found that obeying this final principle amplified my confidence in my ability to hear God's voice so that I could finally live out of His initiatives, naturally and normally. The **fourth key, two-way journaling or the writing out of your prayers and God's answers, brings great freedom in hearing God's voice.**

I have found two-way journaling to be a fabulous catalyst for clearly discerning God's inner, spontaneous flow, because as I journal I am able to write in faith for long periods of time, simply believing it is God's voice through me. I know that what I believe I have received from God must be tested. However, testing involves doubt, and doubt blocks divine communication; therefore, I do not want to test while I am trying to receive (see James 1:5-8). With journaling, I can receive in faith, knowing that when the flow has ended I can test and examine it carefully.

So I wrote down what I believed He had said: "She is insecure."

But the Lord wasn't done. I continued to write the spontaneous thoughts that came to me: "Love her unconditionally. She is flesh of your flesh and bone of your bone."

My mind immediately objected: *She is not flesh of my flesh. She is not related to me at all—she is a foster child, just living in my home temporarily.* It was definitely time to test this "word from the Lord"!

There are three possible sources of thoughts in our minds: ourselves, satan, and Holy Spirit. It was obvious that the words in my journal did not come from my own mind—I certainly didn't see her as insecure *or* flesh of my flesh. And I sincerely doubted that satan would encourage me to love anyone unconditionally!

OK, it was starting to look like I might have actually received counsel from the Lord. It was consistent with the names and character of God as revealed in Scripture and totally contrary to the names and character of the enemy. So that meant that I was hearing from the Lord, and He wanted me to see the situation in a different light. Rachel was my daughter—part of my family not by blood but by the hand of God Himself. The chaos of her birth home had created deep insecurity about her worthiness to be loved by anyone, including me and including God. Only the unconditional love of the Lord expressed through an imperfect human would reach her heart.

But there was still one more test I needed to perform before I would have absolute confidence that this was truly God's word to me: I needed confirmation from someone else whose spiritual discernment I trusted. So I went to my wife and shared what I had received. I knew that if I could get her validation, especially since she was the one most wronged in the situation, then I could say, at least to myself, "Thus sayeth the Lord."

Needless to say, Patti immediately and without question confirmed that the Lord had spoken to me. My entire planned lecture was forgotten. I returned to my office anxious to hear more. As the Lord birthed a new, supernatural love for Rachel within me, He showed me what to say and how to say it in a way that would not only address the current issue of household responsibility, but also the deeper issues of love, acceptance, and worthiness.

Rachel and her brother remained with our family for another two years, giving us many opportunities to demonstrate and teach them about the Father's love, planting spiritual seeds in thirsty soil. We weren't perfect and we didn't solve all of Rachel's issues, but because I had learned to listen to the Lord, we were able to avoid creating more brokenness and separation.

The four simple keys that the Lord showed me from Habakkuk have been used by people of all ages—from 4 to 104—from every continent, culture, and denomination to break through into intimate two-way conversations with their loving Father and dearest Friend. Neglecting any one of the keys will prevent you from receiving all He wants to say to you. The order of the keys is not important, just so long as you *use them all*. Embracing all four by faith can change your life. Simply quiet yourself down, tune in to spontaneous thoughts, look for vision, and journal. He is waiting to meet you there.

You will be amazed when you journal! Doubt may hinder you at first, but throw it off, reminding yourself that journaling is a biblical concept and that God is present, speaking to His children. Relax.

When we cease our labors and enter His rest, God is free to flow (see Heb. 4:10).

Why not try it for yourself right now? Sit back comfortably, take out your pen and paper, and smile. Turn your attention toward the Lord in praise and worship, seeking His face. Many people have found the music and visionary prayer called "A Stroll Along the Sea of Galilee" helpful in getting them started. You can listen to it and download it free at www.CWGMinistries.org/Galilee.

After you write down your question to Jesus, become still, fixing your gaze on Him. You will suddenly have a very good thought. Don't doubt it; simply record it. Later, as you read your journaling, you, too, will be blessed to discover that you are indeed dialoguing with God. If you wonder whether it is really the Lord speaking to you, share it with your spouse or a friend. Their input will encourage your faith and strengthen your commitment to spending time getting to know the Lover of your soul more intimately than you ever dreamed possible.

IS IT *REALLY* GOD?

Five ways to be sure that what you're hearing is from Him:

1. Test the Origin (1 John 4:1)

Thoughts from our own minds are progressive, with one thought leading to the next, however tangentially. Thoughts from the spirit world are spontaneous. The Hebrew word for true prophecy is *naba,* which literally means "to bubble up," whereas false prophecy is *ziyd,* meaning "to boil up." True words from the Lord will bubble up from our innermost being; we don't need to cook them up ourselves.

2. Compare It to Biblical Principles

God will never say something to you personally that is contrary to His universal revelation as expressed in the Scriptures. If the Bible clearly states that something is a sin, no amount of journaling can make it right. Much of what you journal about will not be specifically addressed in the Bible, however, so an understanding of biblical principles is also needed.

3. Compare It to the Names and Character of God as Revealed in the Bible

Anything God says to you will be in harmony with His essential nature. Journaling will help you get to *know* God personally, but knowing what the Bible says *about* Him will help you discern what words are from Him. Make sure the tenor of your journaling lines up with the character of God as described in the names of the Father, Son, and Holy Spirit.

4. Test the Fruit (Matthew 7:15-20)

What effect does what you are hearing have on your soul and your spirit? Words from the Lord will quicken your faith and increase your love, peace, and joy. They will stimulate a sense of humility within you as you become more aware of who God is and who you are. On the other hand, any words you receive that cause you to fear or doubt, bring you into confusion or anxiety, or stroke your ego (especially if you hear something that is "just for you alone—no one else is worthy") must be immediately rebuked and rejected as lies of the enemy.

5. Share It with Your Spiritual Counselors (Proverbs 11:14)

We are members of a Body! *"A cord of three strands is not quickly broken,"* and God's intention has always been for us to grow together (Eccles. 4:12 NIV). Nothing will increase your faith in your ability to hear from God like having it confirmed by two or three other people! Share it with your spouse, your parents, your friends, your elder, your group leader—even your grown children can be your sounding board. They don't need to be perfect or super-spiritual; they just need to love you, be committed to being available to you, have a solid biblical orientation, and most importantly, they must also willingly and easily receive counsel. Avoid the authoritarian who insists that because of their standing in the church or with God, they no longer need to listen to others. Find two or three people and let them confirm that you are hearing from God!

NOTES

1. Phil Mason, *Quantum Glory: The Science of Heaven Invading Earth* (Maricopa, AZ: XP Publishing, 2010), 121.

2. Myles Munroe, Rediscovering the Kingdom: Ancient Hope for Our 21st Century World (Shippensburg, PA: Destiny Image, 2014), 32.

3. This phrase is a refrain in C. S. Lewis' *The Last Battle* (New York: HarperCollins, 1984).

4. Bill Johnson, *Dreaming with God: Secrets to Redesigning Your World Through God's Creative Flow* (Shippensburg, PA: Destiny Image, 2006), 24.

5. This comment refers to C.S. Lewis' *The Lion, The Witch and the Wardrobe* (New York: HarperCollins, 1984).

6. *August Rush*, directed by Kirsten Sheridan (2007; Burbank, CA: Warner Home Video, 2008), DVD.

7. Murray Dueck, *If This Were a Dream, What Would It Mean?* (Amazon: CreateSpace Independent Publishing Platform, 2005), 111.

8. Emotion. Dictionary.com. Dictionary.com Unabridged. Random House, Inc. http://dictionary.reference.com/browse/emotion (accessed: January 31, 2016).

9. Caroline Leaf, *Who Switched Off My Brain?: Controlling Toxic Thoughts and Emotions* (Dallas, TX: Switch on Your Brain USA, 2007), 36.

10. Thayer and Smith. "Greek Lexicon entry for Eudokeo". "The NAS New Testament Greek Lexicon". 1999. http://www .biblestudytools.com/lexicons/greek/nas/eudokeo.html (accessed February 6, 2016).

11. Jim Richards, *Moving Your Invisible Boundaries: Heart Physics: The Key to Limitless Living* (Travelers Rest, SC: True Potential, 2013), 250.

12. Bert Farias, "Why Billy Graham Considered Himself a Failure". The Flaming Herald, Charisma News. http://www. charismanews.com/opinion/the-flaming-herald/54951-why -billy-graham-considered-himself-a-failure (accessed February 13, 2016).

13. *Compelled by Love*, directed by Shara Pradhan (Iris Global Films, 2014), DVD.

14. Bill Johnson: *Heavenly Dominion* 7/30/2013 https://www .youtube.com/watch?v=7LWGPekG2M8, 30:45

15. Ron Lagerquist, *Fasting to Freedom* (Colorado Springs, CO: International Bible Society, 2003), 28.

16. Ibid., 34.

17. Scott Jeffrey, *Creativity Revealed: Discovering the Source of Inspiration* (Kingston, NY: Creative Crayon Publishers, 2008), 122.

18. "Dream Swing! Nicklaus Find 'Error' in Sleep." *The Milwaukee Journal* – June 27, 1964, page 14

19. "How the Eye of the Sewing Machine Needle Was Located," in *Popular Mechanics* 7, no. 5 (May 1905): 560, accessed January 20, 2016, https://books.google.com/books/about/Popular _Mechanics.html?id=oN8DAAAAMBAJ.

20. Sarah Arehart, "Exhibit Review: George Washington Carver" in *CRM: The Journal of Heritage Stewardship*, volume 5 number 2 (National Park Service, summer 2008), accessed January 30, 2016, http://www.nps.gov/history/crmjournal/Summer2008/reviewexhibit.html.

21. William J. Federer, *George Washington Carver: His Life & Faith in His Own Words* (St. Louis, MO: Amerisearch, Inc., 2003) 36.

22. Jill Morris, *The Dream Workbook* (New York: Little, Brown and Company, 1985), 125.

23. Lenore Skenazy, "Is It Just Me?" *Reader's Digest* Volume 185, Issue 1111 (June 2015): 83.

24. Ben Carson, untitled speech (National Day of Prayer, Washington, DC, May 7, 2015), quoted in Jeremy Burns, "Ben Carson: God Gave Me a Prophetic Dream That Changed Everything," in *Charisma News* (May 12, 2015), accessed January 20, 2016, http://www.charismanews.com/us/49604-ben-carson-god-gave-me-a-prophetic-dream-that-changed-everything.

25. E.C. Barton, "Handel" (*London Quarterly and Holborn Review*, Volume 58, 1882), 320.

26. James and Michal Ann Goll, *Dream Language: The Prophetic Power of Dreams, Revelations, and the Spirit of Wisdom* (Shippensburg, PA: Destiny Image, 2006), 53.

27. "How Can I Pray?," *Ignation Spirituality*, accessed January 20, 2016, http://www.ignatianspirituality.com/ignatian-prayer/the-examen/how-can-i-pray.

28. "Dog," *Dream Moods*, accessed January 20, 2016, http://dreammoods.com/cgibin/dreamdictionarysearch.pl?method=exact&header=dreamsymbol&search=dog.

29. Ibid.

30. Dutch Sheets, *The Pleasure of His Company: A Journey to Intimate Friendship with God* (Bloomington, MN: Bethany House, 2014), 36.

31. Augustine, *The City of God against the Pagans* 15.23.

32. Sherrie Rice Smith, *EFT for Christians* (Fulton, CA: Energy Psychology Press, 2015), personal correspondence with the author.

33. Schweitzer Quotes in Brief: Quotes by Albert Schweitzer. http://www.schweitzerfellowship.org/about/albert-schweitzer/quotes-by-albert-schweitzer/ (accessed February 6, 2016).

34. Mike Murdock, *Dream Seeds* (Ft. Worth, TX: The Wisdom Center, 2002).

ABOUT THE AUTHORS

Dr. Mark Virkler has written more than fifty books in the areas of hearing God's voice and spiritual growth. He is the founder of Communion With God Ministries (www.CWGMinistries.org) and Christian Leadership University (www.CLUOnline.com), where the voice of God is at the center of every learning experience. Mark's teachings on developing intimacy with God and spiritual healing have been translated into over forty languages, and he has helped to establish more than 250 church-centered Bible schools around the world.

Dr. Charity Kayembe earned her Master of Divinity and Doctor of Biblical Studies through Christian Leadership University. She is ordained through CWG Leaders Network and has worked alongside her parents in ministry for twenty years. Charity is passionate about bringing Heaven to earth through restoring the supernatural to believers' everyday lives. Her international outreach has taken her to all corners of the globe, traveling to over fifty nations on six continents. She and her husband live in upstate New York.

Discover More from Mark Virkler

YOUR HOW-TO COACH FOR THE SPIRIT-LED LIFE

Mark and Patti Virkler have *written 50 books* demonstrating how to take God's voice into area after area of life. These are available at CWGMinistries.org/catalog.

They have also developed *over 100 college courses* for Christian Leadership University that put the voice of God at the center of your learning experience. These classes can all be taken from your home. View the complete catalog online at CLUOnline.com.

Would you allow the Virklers to *recommend a coach to guide you* in applying God's voice in every area of your life? Information about their Personal Spiritual Trainer program is available at CWGMinistries.org/pst.

You can even host Mark Virkler or Charity Kayembe in your community for *a weekend seminar*. Details can be found at CWGMinistries.org/seminars.

Mark Virkler and Charity Kayembe are *blogging regularly* at CWGMinistries.org/blog.

Discover a salvation website that *honors the role of Holy Spirit*: www.BornOfTheSpirit.Today.

Did you know that *Scripture and science agree* on how you can live long enough to fulfill your destiny in vibrant health? Find out how: www.TakeChargeOfYourHealth.Today.

Interactive Online Training from
CLU School of the Spirit

How Far Could **You** Go with a Bible School in Your Pocket?

Can I really experience a "school of the Spirit" in my home?
Yes, you can!

- ☑ You don't have to go away to Bible school or a school of ministry.

- ☑ You can live in any city in any country, attend any church, and still earn a Diploma in Applied Spirituality from Christian Leadership University's School of the Spirit! CLU provides *interactive* Spirit Life Training Modules that feature video training experiences and online quizzes, all of which can be downloaded directly to your laptop, tablet, or smart phone.

Don't you think it's time YOU team up and focus with a coach at your side so you speed forward and enter your Promised Land?

There is no easier way to grow than to get into a group of like-minded people and focus intently, under the direction of Holy Spirit and a coach who is ahead of you in the area you are pursuing. *"A cord of three strands is not quickly broken"* (Eccles. 4:12 NIV). You support one another through the training process and by "focusing intently," you become a doer of the Word and not a hearer only (see James 1:25). No one wants to die in their wilderness so make sure you are taking the proper steps that will allow you to experience your Promised Land!

Learn more and try our
FREE Course Sampler today:
www.CLUSchooloftheSpirit.com

Hear God Through Your Dreams
Interactive e-Learning Course

Coaching speeds you to *mastery*

We guarantee you *will* learn how to recall and interpret dreams! We can teach you in just three months what it took us years to learn because we have gone ahead and prepared the way. And these exercises are so spiritual in nature you can easily complete them as part of your daily devotional time.

When you meditate on revelation truths in the context of a CLU School of the Spirit course, you are required to fully integrate the life-changing principles. Nothing is left to chance. You will learn what you are supposed to learn, and your life will be transformed by the power of the Holy Spirit.

Look at ALL you will receive in this interactive Spirit Life Training Module!

- ☑ Entire series of downloadable videos
- ☑ MP3 audio sessions
- ☑ Complete PDF ebook
- ☑ Complete PDF eworkbook
- ☑ Step-by-step guidance from the Interactive Learning Management System
- ☑ Certificate of Completion awarding 5 CEUs
- ☑ Coaching

**Learn more and enroll today at
www.CLUSchooloftheSpirit.com/dreams**